SOCIOLOGICAL THEORIES OF THE ECONOMY

Edited by

Barry Hindess

First edition 1977
Reprinted 1978

Published by
THE MACMILLAN PRESS LTD
London and Basingstoke
Associated companies in Delhi
Dublin Hong Kong Johannesburg Lagos
Melbourne New York Singapore Tokyo

ISBN 0 333 21313 0

Printed in Hong Kong

Contents

Notes on Contributors

LORRAINE CULLEY is Lecturer in Sociology at the University of Hull.

BARRY HINDESS is Senior Lecturer in Sociology at the University of Liverpool.

ALAN JENKINS is a research student in Sociology at the University of Liverpool.

BRYN JONES is Lecturer in Sociology at the University of Bath.

GARY LITTLEJOHN is Lecturer in Sociology at the University of Bradford.

STEPHEN P. SAVAGE is a research student in Sociology at the University of Liverpool.

Introduction

This book contains revised versions of papers originally prepared for a seminar on sociological theories of the economy held in Liverpool in September 1975. The titles of these papers are largely self-explanatory and there is no reason to provide here more than a brief introduction to this collection. With one exception these papers deal with particular theories, the work of particular authors or schools, and between them they provide a substantial critique of the more significant sociological attempts to conceptualise types of economy or of economic action in relation to other areas of social life. A glance at their titles, however, will be enough to show that the title *Sociological Theories of the Economy* may be perhaps unduly restrictive. Chayanov is no sociologist, but the recent growth of interest in the idea of the peasantry as representing some allegedly distinctive type of economic or social life justifies including a study of the most rigorous and systematic attempt to construct a theory of 'peasant economy'. Similarly, it would take a broad definition of sociology to cover both the 'substantivist' work of Polanyi, Dalton, Sahlins and others and the neo-Marxist work of Baran, Sweezy and their associates. Nevertheless, outside of the main streams of Weberian and functionalist sociology, these schools provide the most influential conceptualisations of the economy within contemporary sociology. While it goes beyond the limits of what is conventionally understood by sociology in these respects, this book does not attempt to examine directly either conceptualisations of the economy developed within economic theory or, apart from Baran and Sweezy, those developed within Marxism. An investigation of one or both of those areas would have been outside the scope of our seminar, it would involve problems of a different order from those posed in the papers presented here, and it would result in a different kind of book.

All the participants in the seminar had encountered problems in their own research into attempts by sociologists and others to conceptualise types of economy in relation to other areas of social life, but their interests in these problems came from rather different directions and arose out of rather different areas of investigation – studies of structuralism in anthropology, of the work of Talcott Parsons, of sociological theories of economic development, and so on. The seminar provided each participant with the opportunity to raise such specific problems and to discuss them in more general ways. The papers have been corrected by their authors to take account of points made during the seminar or subsequently and they have been further revised for publication, but they do not present an agreed or collective position. Each author is responsible for the argument of his own paper and, although these papers share a general critical and theoretical objective and are interdependent in certain respects, the positions advanced by any one author are not necessarily accepted by the others.

All the papers are critical and theoretical in approach: they are concerned to investigate theories as theories, to analyse the internal structure of their concepts and arguments. The principal mode of critique in these papers is therefore directed at the internal, logical and conceptual, problems and inadequacies of the theory concerned. It is not a 'realist' or an 'empirical' mode of critique in which theory is alleged to be measured against the real as represented in empirically given facts or encapsulated in some other more favoured theoretical discourse. Thus, to take just one example, while the work of Baran and Sweezy is shown to diverge significantly from classical Marxist theory, the major criticism of their position is not directed at the divergence, for the mere fact of a difference between two positions can provide no grounds for accepting one and rejecting the other. Rather the critique is concerned with the evolutionist and ultimately incoherent character of their conceptualisations of 'mono-poly capitalism' and 'underdevelopment'. The dogmatic and theoretically ineffective character of 'realist' and 'empirical' modes of critique has been established elsewhere and they need not be considered here (see Hindess, 1977, chap. 7; Savage, forthcoming, chap.1).

Finally, and in order to avoid any possible misunderstandings, it is necessary to comment briefly on the only paper in this collection which is not primarily concerned with the works of one particular author or school. In the context of our seminar, 'Humanism and Teleology in Sociological Theory' was presented as one paper among others. It did not provide and it was not intended to provide a framework for analysis to be adopted in the other papers. Rather it provides a general discussion of issues which were bound to arise in one form or another in connection with many of the other papers. As its title suggests, 'Humanism and Teleology in Sociological Theory' deals with the conceptual structure of two types of con-ceptualisation that are ubiquitous in the academic social sciences, namely, theoretical humanism and related positions on the one hand and teleology on the other. It investigates the general structure of both types of conceptualisation and attempts to provide a rigorous theoretical critique of both of them. The scope of that paper therefore goes beyond the formal limits of a seminar on theories of the economy. Its conclusions are certainly intended to have a more general significance for social theory, but its arguments are developed with particular reference to the writings of Parsons and Weber on the economy and on economic change. The inclusion of such a paper is justified because of the crucial role that theoretical humanism and related positions play in sociological attempts to conceptualise economic action, the economy and economic change and of

Introduction

the manifest significance of the economy as perhaps the principal location of teleological conceptions in contemporary social theory. The paper examines the properties of these types of conceptualisation and it argues, in particular, that they are fundamentally and inescapably incoherent. It does not attempt to establish that particular theoretical discourses are in fact dominated by either theoretical humanist or teleological conceptualisations and it refers to the works of Parsons, Weber and others solely in order to illustrate its general arguments. It is therefore neither a substitute for nor a résumé of the analyses of particular authors or schools provided in the other papers.

I, and the publishers, wish to thank the following who have kindly given permission for the use of copyright material. Richard D. Irwin Inc., for a table by A. V. Chayanov and short extracts from *The Theory of Peasant Economy*, edited by D. Thorner, B. Kerblay and P. E. F. Smith (1966). Routledge & Kegan Paul Ltd and Macmillan Publishing Co Inc., for the extract from *Economy and Society*, by T. Parsons and N. J. Smelser. Copyright © 1956 by The Free Press. The publishers have made every effort to trace the copyright-holders but if they have inadvertently overlooked any, they will be pleased to make the necessary arrangement at the first opportunity.

1 Talcott Parsons and the Structural-Functionalist Theory of the Economy

STEPHEN P. SAVAGE

INTRODUCTION

The objective of this paper is to discuss Talcott Parsons' theorisation of the economy or the economic on the one hand, and the social-structural or non-economic spheres in general on the other; as such its main object will be the text *Economy and Society* (Parsons & Smelser, 1956)

Parsons' own mode of conceptualisation and theorisation, i.e. according to the concepts of the action frame of reference and the theory of social systems, seems to pose three sorts of issues for this paper. Firstly, it will be necessary to elaborate the distance that Parsons establishes between the theory of social systems and its derivate concepts on the one hand, and attempts made at various levels in economic theory to handle concepts of the non-economic on the other. Secondly, it will be necessary to measure further the theoretical distance between the theory of social systems and approaches from *within* sociology to conceptualise the economic and non economic; in this context of particular concern must be Max Weber's sociology of action and Parsons' own earlier attempts at such a theory in *The Structure of Social Action (SSA)* (Parsons, 1949a). The third issue, and the major one for this paper, concerns the theoretical issues raised by the most elaborate theoretical position on this area taken by Parsons in *Economy and Society* – the problem as to whether or not the Parsonian approach does indeed overcome the problematic features of previous attempts, within and without of sociology, to theorise the economic/non-economic relation, features which Parsons himself has subjected to telling criticism. Parsonian theory has elaborated what is undoubtedly the most rigorous and systematic analysis of the economic/non-economic relation that has been produced from within sociology.[1] A critique of such a theory is thus doubly significant, not only as a comment on Parsons but on sociological theory in general and its capacity to theorise the economy.

The structure of the paper is as follows. Part I will elaborate on two issues: on the one hand, Parsons' critique of the mode in which economic theory itself has approached the problem of its periphery – the non-economic areas of the 'social', to 'wants', preferences, propensities and so on; on the other, the distance between previous attempts from within sociology to theorise such issues, and Parsons' own concept of structural-functionalism. This includes his own earlier approaches but in particular the important theses of Max Weber on economy and society. Following this, Part II will direct a critique at the structural-functionalist theory of the economy itself. Two areas are of particular concern in this respect, both of which constitute focal points of Parsons' thesis: on the one hand the concept of 'structural differentiation', on the other that of 'functional sub-system'.

It will be argued that, despite the level of rigour that Parsons attains, the structural-functionalist theory of the economic/non-economic relation falls down at two decisive junctures. On the one hand it is argued that this theory depends on a confusion and conflation of two orders of concepts, those concerning the notions of 'cultural directionality' and 'structural differentiation', orders which, it is shown, are theoretically incompatible. It is also shown that both notions, taken independently or together, involve assumptions which are strategically teleological, despite claims to the contrary. On the other hand, this paper locates a number of crucial theoretical problems which surround the concepts of the 'functional prerequisites' and 'functional sub-systems'. These concepts, which most characterise the structural-functionalist mode of analysis, are shown in the last analysis to reproduce the ambiguities and arbitrariness which they at one level appear to surpass. Central in this respect is the notion of the human 'subject' and the humanist way in which the relation between subject and situation (system, requirements of the system, etc.) is elaborated. These theoretical problems are shown to render the project for a coherent mode of analysis of the economic/non-economic relation on the lines of structural-functionalist theory impossible to achieve.

PART I

ECONOMIC THEORY, ACTION, AND THE THEORY OF SOCIAL SYSTEMS

Economy and Society represents a distinct theoretical position at two levels; it is distinct from the mode in which economic theory has itself approached the problem of its non-economic periphery on the one hand, and it is distinct from the mode in which 'action theory' proper, i.e. Weber's sociology, has conceived this relation on the other. This part of the paper will consider these issues and their significance.

ECONOMIC THEORY AND SOCIOLOGY

Economy and Society (ES) elaborates a critique of economic theory much of which has been the continual concern of Parsonian theory from even its earliest theses, culminating in *SSA*.[2] Here the major objective is to demonstrate that the voluntaristic theory of action is the only truly general formulation of the economic/non-economic relation, one which incorporates all the analytic elements of the action frame of reference. In respect of this, *SSA* argues that previous attempts have ignored or suppressed at least one of these elements. One such attempt, Parsons argues, is utilitarian theory which, it is argued, is characterised by atomism, rationalism and empiricism. It is utilitarianism that is seen to constitute the basic conceptual apparatus of both classical and neo-classical economics in its conception of the non-economic periphery of economic processes.

Two general criticisms are levelled at classical economic theory: either it has tended to depend entirely upon the postulate of the intrinsic rationality of action in which the means – end relation is conceived in such a fashion as to obliterate the investigation of ends altogether, i.e. ends become random, or it has formulated the determination of ends in a metaphysical and/or positivistic manner as the 'natural identity of interests', 'needs', hedonism, etc.[3] The critique of economic theory is thus posed in terms of *absences*, either the absence of *any* determination of ends or more generally of the non-economic sphere, or the absence of a particular type of determination, viz. its voluntary element – action oriented to sets of 'ultimate' ends and values.

At the level of *SSA*, however, the critique of economic theory is very limited: there is little or no theoretical demonstration that such absences are theoretically damaging,[4] and there is little offered in terms of an alternative formulation of the economic/non-economic relation. It is not until *Economy and Society* that the problems of economic theory are rigorously posed.

In this text Parsons refers to the tendency within economics of 'resting on *ad hoc* hypotheses about "human nature" which are psychologically and sociologically dubious if not downright untenable' (*ES*, p. 184). In particular, he locates three primary tendencies in economic theory in its handling of the non-economic realm[5] which go beyond the mere issue of 'ends'. The first is the use of vague, often anthropological, notions of 'homo oeconomicus', of 'human nature', and so on. Second is the tendency to *reduce* the non-economic to the status of a random variant, i.e. a purely dependent variable and thus empirically a contigent one (Parsons cites Schumpeter's concept of a hypothetical economy, from which deviations are to be measured). The third tendency is to conceptualise the non-economic in terms of an 'empirical generalisation', i.e. as a 'given', an example being Keynes' notion of 'psychological laws'.

As well as the general problem of ambiguity, the effects of such tendencies are in the direction of an indvidualism – particularly the theory of marginal utility, but also in such apparently non-individualistic areas as welfare economics[6] – a rationalism in which all action that does not come directly within the scope of economics is defined as somehow 'irrational', and the overall theoretical barrier to the formation of a truly *general* system of concepts for the analysis of the economic/non-economic relation. Such consequences Parsons attempts to demonstrate by means of several examples; I shall cite the two most effective.

The first and most extensive is the Keynesian concept of the 'consumption function' and its reliance on the notion of 'propensity'. For Keynes the problem of the aggregate demand function requires that some explanation be given of the general relation between consumption on the one hand and savings and investment on the other: the objective is thus to formulate a general thesis concerning the factors which determine the sum which is to be spent on consumption when employment is given. Two broad classes are differentiated, the 'objective' and 'subjective'. The former includes such factors as changes in the wage-unit, in the difference between net income and income in general, in capital values, in fiscal policy, and so on;[7] the subjective factors are seen to be general subjective dispositions and social 'incentives'. Within both classes and in the relation between them is the assumption of the operation of a *psychological* mechanism, seen by Keynes to be a 'fundamental psychological law' – the 'propensity'.

Parsons considers such a thesis to be inadequate on both theoretical and empirical grounds. The concept of propensity reduces the non-economic world to a single variable, which is itself an expression of a psychological tendency; consumption and savings are conceived in terms of the unidimensional relation between level of income and the psychological expression of it. The problem with such an argument lies at two levels: on the one hand it depends upon a totally unfounded presupposition as to a psychological law, on the other it involves the total absence of any theorisation of the conditions of existence of the non-economic sphere itself, a sphere which Parsons argues is a *socially determinate* realm. The ambiguity and reductionism inherent in the concept of 'propensity' to consume is seen to derive from the absence of the concept of the social conditions of existence of the consumption function:

What does this function imply about the social structure? In the first place, the only two terms in the consumption function relation – the consumers and their incomes – are linked by the principle that consumption rises as income rises, though not so rapidly. If this principle is all that is given, what are the reasons why the principle should hold? (*ES*, p. 229)

Essentially similar features are seen to be operative in the economic analysis of 'imperfect competition', although more acute because of its wider referent. The tendency in this case is to *reduce* the non-economic to an economic object. The theory of imperfect competition refers to a situation in which the assumptions of the perfect market no longer apply – there exists an imbalance of advantages and power on one side of the market. Such imbalances are, however, conceived in purely economic terms – supply and demand (number of sellers, elasticity), cost curves, monopolistic competition, and so on. The problematic issue is again one of determinacy:

> But what are the *conditions* of imperfection? What are the *sources* of the power imbalance? In terms of our paradigm, what are the conditions to which either ego or alter (or both) must adapt which lead to the relative advantage or disadvantage in the market situation and to the development of features of the market which are not obvious cases of economic rationality? (*ES*, p. 145)

In these and many other areas of economic analysis (the theory of labour supply, trade-cycle models, etc.) Parsons locates a primary problem: the theorisation of the non-economic conditions of existence of the economic sphere remains at a level that is unsatisfactory or non-existent. It is in respect of this critique that he proposes the theoretical 'synthesis' between economic theory and sociology.

In this case Parsons must demonstrate that it *is* sociology and not psychological theory, political science, or any other body of theory that must undertake this regeneration of economics. He attempts this through reference to the apparently 'fundamental' nature of its object – human action. As an effect, Parsons claims a set of theoretical 'congruences' between economics and sociology: these relate to the apparent complementarity of their respective 'frames of reference' which is seen to be effective at several levels. Firstly, it is claimed that the economist's conception of supply and demand can be viewed as a special case of the general concepts of performance and sanction, i.e. as a part of the theory of action; secondly, that the distinction between goods and services is a logical equivalent to that of social and non-social objects; thirdly, in both disciplines there is a notion of 'exchange' or mutual advantage, which in both cases is a central organising postulate; and finally, there is the reference in both sociology and economics to some mode of organisation or 'system'.

On the issue of this demonstration it might be worth while to pose one or two doubts concerning this attempt. For example, the parallel between supply – demand and performance – sanction would appear to disregard the essentially *marginal* determination of choice in the former as opposed to the cultural (value-orientational) determination of choice in the action-conception. Or again, the congruence between the distinctions between social and non-social objects and goods and services pays little or no concern to the theoretical differences that hold between the notion of *interaction* on the one hand and *utility* on the other. What Parsons offers by way of theoretical proof of compatibility is hardly sufficient to bridge the gap created by these conceptions; if this is the case then no amount of word-play can rescue the project from eclecticism.

The project itself is to reformulate certain features and parameters of economic theory according to the exigencies of sociological theory; the objective is to maintain the major categories and concepts of formal economics[8] – in particular its essential feature of measurement in mon-etary terms – but to subsume them within a specifically *sociological* frame of reference. For example,

> the imperfection of markets differs not only in degree *but in sociological type*. The market for consumers' goods differs from that for labour, and both differ from that for capital funds. These markets differ in type primarily because the different markets connect the economy with *different* sectors of the society: these connections enforce qualitatively *different* limitations on the respective market conditions. (*ES*, p. 3; emphasis in original)

The origin of the intervention of this explicitly non-economic referent Parsons locates in Marshall's notion of 'human services', which includes a referent to both the marginal response to the rate of remuneration *and* to a more general 'underlying willingness to work'.[9] In addition, Marshall supplements the orthodox economic classification of the factors of production (land, labour, capital) with an additional factor – that of organisation, a referent to the non-economic sphere of contract. These notions are, however, of an elementary character; the synthesis between sociology and economics in *ES* is of a more elaborate form.

THE ECONOMY, ACTION, AND THE THEORY OF SOCIAL SYSTEMS

It is generally recognised that *Economy and Society* offers a difference in 'emphasis' from the position taken in *SSA* concerning the economic/non-economic relation. In the latter, the prime objective was to construct a position mid-way between both forms of theoretical 'imperialism', econ-omic and sociological, i.e. to include all the analytical elements. The prime example in this respect is the thesis of Pareto; here primary reference is given to 'economic rationality' in the form of the marginal subject, but in *addition* to a sphere of 'residues' – non-logical action, the object of sociology rather than economics. This distinction is elaborated by Parsons into that between rational action and action oriented to 'ultimate ends', i.e. the position taken by Weber. The complete analytical prgoramme is thus one of economics *plus* sociology.

In *ES* however, Parsons claims: 'Our view now is distinctly different…' (p. 6). The distinctiveness of the later position is seen to lie in the conception that economic theory is not merely the organisation of a distinct class of 'variables' to which a further set is to be added; what is seen to demarcate the two spheres is not the variables but the *parameters* which the two disciplines must conceptualise, parameters seen in terms of relations of *functional sub-systems*:

> Economic theory should, according to this view, be regarded as the theory of typical processes in the 'economy', which is a sub-system differentiated from other sub-systems of a society. The specifically economic aspect of the theory of social systems, therefore, is *a special case of the general theory of the social system*. (p. 6; emphasis added)

But what is the *significance* of this transformation of the theoretical mode in which the economic/non-economic relation is to be conceived? It would appear to be much greater than Parsons himself has made explicit and concerns the implications of the concepts presented in *ES* for a critical reading of *SSA* and indeed of Weberian economic sociology. A few comments on both Weber and the theoretical means of *SSA* would appear to be in order.

As Parsons points out in his introduction to Weber's *Theory of Social and Economic Organisation* (Weber, 1964a), it was not Weber's objective to replace economic theory but to add to it an area of relatively under-developed conceptualisation – the major one being, for Parsons, the theory of institutional structure. Institutions are seen as the social form of orientational modes, of *types* of action. One such mode is that pertinent to the economy, economically oriented (rational) action:

> Action will be said to be 'economically oriented' so far as, according to its subjective meaning, it is concerned with the satisfaction of a desire for utilities. 'Economic action' is a peaceful use of the actor's control over resources which is rationally oriented, by deliberate planning, to economic ends. An *'economic system'* is an autocephalous system of economic action. (Weber, 1964a, p. 158; emphasis added)

What is of particular significance in such a thesis is that the 'economy' is defined not as a mode of organisation or a structure but in terms of an *orientation*: the economy has an *essence* which is the form of action that it embodies. The distinction between the economy and non-economic spheres is thus in terms of distinctions between *types* of action. This is clear in his distinction between 'market' and 'planned' economies: these are differentiated in terms of the relative presence of two polar types of meaningful orientation, budgetary and profit-making, the former oriented to 'the security and increase of resources and income', the latter 'to maintaining and improving profitability and the market position of the enterprise' (Weber, 1964a, p. 199). The economy is thus conceived in terms of the combination of an individualist referent – the vehicle of the economy is the individual actor and his orientations (to profit or towards 'irrational' considerations) – and ideational or 'value' elements which constitute those orientations. The determinations of the society – economy relation lies essentially in the realm of values and their effectivity. Weber provides no concept of this relation in terms of determinate totalities, structures or systems.

Parsons' own *SSA* remains, on the whole, little removed from Weber's formulation. There is, however, one major distinctive referent, albeit a rather formalist one: this concerns the epistemological concept of 'emergent properties'. Thus economic rationality is not to be seen simply as the orientation of an individual as in Weber's notion, but rather, 'Economic rationality is...an emergent property which can be observed only when a plurality of unit acts is treated together as constituting an *integrated system of action*' (*SSA*, pp. 739-40; emphasis added).

The concept of emergent properties signals the theoretical pertinence of the concept of a system of action, which is more than a simple aggregate of individual actions and distinct from a simple mode of orientation, but which involves the concept of a *mode of organisation* of action elements and consequently a set of situational exigencies. But beyond this formal notion *SSA* provides no *specific* concept of the social or the economic system; this is clear in the essay written shortly after this text, 'The Motivation of Economic Activities',[10] in which the economy is still conceived solely in terms of an *institutional* form determinate according to the value-patterns which it represents rather than as a discrete *system* of action. It is the objective of *Economy and Society* to pose precisely this problem and implicitly to overcome the idealism apparent in the earlier position and in the theses of Weber.

We now find a distinct mode of theorisation of the economic/non-economic relation: 'In defining production, utility, wealth and income, the focal point of reference is for us *society* as a system' (*ES*, p. 21). The objective is no longer to supplement economic theory but to subsume it within the theory of social systems; it involves not the extension of the theses of *SSA* but transformations of the problem itself.[11] The crucial concept is the notion of the *social system* and its distinction from both the personality and cultural systems. This transforms the conceptualisation of the determination of the social sphere from the orientational reference of *SSA* (social=a type of action) to the boundary reference of the later works in which the social is defined as a collective *actor*:

A social system having the three properties of collective goals, shared goals, and of being a single system of interaction with boundaries defined by incumbency in the roles constituting the system, will be called a collectivity (*Parsons & Shils, 1962*, p. 192)[12]

Given the differentiation of the cultural and social systems, the status of values is displaced: they no longer constitute the social but become *mechanisms of its functioning*.[13] This is clear in the case of economic rationality:

> the concept of economic rationality may designate either a property of a social system or a property of a personality system; but these two references must not be confused. In either case, however, the concept refers to the mode of organisation of the system relative to its values. (*ES*, p. 177)

Economic rationality is not the *essence* of the economy, as in the case of Weber, but is a mechanism of its functioning and is thus secondary to the exigencies of the boundaried system. The economy is defined as a boundary-maintaining system and as such is subject to two related forms of processes, those relating to the appearance of that system and those concerning its pertinence as a system.

The first process is that of 'structural differentiation', and accounts for the actual presence of the 'economy', defined in the strict sense as the predominantly *market*-based means of fulfilling consumption needs. This process refers to an evolutionary tendency of social systems to fragment along functionally beneficial lines – Parsons' version of the traditional approach to the division of labour. That the economy as such exists as a specific totality is due to a sequence in which all social systems are constrained to comply with certain internal and external requirements. These lead into the second order of process: the synchronic sphere of 'functional imperatives'.

There are four functional imperatives: adaptation, goal-attainment, integration, and pattern-maintenance/management (referred to as A, G, I and L, respectively). The first two concern the relation between the system and its situation: A refers to the capacity of a system to control its environment for the purpose of achieving certain goals; G refers to the establishment of a relation between the system and its situational objects in terms of the formulation of a specific 'goal-state' in the direction of gratification of the system as a whole. The other two relate to the internal mechanisms of the system: I involves the maintenance of solidarity between the units of the system in the interest of its effective functioning, and L the maintenance of a stable value-system (cultural consistency) and the control of endemic motivational strains (Parsons *does* refer to inherent conflict), which are potentially disruptive of the system. For Parsons, 'Any system of action can be described and its processes analysed in terms of these four functional prerequisities' (*ES*, p. 18).

It is at this level that the concept of 'functional sub-systems' emerges. Given these imperatives, Parsons argues, systems will tend to produce sub-systems which will be constituted with primary reference to one of the four requirements. Each sub-system may be seen as a boundaried mode of organisation which articulates with its environment through certain 'boundary interchanges'. The pertinence of the concept of functional sub-system for the Parsonian theory of the economy is obvious – it represents the double referent by which the economy is theorised in *ES*: on the one hand as a sub-system of the total social system, on the other as a social system in itself in which the different economic processes are conceived as differentiations of functional primacy. The schema of functional problems/ functional sub-systems is applied at both levels of the economic/non-economic relation. A brief exposition of the two levels, the functional differentiation of *society*, and the functional differentiation of the *economy*, will be given by way of illustration.

The theory of the functional differentiation of society is Parsons' most distinctive and famous contribution to sociological theory; in particular it serves to distinguish his theory of the economic/non-economic relation from other attempts from within sociology to handle the problem.[14] At this level the non-economic sphere is explicitly conceived as a *situation* to the economy – not as a 'given' nor as an 'empirical generalisation', but as a functionally determinate system of boundaries and interchanges. The economic and the non-economic are thus viewed as different modes of *organisation*, centred around the differentiation of functional problems. This constitutes the well-known formula of the structure of society: the economy is the sub-system primarily concerned with the problem of A, its goal being the *production* of generalised facilities for the disposal of the society; the polity involves the G function in that it mobilises societal resources for the attainment of given collective goals; the I sub-system is concerned primarily with solidarity, or the co-ordination of units in the direction of 'harmony' and control of deviance; finally, the L sub-system is differentiated according to the problem of intra-unit states and processes, with maintaining conformity to the dominant values and with developing sufficient motivation (primarily at the level of personality).

The assertion of functional primacy constitutes the conceptual *autonomy* of each system but it also presupposes a mode of *relationship* between each system, or their functional interdependence. Parsons handles this in terms of the notion of interchange, the mutual exchange of generalised facilities between the systems in the direction of an overall contribution to the system as a whole.[15]

The contribution of each sub-system to the social system is thus conceived in terms of output or products which flow into the three situational sub-systems in the form of generalised facilities; at the societal level the economy produces wealth, the polity produces political power, the I sub-system produces solidarity, and the L sub-system produces prestige (which relates motivational factors to the common-value system). A further specification (and, as will be seen, a significant one) is that such facilities are processed through the further differentiation of the sub-systems themselves according to their own functional primacies. Outputs are thus always directed at specific branches of each sub-system and are not distributed by a simple spreading of resources across the board.

Given this theoretical basis, Parsons elaborates the second major level of functional theorisation to be found in *Economy and Society*, the functional differentiation of the economy itself. Very briefly, the economy is conceived in terms of the four universals outlined above such that its structure is broken into four sub-systems whereby the A function is fulfilled through capitalisation and investment, the G function by production (including distribution and sales), the I function by 'organisation' and the L by what Parsons calls 'economic commitments' (cultural, motivational and physical resources). These sub-systems are made parallel with the more orthodox classification of the 'factors of production', labour, organisation and land respectively – the generalised facilities accompanied by their products, profits, wages, rent and interest. The schema is exemplified by Parsons' treatment of consumption.

Consumption, it is argued, must be conceived in terms of *boundary processes*: the relations between this sphere and its periphery must be seen as a process of 'double interchange', the reciprocal distribution of facilities between sub-systems which is rigorously governed by the functional requirements of the total system. Consumption is not to be conceived in mechanistic fashion as the mere expression of income or of market position but as a boundary process between the A and L sub-systems, primarily between the institutional representations of these sub-systems located in the household and the enterprise. The whole process is mediated by the value-system (internalised and institutionalised) and as such it is claimed that the economy offers consumer goods and services 'in return for which' it receives motivated labour, and conversely the household offers consumer spending and labour services as its main goal in the reciprocal relation.

It is only in terms of such a schema, Parsons argues, that the conditions of consumption patterns can be analysed. Economic processes and their non-economic relations must be seen as boundary relations, relations which are subject to both levels of systemic effectivity.

It is clear that Parsons' attempt in *Economy and Society* to theorise the economic/non-economic relation is significantly distinct not only from the way in which economic theory handles this problem but also from the orthodox sociological conceptions often presented in some form as the relations between rational value-based action, or between *Gemeinschaft* and *Gesellschaft*, distinctions which are common coin amongst idealist sociologies. The major concepts in Parsons' case are those of functional prerequisites, modes of organisation, sub-systems, boundary interchange, structural differentiation, and so on. But what of the status of *these* concepts?

PART II

THE THEORETICAL STATUS OF THE PARSONIAN CONCEPTION OF ECONOMY AND SOCIETY

If Parsons' theory of the economy is to be seen as a theoretically elaborate attempt to conceive the economic/non-economic relation as compared with other attempts, both from within economic theory and sociology, to handle the problem, then it is due primarily to two orders of concepts (both related): on the one hand the notion of 'structural differentiation', on the other that of 'functional sub-systems'. In this section the theoretical character of these concepts will be interrogated.

THE CONCEPT OF STRUCTURAL DIFFERENTIATION

As will be demonstrated shortly, the concept of structural differentiation occupies a particularly strategic position in the Parsonian theory of the economy: it supplies the means of establishing the 'economy' as a distinct object for the theory of social systems, of accounting for the processes which articulate with the economy, and in a general sense of explaining the apparent significance of the 'Western' form of economy. This section will argue, however, that this concept is a highly problematic one on two levels: firstly, that Parsons includes within the one concept *two* processes which are not only confused and conflated but which are theoretically incompatible—these are on the one hand the concept of functional differentiation, and on the other the notion of cultural directionality; the two concepts are theoretically necessary to Parsons' project but are logically incompatible. Secondly, it will be further shown that both referents of structural differentiation involve theoretical properties which are in fact *teleological*, the postulate of an immanent tendency whether in the realm of value-systems or in the sphere of systematic 'advance'. As a consequence, it will be claimed that this decisive concept is without any coherent foundation.

One of the major concerns of *Economy and Society* is to approach a problem essentially similar to that posed by Weber in *The Protestant Ethic and the Spirit of Capitalism* (Weber, 1930): the nature, significance and genesis of the 'Western' or 'market' form of economy. In both cases the thesis is that such an economy is of 'universal' significance, and that more generally the Western form of society is a decisive landmark in human history,[16] and that therefore its analysis is of central concern for sociological theory.

For Weber the market form of economy represents the dominance of specifically *economic* relations, the dominance of formal over substantive rationality (the latter remain, of course, a persistent element). The market economy, distinguished by the presence of a 'market situation' (exchange for money), 'marketability' (regularity with which objects are exchanged), and 'market freedom' (autonomy of parties in the sphere of price competition), is contrasted to what in many ways is its opposite – the planned economy in which these essential elements are non-existent or 'regulated'. In these cases the major conditions of existence of the capitalist economy are reducible to the regulation or freedom of an *orientation* of individual actors, the rational pursuit of self-interest on the basis of monetary (marginal) calculation, i.e. economic rationality. Therefore what is of prime significance is the *determination* of this orientation, which for Weber lies above all in the realm of 'ultimate values' and in particular the form of values present in the Calvinist branches of the 'Protestant ethic'.

It is clear then that the primary concept in the theory of the market, the concept that is offered to account for the *appearance* of the market form of economy, is the notion of *cultural directionality*. It is at this level that the very basic tendency that constitutes the great bulk of Weber's work becomes pertinent: the so-called 'process of rationalisation'.[17] In relation to this process, a cultural one, the non-cultural conditions of existence of the development of the market economy are little more than supports or obstacles to the domination of rational orientation, concrete elements which may allow or prohibit the expansion of formal rationality as opposed to substantive rationality. What is significant here is that the conditional, or in Parsons' terms the situational, features of the economy and society are not theoretically effective but are merely secondary to the overall notion of an ideational process – hence the study of the world religions. The idealism of this thesis is evident.

If Parsons adopts a similar problem, the means of theorisation contain significant distinctions from Weber's formulation. The major referent used to account for the market form of economy in Parsons' case is one absent in Weber – the concept of *functional differentiation*: 'Societies differ from each other in the degree to which the collectivities of which they are composed are differentiated in terms of functional primacy' (*ES*, p. 16).

The central feature of the concept of functional differentiation is the postulation of a general tendency towards increasing efficiency of the system – a tendency later specified as the 'enhancement of adaptive capacity'.[18] Smelser's work on one concrete example of this process is perhaps most explicit on this issue.[19] For Smelser, the essential elements of a theory of social change are the notions of 'complexity' and differentiation; the former implies the 'splitting' of simple structures into more complex organisations, the latter supplies the *significance* of this process, the directionality of *advance*:

The model of structural differentiation is an abstract theory of change. When one social role or organisation becomes archaic under changing historical circumstances, it differentiates by a definite and specific sequence of events into two or more roles or organisation. (Smelser, 1959b, p. 2)

This general formulation is illustrated for Parsons by the case of the break-up of the European medieval manor. The manor had traditionally been characterised by the unification in it of both economic and non-economic functions, i.e. it occupied the central organisational position with regard to political, social and economic processes. As an effect of the tendency of systems to differentiate, however, the manor was subject to diversification and fragmentation, resulting in the enclosure movements and the development of handicraft. This process of break-up created the conditions for the beginning of a new era of economic development in Europe.[20]

The concept of structural differentiation, the tendency of systems to develop into more advanced structures, is one of the central theses of Parsons' theorisation of the appearance of the market: the market represents the sphere of social relations which have become *specifically* economic (hence one of the conditions of existence of formal economic theory itself, for the latter, grounded in the technique of measurability, is seen to depend upon the *prior* existence of money and markets) – the market is the differentiated structure of action representing the process of increasing adaptive capacity, it signifies the real differentiation of the *economy* from non-economic structures (the obvious implication being that non-market economies are relatively less advanced and efficient).

However, in itself this concept is inadequate, for some other concept is required to explain why some societies are more differentiated than others, i.e. which invokes a process operative at an even more fundamental level in that it provides the conditions of *success* of the process of structural differentiation itself. Such a concept is to be found in fact in the conception of the effectivity of the cultural realm and in the notion of *cultural directionality*,[21] and bears a close relationship to Weber's conception of the evolution of value-systems or the 'process of rationalisation' (as Parsons himself claims in his introduction to 'Culture and Social Systems' in *Theories of Society* (Parsons, 1961)).

The double referent, however, involves major theoretical problems. Parsons appears to operate with the concept of two developmental processes, the functional process of structural differentiation and the ideational processes of cultural directionality. He presents their relationship in terms of the hierarchical effect of the latter in creating the conditions of existence of the former; for example, in the attempt to theorise the appearance of the market economy, the latter is held to be the most advanced and differentiated form of economic activity, but its *appearance* in one society rather than another is subject to the requisite development of adequate value-systems. However, this hierarchy in itself does not escape the central issue of the *theoretical* relationship between the two concepts, for despite expositional attempts to account for their combination (in particular the epistemological relationship between analytic and concrete), the basic problem remains: *the concept of cultural directionality is not logically compatible with the concept of structural differentiation.* In order to demonstrate this point I shall refer again to certain of Weber's theses on the matter in question, and relate them to Parsons' parallel arguments.

Weber's *The Protestant Ethic and the Spirit of Capitalism* is a thesis which is centred around the role of a specific cultural pattern in determining modes of orientation of action, which in turn are seen to be determinant of the forms of economy adopted by different societies – here the case of the Calvinist variant of Protestant theology. The problems with such a thesis have already been noted, but of particular significance here is the absence of any elaborate theory of the extra-cultural relations of the value sphere; the latter in fact effectively *constitutes* the former. It is the distinction between such a thesis and Parsons' mode of theorisation that is pertinent, for in Parsons' case the concept of the social level involves not only a reference to the process of cultural directionality but to a very definite extra-cultural realm of determination absent in any rigorous form in Weber. Thus although Parsons reproduces the Weberian insistence on the effectivity of the Protestant type of value-attitude for the development of the market economy, he is at pains to supplement the ideational level of effectivity with a theoretically distinct one – the effectivity of structural differentiation.

In the case of the latter there is clearly a notion of directionality, but it is, or must be, distinct from a simple cultural directionality: it has a reference to a different system of action, the social system, and the divisions or sub-systems within it. The essential issue here is the notion of increasing efficiency of systems to cope with their situations and environments. The relationship between system and situation is not reducible to that between values and orientations but involves the theoretical significance of *determinate levels of organisation*, the notion of functional prerequisites, and so on. Values are not expressed in action apart from their relation to the given organisational forms. In short, the cultural level is *functional but not determinant* of the social. In this case the difference between primitive and advanced societies is not, as is the case for Weber in his analysis of the 'East' and 'West', primarily a difference of cultural/orientational forms, but of differences in the capacity of systems in a functional sense. One or two examples will illustrate the crucial point that the two processes of directionality are distinct.

First, take the discussion of the Soviet Union. It is argued that as a form of social system it must be considered a relatively undifferentiated structure compared with, say, the United States. In particular there is apparently a 'fusion' of two major spheres of action – the polity and the economy. Parsons' comment on this situation is illuminating:

> How stable, beyond the period of 'forced draft', such a fusion may be is a crucial question about such societies; *will certain 'natural' tendencies* for the economy to differentiate from the polity appear or will they be inhibited? (*ES*, p. 83; emphasis added)

A clear distinction is thus made between the inherent tendency of social systems to differentiate and the value-system within which that system operates; in this case the values of 'Marxism-Leninism' are seen to be in conflict with the natural forces of social development. Conversely the case of the 'Western' societies is an example of a unitary relationship between the two levels, cultural and social; that is, the value-system is seen to be highly adaptable to the demands of structural differentiation. Even in this case, however, the two realms are theoretically discrete.

The second example of this feature of Parsons' thesis has already been referred to above: the treatment of the crucial status of economic rationality shows that orientational patterns in themselves cannot constitute an economy but are only mechanisms of its functioning. Economic rationality is not the essence of the economy but is *embodied* at specific systemic levels.

The significance of the distinction between the cultural and social levels in social development for this discussion is that at the level of the theory of the market economy the two spheres are conjoined: the market form of economy is seen to be the product of the joint operation of the processes of cultural directionality and structural differentiation, as is clear in this comment on Weber: 'We would like to reformulate the process of rationalisation as the tendency of social systems to develop progressively higher levels of structural differentiation under the pressure of adaptive exigencies' (*ES*, p.292).

This reformulation is central to the thesis of *Economy and Society* concerning the market economy: it refers to the *unification* of the two processes, the complementary relationship between cultural and social processes. Parsons needs to argue both that the two are discrete (the social system has a functional, not a simple ideational, reference) and also that at some stage they can be united (in order to explain why the tendency has been realised in some cases and not in others). I argue that this cannot be coherently achieved, that it is theoretically impossible to maintain both the distinction and the unity of the two processes of cultural directionality and structural differentiation.

Why should a rationalistic orientation to action be equivalent to the functional capacity of systems of action? If the concept of system is to be defined in consistent fashion as a discrete level of organisation with *its own* conditional requirements, why should this cultural object be seen as complementary to a systemic referent? Not only does Parsons offer no elaborated account of exactly how and why the processes of directionality and differentiation can be at some level conjoined – indeed, they are often presented as expressions of the same process (the 'reformulation' of the process of rationalisation referred to above) – but there are indications that the thesis *cannot* be rigorously maintained.

This is so on two grounds. At a very general level, the relation between 'action' defined as a process of orientation towards meaningful objects (primarily values) and the concept of *systems* of action is a problematic one. As has been demonstrated in another paper,[22] Parsons cannot coherently maintain both the determinacy of value elements in action and the notion of discrete modes of organisation of action elements into systems. Consequently the rigorous coexistence of the double reference of cultural directionality and structural (systemic) differentiation is not theoretically possible. At the level of both the action/system relation and of the two realms of social evolution, cultural and systemic, it is theoretically impossible to resolve the contradiction between the distinct forms of determination.

Another way of making this point with specific reference to the problem of directionality is to consider the effect of the extension of either process in relation to the other. Thus in the case of the process of rationalisation, just which referent is dominant, the orientational aspect of rationality or the system within which rationality is embodied? If it is the former then the specificity of systems is denegated, the effectivity of systemic requirements is suppressed and they can no longer be considered as 'independent foci of organisation' (Parsons, 1951, 6). If it is the latter, then why should culture be held as a unique sphere of determination of action, as indeed it is in the theory of the development of the market economy? It is clear that the effectivity of one precludes the effectivity of the other, that the processes of cultural directionality and of structural differentiation, despite the claim that they are concretely co-operative, are *theoretically* incompatible. Parsons' attempt to unite the two processes in *Economy and Society* has no logical foundation; as such it can result only in contradiction or incoherence.

The duality of reference is not the only problem; both processes in themselves are theoretically unacceptable. In the case of cultural directionality the problems are obvious, for the determination of this sphere itself is a non-problem for the theory of action. Its dominant component – ultimate reality – is a realm explicitly conceived as beyond 'natural' determination and thus beyond rational explanation.[23] Thus in order to account for, say, the development of the value-system of Protestantism out of more traditionalistic ethics, Parsons is faced with a major dilemma: to avoid a conception of cultural development which postulates a random order of appearance of ultimate ethics while remaining firm that such an order is beyond rational explanation. Consequently the process of cultural directionality can only be conceived as some form of absolute realisation of a human essence – the process of rationalisation becomes the realisation of the true nature of 'man'. The problems of such a thesis, problems which are more apparent in the later works (in particular, the text *Societies* (Parsons, 1966)) must be evident.

The concept of structural differentiation is more complex in a theoretical sense but nevertheless does have one property in common with the notion of cultural directionality: it is *teleological*. The notions of 'differentiated/undifferentiated', related notions of 'advanced/backward', 'developed/underdeveloped', 'complex/simple', and so on, are theorised in a teleological mode with the central property being that of an immanent tendency: 'Our most general proposition is that total societies tend to differentiate into sub-systems (social structures) which are specialised in each of the four primary functions' (*ES*, p. 47).

These oppositions, common coin in the sociology of development, are defined in terms of a 'future anterior';[24] the past – simple, primitive, undifferentiated, etc. – is conceived purely in terms of its *distance* from, and as an expression of, the future (the present). In Parsons' case, for example, medieval society or Communist societies are conceived of as in certain respects 'undifferentiated' *in relation to* that which is differentiated. The conception of the United States and of Western democracy in general provides the theoretical instruments for the explanation of less differentiated societies: the differentiated society (separation between the market economy, democratic government, nuclear family, etc.) and the differentiated economy (separation of production, consumption, etc.) provide the indispensable means of theorisation of distinct forms of economy and society. The market form of economy is thus the optimum mode of economic process from which all other economies are read off and judged.

This is clearly a case of theoretical *expressivism*: the concept of the differentiated society is the origin from which all other societies are *more or less realisations* of it. The process of social evolution involves a hierarchy (primitive – intermediate – modern) which signifies the phases of realisation of an essence, moments in the movement of the whole. Each stage in the process of structural differentiation is not conceived as a *determinate structure* but rather as a phase in the realisation of the differentiated social system. This concept is thus antithetical to Parsons' own requirements for a concept of the social system.

As well as a conceptual expressivism, the notion of structural differentiation must supply history with a purpose (consistent with the classical philosophies of history). Now although many theories of the economy/society relation invoke this teleological postulate at some level,[25] Parsons' particular attempt involves a more acute property: not only is history the site of the general tendency towards increasing complexity, but this complexity is itself governed by the more fundamental issue of the *increasing adaptive capacity* of systems. In short, complexity is attained *because* of its future effect. This is more explicit in the case of Smelser: 'when one social role or organisation becomes archaic under changing circumstances it differentiates by a definite and specific sequence of events into two or more roles or organisations' (Smelser, 1959b, p. 2). Social change is thus a linear order of advance; complexity and differentiation are the means by which this advance is attained. Smelser makes this point clear: 'Empirically we may classify underdeveloped or semi-developed economies according to how far they have moved along this line of differentiation' (Smelser, 1963, pp. 107 – 8).

The concept of structural differentiation thus requires that the historical process is assigned the status of the support of an essential principle, the immanent tendency towards the increasing adaptive capacity of social systems. Such a teleology cannot provide the means of theorisation of the economy/society relation as determinate structures and processes, for the teleological element in itself is antithetical to this requirement.

THE CONCEPT OF FUNCTIONAL SUB-SYSTEM

If the concept of structural differentiation supplies the means of theorisation of the specificity of the 'economy' in relation to other systems, a further concept is necessary through which to think the relations *between* the systems. This is to be found in the notion of functional interdependence and in the concept of functional sub-systems in particular.

Parsons' opposition to previous formulations of this problem of intra-social process has already been noted: in particular, the attempt from within economic theory to explain the exchanges between the economy and the society and indeed to explain economic processes themselves was claimed to be unacceptable in its reliance on ambiguous notions of the economic subject. Parsons' critique of Homans' exchange theory illustrates both the general strain of the opposition and the nature of the alternative.

Homans argues that concepts such as 'social system' or the 'economy' must be seen as extrapolations from a few well-trusted psychological processes – they must always be explicitly reducible to psychological propositions, e.g. 'man is a reward-seeking animal'.[26] The immediate problem of such an absurd thesis is recognised by Parsons: how, given a set of essential characteristics of the human subject, is it possible rigorously to conceptualise different economies and different social structures? The starting-point of the theory of the economy and society cannot be the properties of the individual human subject, whether they be those postulated by marginalist economics, behaviourist psychology or any other essentially individualist conceptions. On the contrary, a distinct referent is necessary in order to allow the theorisation of the economy/society relation: 'Concrete behaviour is not a function simply of elementary properties, but of kinds of systems . . . their various structures of the processes taking place within them' (Turk & Simpson, 1972, p. 35).

Parsons' distinction between elementary properties and 'kinds of systems' is quite clearly an attempt to avoid the reduction of the latter (and subsequently the economy and society) to the former. The concept of functional system and sub-system is the means by which Parsons attempts to surpass the reliance on any ambiguous notion of the economic 'subject'. The question posed in this section concerns the effectiveness of this project. To be precise: does the concept of functional sub-system overcome the obvious problems of the postulate of the economic (or any other) 'subject'? It will be argued that in fact the distinction between 'elementary properties' and 'kinds of systems' collapses at certain crucial junctures and that consequently Parsons does not achieve the objective necessary to his theory of the economy.

In order to demonstrate this point I shall return to the formulation of the functional prerequisities and in particular to the function of goal-attainment.

The functional prerequisites refer to the relation between the system and its situation: they concern the internal problems of the system on the one hand the relation between it and its environment on the other. Thus I involves the internal cohesion of the system, L the stability of units and pattern, whereas A concerns the control of the environment for the purposes of the system and G the establishment of that state and the mobilisation of resources necessary for its fulfilment. It is obvious that the functional requirement of goal-attainment and its correspondent sub-system occupy a unique position in relation to the other functional imperatives: whereas the I, L and A prerequisites may be seen as relatively 'automatic' processes of adjustment within the system and between it and the environment, the goal-attainment function involves the *establishment* of the relation between system and environment and the *mobilisation* of the system as a whole in a certain direction – in short, it constitutes the 'vital principle' of the system. It is not surprising then that it is at this juncture that the mode of theorisation is most problematic, for when we turn to the conceptualisation of the *mechanisms* by which the functions are realised (establishment of a 'goal-state', mobilisation of resources) it becomes apparent that theoretical ambiguity plays a strategic role. Consider the following argument:

> A goal-state, for an individual actor or for a social system, is a *relation* between the system of reference and one or more situational objects which (given the value-system and its institutionalisation) maximises the stability of the system. Other things being equal such a state, *once present*, tends to be maintained, and if absent, tends to be 'sought' by the action of one or more units of the system. (*ES*, p. 17; latter emphasis added)

The ambiguity surrounds this reference to a relation 'once present', for beyond reference to the given value-systems Parsons offers no concept or theory of the precise mechanisms and processes by which this relation between system and situation is to be established. The role of the culture is misleading here, for although it is functional in this respect it can only supply the particular 'contents' of goal-states and/or maintain a given goal-state. If Parsons is to avoid an idealist-emanationist thesis, then some distinct concept is required of the mechanisms by which one value-pattern is adopted and not another and by which these value-patterns are made functional in a certain direction.

If Parsons offers no such concept, then what processes *are* implied? The definition of goals and goal-states supplies some indication, for it implies on the one hand the capacity to *desire*:

With respect to any boundary interchange . . . each participating system pursues a *goal* which is the establishment of a desired or needed relation between the acquisition of input (with due regard to quality and amount) and the corresponding output. (*ES*, p. 108)

On the other hand systems have the capacity for *gratification*:

Goal-states may be negative, i.e. noxious situational conditions, or positive, i.e. a maximisation of favourable or 'gratifying' conditions. (*ES*, p. 17)

It becomes clear that these two capacities are attributes commonly assigned to the *human subject*; taken together they must imply two more definite mechanisms, *recognition mechanisms* and *gratificational mechanisms*. Both features are theoretically problematic.

To take the first, if a system is to have a 'desire' or a need and if these are to be at some level effective (as functionalism requires) of processes within the system, then some feature of the system must be supplied with the means to recognise these needs and further to recognise the structure of the situation in order that a goal-state may be established. For example, if the goal of the economy as a social system is the production of goods and services, then a mechanism is required by which the economy can become conscious of its goal and by which it can conceive the way in which the situation may be manipulated in order to achieve this imperative. Each sub-system and system must thus have a *consciousness*, a means by which systemic needs, situational object and value-patterns can be sifted and arranged in a particular order or pattern. Functional sub-systems are therefore conceived as *human subjects*, they are supplied with the capacities corresponding to those offered in the humanist formulation of the individual human actor.

Can the fact that sub-systems have capacities normally assigned to individual human subjects be made theoretically consistent with Parsonian discourse? Two forms of reconciliation might be offered. Firstly, it might be argued that the concept of 'cybernetic hierarchy', already introduced in *Economy and Society* and of great significance in the later texts, overcomes the problem of postulating a recognition structure in so far as the process of inter-system relations can be reduced to 'information – energy' interchange, i.e. an automatic process. Such a thesis is hardly successful in avoiding the consequences outlined above, for either the effectivity of culture is defined in the relatively loose sense as a mechanism of functioning of the system (as is the case in *ES*), and then the problem remains as before – some mechanism must exist which can interiorise culture patterns, i.e. a recognition structure – or culture is conceived in the later sense as *constitutive*, in which the systems of action become in the last analysis mere 'slices' of an idealist hierarchy of effectivity. This alternative only overcomes the inconsistency of the earlier position in so far as the claimed autonomy of the systems of action is denegated in favour of a full-blown idealist theology.

The second form of reconciliation is no more successful than the first. In this case the claim that the sub-systems must involve the capacities of human subject might be seen as perfectly consistent with the general theory of action in that it has always been made explicit that social systems are 'actors'. But it is necessary to distinguish, as Parsons indeed does, between the concrete individual actor and a *system* of action; the latter is, of course, 'made up' of individual actors but it is not a mere aggregate of actors (or in the case of the personality system not a concrete human individual) but a theoretically *specific* object. In ambiguously transporting capacities of the individual human subject to the level of the systems and sub-systems, Parsons contradicts the definition of the systems of action as 'analytically discrete'. Totalities such as the polity, the economy, and more generally the total social system, are thus conceived as human subjects or 'society-subjects'. At the level of the polity this leads Parsons to adopt a thesis central to much classical political philosophy: the polity/state as the collective mind of the society, the neutral body above society which operates for the 'good of all', or in Parsons' case for the fulfilment of collective goals. Each and every structure of society is provided with a human consciousness and the capacity to act on the basis of that faculty.

The ambiguity surrounding the mechanisms of recognition is confounded with the second general feature implicit in the concept of functional sub-system: the capacity to obtain *gratification*. Sub-systems are seen to relate to each other, and ultimately to the system as a whole, through a process of reciprocal exchange; the contribution of each sub-system to the functioning of the system is not conceived in terms of a general 'spreading' of products and facilities to all other sub-systems but rather in terms of specific matching – input – output relations are such that the products of one branch go primarily into one other branch. Why, it might be asked, must the functional process take this form? Although the notion of 'spreading' would not be altogether inconsistent with the concept of system, Parsons is emphatic that the process of functional contribution does not operate in this way. This can only be because sub-systems are maintained as essentially *human* entities, they operate on the basis of human desires gratifications; for example, the household receives goods and services for which *in return* it provides labour services for the economy.

Such a thesis is interesting in relation to Parsons' critique of Homans. Homans' form of 'exchange theory' is attacked for several reasons, but one in particular concerns its *psychologism*, the reduction of social processes to psychological processes (for example, the explanation of economic mechanisms in terms of 'reward-seeking'). Now although the alternative to a reductionism is, as has been seen, the concept of system and related concepts, when it comes to the problem of the *mechanisms* by which the systems and sub-systems articulate and function, it is apparent that Parsons depends upon precisely the ambiguous psychologism and humanism explicit in the positions he criticises. In short, *Parsons is forced to assign to the mechanisms of the systems capacities he refuses to assign to the systems themselves.*[27] The exact status of these mechanisms becomes theoretically problematic: they are situated mid-way between two forms of determination, the effectivity of culture on the one hand and the conditional exigencies of systems of action on the other. The ambiguous nature of the recognition and gratificational mechanisms is inflated with this contradictory mode of double determination: the crucial role played by these components of the sub-system is conceived in terms which have no coherent theoretical foundation.

In addition to this order of problems, a more concrete set exists over the concept of functional sub-systems: this concerns the mode in which economic categories are interiorised within the theory of social systems. It has already been noted that Parsons' claim concerning the 'congruences' between economic theory and the theory of action is devoid of sufficient demonstration and indeed appears to operate on the basis of word-play; the actual theoretical link offered is no more convincing.

The articulation of the theory of social systems and economic theory is made at two levels: on the one hand the economy is conceived as both a social system (in which the differentiated sub-systems are made cor-respondent with the factors of production, land, labour, capital and organisation) and as a sub-system of the total social system; on the other, the factors themselves are seen to be 'concretely' represented in basic economic *institutions* – enterprise, occupation, contract and property. Both levels are problematic.

In the first case the parallel between the functional problems and the factors of production has no determinate basis, for there appears to be no rigorous foundation on which to make each parallel between sub-system and factor of production. Why, for example, must the integration of the economic process be fulfilled through the enterpreneur? Why, indeed, should Parsons adopt the orthodox economic set of categories to begin with? There is no theoretical demonstration why one factor should occupy any particular functional role and not another, nor is there a rigorous justification for accepting concepts produced externally to the theory of social systems to begin with.

The second step of interiorisation of economic categories is perhaps more problematic in so far as it involves a more fundamental order of problems. Functional sub-systems are 'concretised' through the merger with economic institutions (property, contract, etc.) – concrete economic behaviour is functionally determinate only given its mediation by economic institutions; these represent the dominant value-patterns at the social level, and in particular, economic institutions embody and reflect the value of economic rationality. The major ambiguity here surrounds the relation between institution and functional sub-system, for this relation is another example of *double determination*: institutions are governed by cultural configurations of which they are an expression (hence their close relation to the 'pattern variables'), whereas systems of action are governed by the organisational exigencies of their internal constitution; *the concept of institution is logically incompatible with that of functional sub-system*.[28] There are no consistent theoretical grounds for interiorising economic institutions within the functional sub-systems.

Given these features of the concept of functional sub-system, it is impossible to consider it as a theoretical alternative to existing attempts to conceive economic and non-economic relations; in the last analysis this concept is no less problematic than those it attempts to surpass. It cannot provide a coherent means of theorisation of the economy/society relation.

CONCLUSION

This paper has attempted to consider the extent to which the structural-functionalist theory of the economy, most clearly represented in Parsons' and Smelser's text *Economy and Society*, provides a distinct and coherent theoretical apparatus for the analysis of the economic/social relation. It has intended to show that there are a number of conceptual levels at which structural-functionalism not only distinguishes itself from other attempts from within sociology and economic theory to pose the problem, but in fact surpasses such attempts in respect of the problems it explicitly approaches and the theoretical means it supplies. Beyond this, however, it has been argued that structural-functionalism does not in the final analysis overcome the theoretical obstacles presented by teleological theories of society and humanistic conceptions of action.

On this point it should be borne in mind that this paper has chosen to analyse only certain of the points which are pertinent to the Parsonian theory of the economy. There are two levels of argument which may have been made but which have not been subjected to an elaborate investigation in this particular context, arguments which are in no sense irrelevant to the issue at hand. Firstly, there are the more general theoretical conceptions central to the Parsonian schema, such as the notion of the action frame of reference, the theses on epistemology and 'analytical realism', the conceptions of values and 'ultimate reality', the abstract concept of 'system', and so on, all of which are presupposed in the concepts dealt with here. Secondly, there are the numerous 'concrete' and 'empirical' theses which are presented within the theory of the economy and which represent Parsons' attempt to demonstrate the applicability of structural-functionalist analysis to certain well-established debates in the area – for example, the separation of ownership and control in joint-stock enterprise, the 'entrepreneurial function', problems of economic gorwth, etc.

With reference to the first area it is clear that any elaborated discussion of the basic concepts of action, system and so on would not have been possible in view of the specific problem at hand; these issues have, however, been dealt with elsewhere.[29] The omission of any extensive discussion of Parsons' empirical analyses requires more justification. The fact that the analysis of the sub-systems of the economy, their breakdown into smaller analytical objects, and arguments of a similar standing have received only brief consideration can be justified with reference to the particular objective which governed this critique. An assessment of the distinguishing features and specific potentialities of structural-functionalist theory requires an investigation into what are the theoretically decisive concepts of that theory vis-à-vis other modes of analysis, particularly from within sociological theory. The position taken here is that the really crucial concepts of functionalism,[30] those which serve most to distinguish it as a form of theorisation and upon which its ultimate success rests, are those of structural differentiation and functional sub-system/functional prerequisites. Without these concepts the designation 'structural-functionalism' would be strictly meaningless and the structural-functionalist theory of the economy indistinguishable.

It is for this reason, therefore, that this paper has chosen to direct its critique towards these two orders of concepts in particular. Parsons' various arguments on the economy and the empirical theses which stem from the functionalist schema are theoretically subordinate to these conceptual forms and cannot be adequately dealt with independently of an analysis of them. It is on this basis that the critique developed here claims to be conclusive, that the structural-functionalist theory of the economy and society can be said to devoid of a theoretically consistent and coherent foundation.

NOTES

1. The term 'Sociology' as used here is not intended to cover Marxist theory which, in terms of its basic concepts, remains external to sociological discourse.
2. Parsons' early theses on economics and sociology centre around two major areas: the conception of capitalism in Weber and Sombart, and the theories of Alfred Marshall (cf Parsons, 1932). *SSA* represents the most general summary of such theses, but since this text the only significant paper prior to *Economy and Society* is 'The Motivation of Economic Activities', published in *Essays in Sociological Theory* (Parsons, 1949b).
3. *SSA*, pp. 699–700.
4. The 'proof' of the validity of the voluntaristic theory of action oscillates between dogmatic assertion and the ambiguous and teleological postulate of an immanent progress in the development of theoretical systems. The whole analysis of the 'analytical elements' depends on this thesis.
5. Cf. *ES*, p. 91. See also Smelser (1963) chaps. 1 and 11, and Parsons' reply to Morse's paper in Black (1961), in the essay 'The Point of View of the Author', p. 351.
6. This is seen to be so because despite the reference in welfare economics to 'social' utility, the social is conceived as no more than an aggregate of individual utilities; cf. *ES*, p. 32.
7. Cf. Keynes (1936) pp. 91–5.
8. For example, with reference to labour supply, Parsons argues that there is still a great significance in the traditional practice of drawing labour supply curves. What must be formulated, however, is a specification of the conditions of the labour market which does not collapse into the orthodox reductionism and psychologism common to economic theory; 'our purpose here is not to establish the facts of the market in the narrow sense but to provide determinate sociological standards whereby the facts of the market may be established before rather than after the fact' (*ES*, p. 156).
9. e.g. 'the two great forming agencies of the world's history have been the religious and the economic' (Marshall, 1925, p. 1). See also pp. 752 ff. for Marshall's notion of the two parameters to economic life—the sphere of 'satisfaction' and the realm of 'ideals'.
10. Parsons (1949b); also in Smelser (1965).
11. It is thus not a mere extension of analysis from 'micro' to 'macro' levels as claimed by Martindale (1961, pp. 421–5).
12. Although it must be emphasised that not all social systems are collectivities; the latter are those systems characterised by solidarity (shared value-orientations). However, see later for comments on this issue.
13. Cf. Parsons (1951) p. 201
14. This includes the 'substantivist' conception of the economy as represented in Polanyi *et al* (1957). Although there may be a level of similarity between Parsons' conception of the economy and the substantivist notion of the market as formal economising, the determination of this sphere in the latter is not approached by means the concept of structural differentiation but in altogether more ambiguous terms (see the paper by Jenkins, below).
15. Although this is an exchange process distinct in major respects from so-called

'exchange theory'. For a discussion on these distinctions, see the various arguments in Turk & Simpson (1972).

16. Parsons (1971) pp. 139 ff.
17. For a discussion of this concept, see Kolko (1959).
18. Cf. Parsons (1966, 1967).
19. Smelser (1959b).
20. Cf. *ES*, p. 82.
21. For brevity, the concept of structural differentiation will be referred to as 'differentiation' and the concept of cultural directionality as 'directionality'.
22. Hindess & Savage (forthcoming).
23. The unique character of the cultural realm has, of course, always been a central postulate of Parsons from his earliest writings, but the only really elaborate attempt explicitly to confront the problem of culture and its primary element, 'ultimate reality', is his introduction to the section 'Culture and Social System' in *Theories of Society* (Parsons, 1961).
24. This is a concept used by Althusser to designate the mode of reading dominant in readings of the relationship between the 'Young' and 'Old' Marx (Althusser, 1969, pp. 54, 54n.). Althusser has demonstrated the expressivist and teleological character of such a formulation.
25. It might be worth while to note the existence of a theoretical position which does not, at least in certain of its formulations, define the economic-societal relation in a teleological fashion; this is a position the outlines of which are given in Marx's 1857 introduction to *A Contribution to the Critique of Political Economic*. See in this respect Marx's opposition to the notion of production-in-general and the alternative concept of *modes* of production. For a recent elaboration of these points, see Hindess & Hirst (1975).
26. Cf. 'Bringing Men Back In, in Turk & Simpson (1972).
27. For a detailed analysis of systematic relations in Parsons' work, see Lessnoff (1968). It should be noted that Lessnoff's critique of Parsons is distinct from that advanced here in so far as a crucial role is played in the former by substantive counter-conceptions – it is not, that is, a strictly *internal* analysis.
28. This point is another way of showing that there is a fundamental inconsistency between the conceptions of the functional prerequisites and the famous 'pattern variable' schema which plays such a decisive role in Parsons' empirical classifications of concrete societies. This argument is presented elsewhere in Savage (forthcoming).
29. Ibid.
30. It is important to register the major differences within what is arbitrarily referred to as 'functionalism'. In particular, there are major distinctions between Parsons' structural-functionalist theory and the 'functional paradigm' of Merton and Davis. On this point see Isajiw (1968).

2 Economic Action and Rational Organisation in the Sociology of Weber

BRYN JONES

The influence of the work of Max Weber upon sociological theories dealing with economic phenomena should be appreciated by anyone with a general knowledge of the various branches of sociology. Starting with Talcott Parsons' attempt to integrate aspects of economic and social theory in his *Structure of Social Action*,[1] various judgements and applications of Weber's sociological interpretation of the economy can be traced in theories of development, modernisation, social stratification and industry.

I do not intend in this paper to offer a systematic treatment of all these areas. What I shall be concerned to do is to offer a conceptual analysis of the sources of Weber's interpretation of economic phenomena. Even with such a limited proposal it will not be possible to examine the effects of Weber's basic concepts of economic affairs upon all his substantive applications of these concepts. I shall not, for example, be discussing Weber's treatment of the economy under feudal or ancient social conditions.

Instead I propose to examine Weber's basic distinctions between sociological and economic aspects in terms of his conception of the 'action' paradigm as the means of analysing social phenomena. The particular theoretical areas on which I shall concentrate are the effects upon Weber's differentiation of modern capitalist from pre-capitalist forms. This differentiation is an effect of a conception of economic action as distinguished by various kinds of rational deliberation as to the ends of action that are conceived by individual subjects.

While various commentaries have been made about Weber's emphasis on the uniqueness of capitalism as a type of society in the modern West, and various writers have evaluated Weber's specification of capitalism's economic forms as distinguishable by their 'rationality', the question of the conceptual determination of Weber's capitalism has scarcely been raised.[2]

By emphasising the fundamental concepts at work in Weber's sociology, I hope to show that his attempt to provide a sociological interpretation of economic phenomena in general, and capitalist economic forms in particular, entails serious theoretical difficulties because the conceptual starting-point cannot provide a rigorous specification of the sphere of economic phenomena. This starting-point is a speculative pre-economic one of innate human tendencies of action.

In the first sections of this paper I shall relate Weber's project for a general sociology of subjectively meaningful actions to his appropriation of certain concepts of economic theory. I want to demonstrate here that his attempt to use certain economic categories such as production, consumption and exchange in terms of their sociological significance entails a specification of modes of economic action which are defined according to a dichotomy between economically acquisitive action and economically 'budgetary' action.

In the later part of the paper the basis for, and implications of, Weber's conceptualisation of economic activity will be related to his discussion of modern capitalism. It will be argued that the famous distinction between the rationality of market-oriented capitalism and preceding forms is not one which can be seriously related to objective conditions of economic systems. Rather, as with the much emphasised formal rationality alleged to dominate modern capitalism, the demarcation of forms of economy results from, and is limited by, the manner in which the human subject reduces to an ideal essence. This essence Weber posits as the source of different actions, and is classified according to differences in subjective meanings as variations in the ideal essence of actions. Weber attempts to combine an individualism of the same level as a vulgar 'homo economicus' with a construction of social relations and social structures from the ideational influences on human actions postulated by an 'interpretative sociology'. This combination involves Weber in a teleological specification of a 'rational' essence of economic action which is ultimately idealist in its source and effects.

Finally, I shall attempt to demonstrate that Weber's critical appraisal of capitalism's provisioning of human needs by the alleged mechanisms of the market, and capitalism's utilisation of human subjects in a 'rationalised' division of labour and 'bureaucratic' forms of employment, is theoretically unacceptable. These alleged characteristics of capitalism are only problems if one accepts Weber's theoretical humanism and its attendant teleological and idealist modes of explanation.

Before examining Weber's arguments in depth it is first necessary to outline the general problems involved in elaborating sociological concepts of a humanist kind from an apparent and unquestioned similarity in economic theory.

INDIVIDUAL AND STRUCTURE: CONCEPTUAL ELEMENTS IN THE THEORISATION OF THE ECONOMY

A sociological theory or interpretation of what is 'economic' presupposes that there is an area, or set of phenomena, already existent as an economy or economic phenomena which can then be examined from a sociological position. More precisely, for sociological (as distinct from ethical, political or religious) concepts to be involved in producing theoretical statements, the economic 'object' upon which this theorising commences must exist as a conception (or series of conceptions) which can be recognised at the same time as 'economic' and not, for example, as biological or physical or cosmic.

In this way Parsons, for instance, can theorise a conception of the economic aspects of society which are principally distinguished by their maximising of available means to want-satisfactions (Parsons & Smelser, 1956, p. 20). In similar fashion, Pareto was able to develop his sociology upon the predication of economic activity as the outcome of logical implications of, and obstacles to, given 'tastes', while the social basis of these tastes lay in the logical and illogical derivations of subjective 'residues' (Pareto, 1935, p. 1442).

Weber, likewise, does not apply his sociological concepts to thin air. He operates with a very definite conception of what constitutes economic phenomena. Weber almost unreservedly accepts the theoretical basis for the study of economic phenomena in terms of the definitions of neo-classical 'marginalist' theory.[3] Several references indicate his approval of marginalist concepts, as for example in the relation between demand and production: 'For purposes of economic theory it is the marginal consumer who determines the direction of production' (Weber, 1968, p. 92; hereafter cited as (1968).

There must, however, be some congruence or common ground in the concepts involved in both sociological and economic theories. Now the basic concepts for most sociology are those which seek to consider social relations as constituted by the realisation of certain ideal or cultural factors in purposive human actions. Although the human subject may be considered as partly 'natural', i.e. having psychological or physiological characteristics, and the outcomes or means of his action thought to belong to a similar sphere of nature, for actions of such subjects to take place they must be at least conditioned by ideas and therefore human purposes will be in some sense effects of these ideas. Hindess investigates this 'rationalist conception of action' in his paper.

Sociology definitely shares with post-classical economics this fundamental assumption of the rational purposive subject acting upon a realm of nature. The conceptual overlap is definitely there, although economics' human subject may be considered as prone to non-ideal, e.g. psychological, determinations of his deliberations. Weber's sociology takes off from the assumptions shared with economics by the manner in which the ideal elements are involved in the conditions and practices of the subject in nature.

Substantial criticisms have been made from within economics of the relative freedom involved in according a privileged theoretical place to the human subject. Some while ago Dobb pointed out the primacy of this concept in connection with post-classical economic theory:

> Yet the secret assumptions are there all the time, implicit in the very formulation of the question; and even though outmoded 'utility' may be banished from the forestage, the desires of a free-acting individual are still conceived as ruling the market and this sovereignty . . . of the autonomous consumer is still the basis of any laws that are postulated and any forecasts that are made. (Dobb, 1973, pp. 75−7)

Dobb was critical of the primacy of the powers and functions accorded to the voluntaristic conception of the human subject, because such an assumption obscured the significance and source of economic subjects' actions by wider relations of production, distribution and ownership which determine magnitudes of value, prices or costs. A different mode of criticism with essentially the same formal objective, however, was also initiated by Talcott Parsons in *The Structure of Social Action* and made explicit in *Economy and Society*:

> We feel that the prominence of this 'individualistic' strain in the treatment of want-satisfaction and utility is a relic of a historical association of economic theory with utilitarian philosophy and psychology. If pushed to its extreme, it leads to a type of psychological and sociological atomism. . . . (Parsons & Smelser, 1956 p. 23)

And in attacking Robbins as representative of such individualism, Parsons and Smelser make clear the omission which this tendency necessitates:

> Robbins refuses to admit that even the individual has an integrated system of goals or wants − he is motivated by an unorganised plurality of 'conflicting psychological pulls'. . . . Taking this position precludes recognising any *higher order social integration of goals or values.* (ibid.)

Thus Parsons' objection to the reductionist tendency in an individualist economic theory is similar in form to critiques such as Dobb's in so far as both stress the importance of another level of determination of individual economic subjects' requirements and acts. However, there is a distinct difference in the specification of this wider structure. Dobb's social relations of production are specifically economic in nature. Parsons' 'higher order' is by contrast one which attempts to relate individual actions in terms of the effects of an extra-economic cultural and evaluative sphere. In particular, this supra-individual order makes it possible for Parsons to include the sphere of ideal elements which were mentioned above as necessary, along with the individuality of the human subject (or his capacities), to make the action of men possible in the world of nature.

Despite his teleological mode of presenting the concepts of preceding theories, in *The Structure of Social Action* as an inevitable convergence, Parsons' argument that sociology can be considered as sharing certain assumptions of individual conduct with economic theory is worthy of note. Parsons' thesis on this relationship is basically that the elements for a general theory (sociological) of action are present in economic theory. These elements are, in Parsons' terminology: the actor (reducible to the human subject), the situation (obstacles/'external' conditions for human action), the means of action and the ends for action—in terms of which means are defined. Parsons also points out the relative underdevelopment of any 'normative' or value element within the economic conception of action. Ends are given as random, as with the unfortunate Robbins, and not defined by an 'ideal' sphere acting autonomously from the natural and psychological level of needs and desires.

It will be argued below that what characterises Weber's sociological treatment of economic phenomena is precisely the way in which he strives to add this 'ideal' or evaluating capacity to individual subjects who are each similarly rational even though different in the range of their activities. It is in fact the attempt to use the basic conception of the economic subject as a discrete individual and yet at the same time make these subjects responsive to some form of structural determination which characterises both Weber's and Parsons' adaptation of the economic concepts into their sociological theories. Whilst their conceptual specification of this assimilation is quite different in some respects (cf. Parsons' notion of system and function which is absent in Weber), they remain trapped within the same theoretical conception.

Both these authors attempt to generalise upon and elaborate the conceptual elements perceived in the neo-classical economic subject as being endowed with certain unspecified capacities for ordering means or 'utilities' for the fulfilment of ends as desires or needs. Parsons' project of unifying individual subjects' actions in terms of a wider structure of values which can exist over and above the individual economic subject is explicitly denied by Weber, although it functions in a surreptitious manner within his substantive arguments. However, there remains a problem of relating the actions of individuals one to another, actions in terms either of their uniformities or in terms of supra-individual mechanisms (e.g. money) which are structural and not individual. So that to the extent to which the solution of this problem is posed in terms of the agency of the human subject (his place in a sphere of nature and the derivation of his capacities in terms of a sphere of ideas), Weber's sociological treatment of the economy suffers from a similar, but not identical, idealist reduction of economic phenomena. The organising principle of economic activity for Weber is not to be found *outside* of the economic subject with his individual ends, subjective capacities for definition of means, but through an expansion and specification of these capacities as ideal forms.

Throughout this paper it will be argued that Weber only goes beyond an atomistic treatment of economic activities in terms of individual subjects and their pursuit of ends to the extent that he raises rationality (as a subjective capacity for individual pursuit of ends), to the status of an ideational societal mechanism. Since, however, the existence of a supra-individual social form contradicts his insistence upon the object of sociological analysis being the action of individuals or their relations one to another in terms of individual ends and meanings, Weber's explanation of the social pertinence of various economic phenomena continually opposes a supra-individual determination of the ends of economic action to the individual subject's definition of the ends of action. It is important to notice that it is the subjectively held idea of economic relations in Weber's economic subjects that locates types of economic agents and types of economic organisation and defines their differences. Individual economic subjects or distinct groups of these only relate to each other through the ideal sphere.

The objective of this paper is therefore to argue that the Weberian conception of an economy is inadequate because it can only resolve the problem of the relations between the irreducible human components through an elevation of their subjective rational capacities to a supra-individual essence. But this essence is a set of ideal forms which are necessary only to constitute individual subjective meanings. They serve no theoretical purpose other than to constitute goal-oriented actions which are relatively independent of natural forces. The ideal forms of rationality – ethics, etc. – thus have no determinate conditions for their existence. They merely appear from 'on high', and hence cannot constitute an explanation of the causes of forms of economically relevant subjective meanings. The net effect of this formulation is that the essence of ideal forms replaces any possible structure of economic relations within which economic activities can be located.

ACTION, SOCIAL ACTION, AND THEIR SIGNIFICANCE FOR THE ECONOMY

For sociology, Weber tells us, 'the object of cognition is the subjective-meaning complex of action' (1968, p. 13), and similarly: 'sociology is a science concerning itself with the interpretative understanding of social action', where 'Action is social insofar as its subjective meaning takes account of the behaviour of others and is thereby oriented in its course' (ibid).

It is important to notice that Weber can in this way, by insisting upon the element of subjective meaning, contain economic action as a form of social action – 'if it takes account of the behaviour of others'. According to

Weber's protocols, social action may be oriented in definite and discernible forms. Certain requirements must, however, be met, before specific forms of action can be constructed or interpreted. One of these requirements is that action is something that takes place purely at the level of the *individual* subject: 'Action in the sense of subjectively understandable orientation of behaviour, exists only as the behaviour of one or more *individual* human beings' (1968, p. 13). This remains true even of social collectivities existing beyond the individual:

> But for the subjective interpretation of action in sociological work these collectivities must be treated as solely the resultants and modes of organisation of the particular acts of individual persons, since these alone can be treated as agents in a course of subjectively understandable action. (ibid.)

Thus Weber establishes a direct homology with the level of analysis of neo-classical economics: the restriction of *agents* to the 'individual' human subject. (In a similar fashion an economy is 'autocephalous economic action' (1968, p. 63).)

A second requirement for specifying action in terms of subjectively meaningful action is that the actions of these individual subjects take place through *their own* meaningful mediation:

> Thus for a science which is concerned with the subjective meaning of action, explanation requires a grasp of the *complex of meaning* in which an actual course of understandable action thus interpreted belongs. In all such cases, even where the processes are largely affectual, the subjective-meaning complexes will be called the *intended meaning*. (1968, p. 8; emphasis added)

Weber's objective here is to define and specify actions not in terms of any external context or situation, nor by accepting any direct transmission of extra-subjective forces such as anthropological, and given, needs (Parsons' criticism of the utilitarian conception), but in terms of a definite organisation of intentionality from a *capacity*, with which he has endowed this subject. This capacity is the potential for attaching meanings to their conduct.

It is not the actions themselves as acts or observable behaviour which are the crucial aspect of explanation, but the complex of meaning, '*in which* an actual course of understandable action . . . belongs' (1968, pp. 8–9). It is therefore a subjectively internal process which defines 'objectively' recognisable acts and their conditions. The subjective internality of meanings has far-reaching ramification upon the conceptualisation of the conditions and influences upon social relations. The pertinence of certain economic conditions is, for example, how, in relation to action, 'scarcity is *subjectively presumed* and oriented to it' (1968, p. 333).

Weber here detaches the subjective capacity for meanings from their objects in the needs and wants of 'homo economicus' and makes meanings the condition for the formulation of these requirements in ends and preferences. In this way a more comprehensive category is established within which to install economic actions. While 'economic action', as a category, need not be 'social action' in that it need not necessarily take account of the behaviour of others (1968, p. 22), what is decisive for economic action is that 'there is a *desire* (demand) for utilities . . . and . . . that *provision* is being made to furnish the supplies to meet this demand' (1968, p. 64; emphasis in original).

There is then a given end or requirement which, to be met, involves an act of provision. Weber is careful here to assert the importance of the 'provision' requirement's subjective determination. 'Consumption needs' and their 'satisfaction' are not particularly important in the sense of being some form of 'objective necessity of making provision'. What is necessary is the belief in and conscious primary orientation to provision. Objective economic phenomena, in Weber's conception of action, do not determine or define economic categories, but the significance of these phenomena for the faculty of 'meaning' does:

> The production of goods, prices, or even the subjective valuation of goods, if they are empirical processes, are far from being merely psychic phenomena. But underlying this misleading phrase is a correct insight. It is a fact that these phenomena have a peculiar type of subjective *meaning*. This alone defines the unity of the corresponding processes and this alone makes them accessible to subjective interpretation. (1968, p. 64; emphasis in original)

It is necessary now to establish the precise nature of this 'peculiar type of meaning'. What dominates Weber's discussion of the variations in economic action and 'economically oriented action' (in the latter case, economic factors have only to be 'considered' or are pursued by non-economic methods, e.g. physical force) is the relationship between ends and means. More specifically, this relationship is one in which *ends* (interpreted, apparently, in the sense of outcomes of acts) are weighed one with another with respect to the different *means* necessary or believed necessary to the achievement of an end: 'If anything, the most essential aspect of economic action for practical purposes is the prudent choice *between ends*' (1968, p. 65; emphasis in original). And in the discussion of techniques (which are subordinate components of deliberately purposive action) the qualitative difference is that: 'Economic action is primarily oriented to the problem of choosing the *end* to which a thing should be applied, technology to the problem given the end of choosing the appropriate *means*' (1968, pp. 66–7; emphasis in original).

How then is end-selection different from the selection of means in terms of complexes of subjective meanings? The most appropriate meaningful orientation is that which is 'instrumentally rational', 'that is, determined by expectations as to the behaviour of objects in the environment and of other human beings; these expectations are used as "conditions" or "means" for the attainment of the actor's own rationally pursued and calculated ends' (1968, p. 24). The trait of *rationality* is therefore inseparably bound up with economic actions, while another orientation of social action, that which is *value-rational*, may define both its ends and its means by rationally relating them to the criteria of some ultimate values (e.g. duty, honour, religion), but in this case: 'Choice between alternative and conflicting ends and results may well be determined in a value-rational manner. [But] In that case action is instrumentally rational only in respect to the choice of means' (1968, p. 26).

With value-rationality, it therefore appears that the choice of ends, as the essence of economic action, is displaced. This effect of value-rationality appears to be borne out by Weber's further reference to the valuations within instrumentally rational action:

> On the other hand the actor may, instead of deciding between alternative and conflicting ends in terms of a rational orientation to a system of values, simply take them as *given subjective wants* and arrange them in a scale of consciously assessed relative urgency. He may then orient his action to this scale in such a way that they are satisfied as far as possible in order of urgency, as formulated in the principle of marginal utility. (1968, p. 26; emphasis added)

The distinction between rational action oriented in choice and pursuit of means and ends by values, and action which is instrumentally rational with respect to a choice of means for ends (which are ranked as purely subjective givens), thus opens up a space for different meaningful determinations of actions. In particular, it allows for the intrinsically rational choice of ends and means to be further defined by the meaning (*sic*) of certain values. Now the 'marginal utility' principle referred to in conscious but instrumentally rational action is one that Weber considers to be a 'typical measure of rational economic action' (1968, p. 71). This implies that this essence of economic rationality may be diluted if other meaningful elements such as values intervene. Moreover there are degrees of the effectivity of values: 'the more the value to which action is oriented is elevated to the status of an *absolute value* the more irrational in this sense [of "free choice" of ends and means] the corresponding action is' (1968, p. 26). However, 'actual action' will vary away from such a pure type along a continuum, so that 'The orientation of action wholly to the rational achievement of ends without relation to fundamental values is, to be sure, essentially only a limiting case' (ibid).

There is not a radical distinction between choice of means and ends ('instrumental rationality') on the one hand and, on the other, the predetermination of ends by the meanings that Weber implicates in 'values' and 'value-rational' action. Although Parsons (1971, p. 664) correctly points to the possibility of some kind of values being involved in instrumentally rational action as well as value-rational action, his formulation is ambiguous, implying that a choice between values ('ultimate ends') could be made instrumentally by the actor himself. The important point is that it is theoretically possible (and is, as we shall see, substantively argued by Weber) that certain values might allow the selection of ends and means according to the definition of instrumental rationality. This, of course, would not be the case where absolute, i.e. rationally inflexible, values were the standards of rational choice. Weber qualifies his instrumental – value distinction himself by saying that 'choice between alternative and conflicting ends and results may well be determined in a value-rational manner; in that case action is in-strumentally rational only in respect to the choice of means', so that 'Value-rational action may have *various* different relations to the in-strumentally rational action'. But they *can* be related, and from a methodological point of view 'it would be very unusual to find concrete cases of action, especially of social action, which were oriented *only* in one or other of these ways' (ibid.; emphasis in original)

It is to the concepts necessary for the specification of these 'concrete cases' that we must now turn – in particular, the way in which they depend upon, and are restricted by, the emphasis upon individual subjective orientations to ends and means according to values or instrumental choices.

THE SPECIFICATION OF DIFFERENT FORMS OF INDIVIDUAL ECONOMIC ACTION

As we have seen, Weber identifies neo-classical economics' principle of behaviour in terms of individuals' marginal ranking of 'utilities' as one form of instrumentally rational action; he goes further than this in his elaboration of different economically relevant meanings: 'Economic action is a peaceful use of the actor's control over resources which is rationally oriented, by deliberate planning to economic ends' (1968, p. 63). The rational element in this use of 'resources' is paramount as the precise subjective form of 'provisioning' to satisfy needs. Weber uses this rationality to demarcate it from economically oriented action which may be restricted to the 'instinctively reactive search for food or traditional acceptance of inherited techniques and customary social relations' (1968, p. 70). The element of rationality, whether instrumental or value-oriented, demarcates forms of economic actions which are individually conscious and discriminating from *physically* or *traditionally* derived forms of action. In these latter two cases the meaningful element in actions is (i) in the case of physically anchored 'affects': 'on the borderline of what can be considered 'meaningfully' oriented. . . . It may, for instance, consist in an uncontrolled reaction to some exceptional stimulus'; and (ii) in the case of traditional orientations: 'it is very often a matter of almost automatic reaction to habitual stimuli which has been repeatedly followed' (1968, p. 25).

In both these cases, then, the 'conscious primary intentions' of action created by the space for attaching individual subjective meanings and that 'deliberate planning' to specified or chosen 'ends' made possible by the mechanism of rationality, is necessarily inhibited, if not eliminated. Weber is also, however, able to distinguish further between the forms of economic rational orientations by introducing a further quality — *Calculability*:

> The term 'formal rationality of economic action' will be used to designate the *extent* of quantitative *calculations* or accounting which is technically possible and actually applied.

While an action's

> substantive rationality, on the other hand, is the degree to which the provisioning of given groups of persons (no matter how delimited) with goods is shaped by economically oriented social action under some criterion (past, present or potential) of *ultimate values*, regardless of the nature of these ends (1968, p. 85; emphasis added)

This demarcation between formal and substantive rationality allows a more precise specification of the instrumental and value-rational aspects of the economic significance of meanings. It also provides an avenue between the strict essence of economic action as rational choice and the wider social influences conceived as 'values'. The influence of the latter is one where it is not solely

> the purely formal and (relatively) unambiguous fact that action is based on goal-oriented rational calculation with the technically most adequate available methods but [where actors] apply certain criteria of ultimate ends, whether they be ethical, political, utilitarian, feudal, egalitarian or whatever, and measure the results of economic action, however formally 'rational' in the sense of correct calculation they may be, against these scales of 'value-rationality' or *substantive* goal rationality. (1968, pp. 85–6).

The intrinsically formal aspect of economic rationality is here contrasted to potentially wider external determinations that judge formal rationality's processes according to cultural *values*. Weber conceives of these wider values as the social and extra-individual influences upon economically rational actions. It will be argued below that it is the impossibility of adequately specifying the social organisation of an economy in terms of the differences between external evaluations and intrinsically formal rationality which plagues Weber's sociological theory of the economy and renders it unworkable. It must first be noticed, however, that formal and substantive rationality represent a continuation of Weber's basic conceptualisation of the object of sociological and economic analysis.

I ormal and substantive rationality are meaningful elements which are, in principle, definable in terms of their influence in the subjective orientations of *individual* actors as were instrumental and value-rational types of action. But on the other hand, Weber explicitly relates these categories of meanings to *wider* social units. Substantive rationality is the 'degree to which the provisioning of given groups of persons (no matter how delimited) with goods is shaped' (ibid.), while formal rationality is a category applicable to 'a *system* of economic activity' in a 'rational economy' (ibid.). These concepts of formal rationality and substantive rationality are then capable of application to non-individual, collectively defined economic actors. It must be noted, however, that Weber's conceptualisation of economic phenomena in this form of rational individualism does not allow him to depart fundamentally from marginalist economic theory's characterisation of economic relations as determined by uniform processes of human ratiocination.

It is basically the same kind of subjective mechanisms of individually distinct actions that underlie, for example, conventional categories of *social* economic activity such as production, consumption and exchange. With production, only subjective desires on the part of the producer in relation to subjectively assessed sacrifices as 'costs' determine production procedures.[4]

Exchange and consumption also do not entail any basic differences in subjective meanings. Both forms of action, to be rational (and *ergo* truely economic), take place *according to* subjective calculations of the extra benefits and costs involved in the required procedures. They are only distinguishable, therefore, in terms of 'the concluding act', which 'serves as a basis for interpreting the meanings of the action' (1968, p. 90).

Different categories of economic activity can only, therefore, be analysed as *actions* having a subjective structure which is rational. The only distinctions that can be made between them are in terms of the outcome, or 'concluding act'. But since this must be *chosen* by the actor concerned according to internal evaluations, the different forms of economic activity can only be postulated in terms of values shaping such selections and allowing the requisite rational calculations.[5] Different value choices, however, involve refinements in the level of rational calculations. What distinguishes between different forms of economic activity is not the relation to social ends but to personal and individual ends. These are classified by Weber as an essential duality, between '*profit-making*' actions and '*budgetary*' or householding actions, which *precede* economic forms.

Production, consumption, exchange, etc., are merely effects of the existence of these two personal forms of action-goals. Profit-making is not action solely concerned with acquiring sums of money nor is budgetary action limited to maintaining households stocks. What is decisive is that profit-making is acquisitive activity recurrently oriented to gains, which if action is rational must be *calculable* while budgetary or householding activity primarily orders *given* utilities in terms of various subjectively derived needs. It is not therefore the economic objects involved which differentiate between the calculations in production, consumption and exchange but the manner of the orientation – whether it is the acquisition of extra articles or an allocation of existing ones.

It is this demarcation which allows *institutional* economic forms to be classified. Profit-making, for example, is:

> oriented to opportunities for seeking new powers of control over goods, on a single occasion repeatedly. *Profit-making is 'economic'* if it is oriented to acquisition by peaceful methods. It *may* be oriented to the exploitation of market situations. Means of profit-making (*Erwerbsmittel*) are those goods and other economic advantages which are used in the interests of economic profit-making. 'Exchange for profit' is that which is oriented to market situations, in order to increase control over goods rather than to secure means for consumption (budgetary ends). (1968, p. 91; emphasis added)[6]

How these fundamental and pre-economic forms of profit-making and budgeting affect economic situations is therefore in the manner in which their different objectives define the means or conditions: goods, markets, etc.

It is Weber's manner of conceptualising these means to the overriding ends of budgeting and profit-making in terms of subjective rationality (which for him defines economic activity) which results in differences in the historical and institutional forms of economic activity that he postulates.

Institutionally, budgeting and profit-making are crystallised into *household* and *enterprise* forms of economic activity. It is here that distinctions in the composite subjective meanings involved become decisive in order to maintain the orientations to gain and consumption respectively.

THE DEFINITION OF ECONOMIC INSTITUTIONS

While both these budgetary and profit-making institutions may be 'managed' on a rational basis and may involve some orientation to exchange, they may be distinguished by the *ends* that they seek and the *meanings* entailed in these ends:

> The business of a consumer's co-operative, for instance, is normally oriented to the economic provision of wants; but in the form of its activity it is a 'profit-making organisation' without being oriented to profit as a substantive end. In the action of an individual the two elements may be so intimately intertwined, and in the past have typically been so, that only the concluding act – namely the sale or the consumption of the product – can serve as the basis for interpreting the meaning of the action. (1968, p. 90)

It is always the *meaning* of the *action* that is decisive:

> The administration of budgetary wealth and profit-making enterprises may be outwardly so similar as to appear identical. They are, in fact, in the analysis, only distinguishable in terms of *meaningful* orientation of the corresponding economic activities. (1968, p. 98)

These subjective meanings are for Weber necessarily tied to the forms of formal and substantive rationality. It is also at this point that the radical individualism implicit in the end-seeking of the marginal utility kind begins to break down in terms of the complementary functions of the 'profit-making' and 'householding' orientations. While, in principle, institutions, as magnifications of corresponding economic actions, can embody either profit-making or budgetary orientations, the calculation of profit-making in terms of *monetary calculations* as a formally rational activity distinct from ultimate ends imposes a radical separation between the two which is elaborated in different subjective meanings. When any estimation of marginal utilities is made in monetary terms, the subjective process of calculation is enhanced:

> As accounting in kind becomes completely rational and is emancipated from tradition, the estimation of marginal utilities in terms of want encounters grave complications, whereas if it were carried out in terms of monetary wealth and income it would be relatively simple. (1968, p. 88)

If money's appearance makes calculation more effective in the general mode of utility ranking, for profit-making such calculation has even more radical implications:

> There is a form of monetary accounting which is peculiar to rational economic profit-making; namely, 'capital accounting'. Capital ac-

counting is the valuation and verification of opportunities for profit and of the success of profit-making activity by means of a *valuation* of the total assets (goods and money) of the enterprise at the beginning of a profit-making venture, and comparison of this with a similar valuation of the assets still present and newly acquired at the end of the process. . . . (1968, p. 91)

Questions of specifically 'capital accounting' forms of profit-making are therefore made in terms of the values which allow definition of the different ends of profit-making and budgetary action. Consider the example of the co-operative mentioned above where it is difficult to distinguish between budgeting and profit-making orientations.

Formal criteria may define as intrinsically rational any calculating economic procedures. What establishes profit-making as such is the substantive end or value ultimately orienting the different acts. While any action may be considered as instrumentally rational – in so far as it is *individually* constituted – the way in which *external*, 'value' considerations determine the actual choice of outcomes may involve an interference with the essential individual choice between ends.

Similarly with budgetary action limited to the requirements of *consumption*, while there may be a calculation in the 'marginal' manner of the utilities serving ends, these ends cannot necessarily be pursued in terms of a neutral assessment. They may, for example, be quite arbitrarily defined by subjective wants. ('The fortuitious desire of the moment may establish the marginal utility' (1968, p. 101).)

The intervention of money forms of economic means and ends finally establishes the superior calculation of profit-making because of the flexibility of its ends. For profit-making, money sums become ends in themselves while for budgeting they can by definition only be means towards other ends. Orientations to money profits, where capital accounting is present, posits profits as a substantive end. The difference in ends is clearly involved in Weber's disingenuous discussion of the market:

> It is convenient, though not necessary, to confine the term 'market situations' to cases of exchange for money because it is only then that uniform numerical statements of relationships become possible. (1968, p. 636)

Profit-making via capital accounting thus predetermines the kind of relationships required of capitalist society. In order for capitalist profit-making as calculation of means and ends in monetary terms to dominate a market, such calculating orientations must be predominant. With the essence of profit-making now established in these terms, two further problems are logically entailed. Firstly, individual subjects performing profit calculations cannot also be concerned with pursuit of these moneys as means for consumption, otherwise profit-making and budgeting become confused. Budgeting and profit calculating via money categories thus require an *institutional separation*:

> Want-satisfaction through a market economy, normally in proportion to the degree of rationality, presupposes money calculation, where capital accounting is used it presupposes the economic separation of the budgetary unit (household) and the enterprise. (1968, p. 109)

The second problem is the challenge to the individualist conception of economic activity which capital accounting via money exchanges entails. While exchanges take place between individual parties, monetary calculation as an end means that market exchange is now 'directed by the actions of *all* parties *potentially* interested in the exchange' (1968, p. 636). Moreover this sphere of others' actions is not assessed in terms of actual individual actions but as '*uniform* numerical relations'. While these may express individual actions, such uniformities cannot logically be *reduced to them*.

Because profit calculation in monetary and exchange terms *abstracts* from individual considerations, it is possible to consider it as directed by supra-individual forces which *determine* (via calculation) the individual acts of profit-makers.

Strictly speaking, therefore, this characterisation of economic activity contradicts Weber's protocols about the necessary individuality of social and economic affairs as subjectively conceived and executed actions. Surreptitiously, however, it has enabled Weber to discuss economic organisation in non-individual terms and to maintain a notional adherence to an individualist position through the anthropological distinction between 'profit-making' and 'budgetary' forms as universal aspects of human subjects' behaviour. Before examining the further effects of such a conceptual basis for the analysis of capitalism, I want to demonstrate that it is this speculative anthropology which determines a Weberian explanation of the emergence of capitalism, and that these inadequate concepts define capitalism in a teleological and idealist fashion.

THE CONDITIONS OF A CAPITALIST ECONOMY

Capitalism, as a form of economic activity having the procurement of sums of money capital as its goal, has existed throughout history, according to Weber. The decisive difference of the modern form of capitalism is the institutional idea through which it operates. Other types of profit-making, where they were not concerned solely with operating in money markets, operate through political and militaristic channels, as with 'tax farming' in the Roman Empire (1968, pp. 164–5).

However, such profit opportunities 'are irrational from an economic point of view', as are 'speculative profit opportunities and pure consumption credit' from the point of view of want-satisfaction and the production of goods (1968, p. 165). Where profit-making is advanced via the 'organised entrepreneurial production of goods', however, we have the capitalist enterprise typical of the West'. Here there is an orientation to a *market* of consumer wants expressed in money sums, and neither to political opportunites for monetary gains nor to the satisfaction of wants by non-profit-making mechanisms, as in the 'household' form of economic organisation.

The household types of satisfaction of wants are dominated by budgetary rather than profit-making orientations. While budgetary units operate according to the hallowed principle of marginal utility and gear their acquisitions and productive activities to consumption through this principle, enterprises are capable of achieving a higher level of technical and formal rationality because their operations are oriented to profit. Profit-making enterprises are uninterested in substantive ranking of wants and needs. Profit-making oriented to capital sums does not necessarily operate to satisfy needs but according to certain monetary representations of the objectives of action. The satisfaction of needs which does take place where production and consumption are organised according to capital accounting is only an indirect effect of the orientation to profit.

Weber is here claiming a decisive change in the principle by which a modern capitalist economy operates to provision demands as opposed to other non-capitalist mechanisms. We are entitled to ask how the change from the satisfaction of wants via *their* determination of marginal utilities to the satisfaction of wants through the designation of marginal utilities by the profit criteria came about – especially how the specific actions involved in rational profit-making differentiated themselves from actions concerned with consumption.

Simply by sticking to Weber's insistence upon the importance of subjective meanings in differentiating between action-orientations, we should have to accept that in principle the transition must occur through a transformation of ideal categories held by subjects. As the outline of Weber's specification of action at the beginning of this paper and the discussion of a 'rationalist conception of action' in Hindess's paper show this is necessarily the case with Weber since actions are only understandable in so far as they are constituted by subjective meanings as manifestations of ideational elements.

In opposition to such an idealist determination, however, Weber frequently emphasises that historical development proceeds through concrete and unique causal sequences rather than through the evolution of any spirit or ideal essence.[7] He also specifies various objective conditions for modern capitalism. It could possibly therefore be argued that there are distinct sequences of historical events which can be treated as determining necessary conditions for the emergence of profit-making via rational accounting of money sums as predominating over budgetary orientations in the economy.

Methodologically this position could prove absurd since it would, on its own, entail an enormous narrative of singular events in a potentially infinite causal chain. If on the other hand it were argued that there are certain key historical sequences which are typical of the process, then we can only search in vain through Weber's translated works on the subject. The *Protestant Ethic* essay, for example, only treats the process *after* the establishment of the basic organisational separation. The thousand-odd pages of *Economy and Society* accumulate their typological constructions with only cursory references to the process of separation of budgetary from profit-making institutions, other than in terms of the requisite changes in subjective attitudes. Yet the absence of other specific conditions means that an explanation solely in terms of subjective meanings must constitute an essentialism, since the subjective attitudes cannot constitute both a condition *and* a result of capitalist forms of economic activity.

A brief reference to Weber's discussion of the objective economic conditions associated with capitalist forms of organisation will make it clear that it is the requisite subjective attitudes which determine objective economic conditions, and not vice versa. In this limited sense Weber does maintain his basic position that material and objective phenomena are only socially relevant to the extent that definite subjective attitudes define their significance. If this is the case, however, then there can be no question of determinate development of the subjective attitudes peculiar to capitalism. They must be regarded as developing autonomously. The spirit of capitalism not only defines capitalism for its subjects, it also defines itself. Weber's account of the development and determination of capitalism must be regarded as essentialist and idealist.

Now Weber persistently argues that, subjective and ideational elements apart, there are three crucial objective elements in the formation of capitalist forms of organisation. These are market conditions, available forms of capital and supplies of free labour. Market relations, however, do not constitute a sufficient condition for Weber's conception of capitalism:

> For the purpose of the definition of a 'market economy' it is indifferent whether, or to what extent, economic action is 'capitalistic', that is oriented to capital accounting. This applies also to the normal case of a market economy, that in which the satisfaction of wants is effected in a monetary economy. It would be a mistake to assume that the development of capitalist enterprises must occur proportionately to the growth of want-satisfaction and an even larger one to assume that this development must take the form it has assumed in the Western world.
> (1968, p. 113)

Weber makes other remarks about the easy coexistence of budgetary-oriented organisations which can satisfy their requirements quite competently through participation in the market. There is therefore no necessary development of market forces which will promote the separate emergence of the enterprise.[8] More importantly, a conceptual analysis of his specification of economic structures leads us to ask whether specific markets require the development of capitalist enterprises or whether, on the contrary, it is Weber's insistence upon the principle of profit-orientation in these enterprises which requires markets.

What of a labour force and money supplies as conditions favouring the bifurcation of enterprise and budgetary unit? Weber tells us that the emergence of the Western capitalist profit-orientation is distinguished by 'enterprises with fixed capital, free labour, the rational specialisation and combination of functions and the allocation of productive functions on the basis of capitalist enterprises, bound together in a market economy' (1968, p. 165). Clearly, once an enterprise with a rational orientation is established, then the specialisation, allocation and organisation of functions mentioned here is a question that is *internal* to the enterprise, in Weber's terms (of which I shall say more later). The specification of internal organisation is a result of the mode of capitalist orientation. The market economy we have dealt with. Fixed capital and labour remain to be examined.

Fixed capital can, however, only appear if it can be purchased. Moreover as the *Protestant Ethic* essay shows, this can be 'fixed' with the workers in a putting-out system. What *is* essential is that it can be obtained by 'capitalist' methods so that, in the case of 'clan or tribal crafts', such means of production's 'procurement', 'as long as they remain one's own output, are only tools or raw materials but not capital goods' (1968, p. 154). That is to say, fixed capital must first be *purchased* as capital. This in turn of course requires money capital which is listed by Weber as one of the first 'stages' in the development towards capitalism (1968, p. 148). However, he also tells us that money sums have been available, as credit, etc., throughout history to purchase capital goods and labour services; so the question as to why such money sums were not so devolved to a profit-making enterprise in these other circumstances remains an unanswered question.

It has to be recognised that sums of money capital are *not* required for the formation of enterprises. Money sums are only suitable *expressions* 'of a rational attitude': 'Money is . . . a weapon in this struggle [of 'man against man'] and prices are expressions of calculation only as estimated quantifications of relative chances in this struggle of interests' (1968, p. 108). Money's decisive significance in all market relations is as the formal expression of individuals' subjective calculations. It is a 'weapon', in so far as it allows these individuals to calculate their situation, be it in terms of capital goods or whatever. Its function for the capital-accounting enterprise is that money places such objective phenomena as fixed or working capital into a different form of subjective meaning which can, in turn, orient action. A similar conception exists with respect to the role of the labour supply in the transition from the dominance of economic provisioning by budgetary institutions of the household type, to its domination by profit-making enterprises.

Weber lays great stress, both in *Economy and Society* and in *The Protestant Ethic*, on the importance of a freely purchasable supply of labourers for service in capitalist enterprises.[9] But the precise significance of 'free' labour as a condition for organising enterprise-type production does not lie, for Weber, in labour's productive functions or in its costs relative to other methods of applying labour services. Weber quite correctly lays stress upon one of the social advantages of the employment of labour by wage payment – that it makes the worker responsible for his own and his family's reproduction and maintenance (1968, p. 151) yet the ultimate linkage between labour and the enterprise takes place purely at the level of inter-subjective meanings. Capital cannot dispose of labour in the correct manner unless the workers possess the correct meaningful orientations. In the case of workers oriented to tradition, for example, 'it is difficult to manage labour on a rational basis and production cannot be increased by such incentives as piece rates' (1968, p. 151). A certain subjective orientation is therefore required of the workers themselves before their services can be utilised by rational organisation. In discussing the conditions for the generation of such meanings in the work-force, Weber also shows their true pertinence for capitalist organisation. He says of earnings related to performance that this appeals:

> immensely more strongly to the worker's self-interest . . . [and with] . . . freedom of selection according to performance. *In this sense it has a higher degree of formal rationality from the point of view of technical considerations* than any kind of direct compulsion to work. It presupposes the expropriation of the workers fully from the means of production by force. (1968, p. 150)

The 'presupposition' of expropriation of the workers by force is a completely gratuitous insertion on Weber's part. Clearly it does not matter how the workers are separated from the means of production. What is involved is that a formally rational *calculation* of their services is technically easier when they do not have control of these means but strive according to wage-bound 'self-interest' in their work. Such orientations on the part of workers are *conceptually* required for Weber by the designation of the enterprise's utilisation of labour (and indeed other elements in its activities) as an institutionalisation of formally rational calculation. Weber does not really establish *how* formally free labour has historically come to be associated with capital or what its general advantages were, or are. It is only when the form of its employment adjusts to a formally rational perception that it is a favourable condition for the capitalist enterprise. In terms of Weber's position on the exact pertinence of free labour for capitalism, his enterprise does not require independent supplies of labour at all, but only the possibility of calculating labour costs. Enterprises could in theory consist only of single individuals who could calculate their own labour services' costs and offer themselves profitable incentives as labourers.

With all conditions related to the capitalist enterprise it is their suitability for formally rational capital accounting which makes them, in Weber's eyes, elements in the operation of enterprises: 'Exact calculation – *the basis of everything else* – is only possible on the basis of free labour' (Weber, 1930, p. 22). In other words, any economic phenomena may suffice to establish the capitalist organisation of production. The sole criterion is that these phenomena can be subjectively recognised as numerically calculable entities for profits. The true 'condition' for Weber's conception of modern capitalism is the presence of the correct structures of meanings. Weber does indeed in this instance maintain his own protocols about social and economic pehenomena, but only at the cost of a complete circularity. Objective economic conditions do not enforce or facilitate the correct subjective meanings; they themselves can only exist if they are recognised by these subjective attitudes:

> for example, a machine can be understood only in terms of the meaning which its production and use have had or were intended to have; a meaning which may derive from a relation to exceedingly various purposes. Without reference to this meaning such an object remains wholly unintelligible. That which is intelligible or understandable about it is thus its relation to human action in the role either of means or end; a relation of which the actor or actors can be said to have been aware and to which their action has been oriented. Only in terms of such categories is it possible to 'understand' objects of this kind. (1968, p.7)

To the extent to which labourers or capitalist entrepreneurs were 'unaware' of the function of rate of profit or levels of subsistence in determining the economy-wide levels of capital investment and employment, we can only conclude that by his own rubric Weber must also be completely unaware of their significance in the development of the capitalist enterprise. Certainly, if we were dependent upon his narration of this development, then money sums, fixed capital and forms of labour supply must remain 'wholly unintelligible' to us.

In other words, as I have already argued, the emergence of the capitalist enterprise as the distinct form of profit-making peculiar to modern capitalism is not formed by the presence of markets, capital sums or labour supplies. It is necessarily a development that is achieved by the emergence in individuals of the ideas generated by an autonomous sphere of *culture*:

> Even where the household unit remains outwardly intact, the internal dissolution of household communism by virtue of the growing *sense of calculation* (*Rechenhaftigkeit*) goes on irresistibly in the course of *cultural development*. (1968, p. 376; emphasis added)

The emergence of capitalism and indeed the process of succession of economic forms is for Weber solely one in which different *cultural* elements change. Traditional attitudes are replaced by persistently rational calculating ones in a struggle which takes place completely at the level of culture or spirit and which arbitrarily realises itself in individuals who are the mechanism for perceiving and organising economic phenomena.

This idealism also involves a double teleology. On the one hand, at the level of individual economic actions because the economic rationality of profit-making oriented to capital accounting is defined in terms of a *value*—formal calculation of all economic elements in terms of their monetary worth—other forms of rational economic *action*, principally those forms of budgetary action which use monetary calculations for ends of personal consumption, can only be defined in terms of their *difference* from formally rational profit-making having monetary calculation as an end. Different forms of economic action can therefore be arranged hierarchically only in terms of the extent to which their substantive ends inhibit the formal monetary calculation which is at the apex of the hierarchy. Other forms of calculation governed by other ends can only be conceived as so many different ways of interfering with the value of money profits as a substantive end in its own right.

The other teleological aspect of Weber's formulation of the structure of capitalism is that it renders all pre-capitalist economic *systems* less rational in terms of their institutional location of the formally rational pursuit of money profits. In a similar manner to the differences between the ends of individual kinds of economic actions, *economies* can only be compared hierarchically according to their separation of substantive budgetary ends or other 'ultimate' values from the *institutional* autonomy of enterprises.

In both these respects (of distinct economies and forms of individual economic action), the *essence* of formally rational calculation, which Weber modifies from its ubiquitous functions in the marginalist strategies, is teleologically defined since it has no determinate conditions of existence other than its simple difference in terms of ends of action which inhibit or obscure it.

I now want briefly to evaluate the implications of this idealist and essentialist teleology for the analysis that Weber makes about the divisions and inequalities in his conception of capitalism as a rationalised form of society.

THE INEQUALITIES OF THE CAPITALIST MARKET

We have seen how the market is not a sufficient condition for the dominance of economic organisation by capitalist orientations, but that it does provide a secure foundation for profit-making oriented to capital accounting because of the opportunities that the market gives for purchases and sales in calculable money terms. However, this profit-orientation must, conceptually, be complemented by an orientation towards the satisfaction of needs. Economic action in general is that which is oriented to the provisioning of demands and desires through a capacity for disposing of resources. While an orientation to profit-making is certainly concerned with a rational control over certain resources, this is primarily as an acquisitive rather than a want-satisfying activity. In terms of the total economic situation there must be some place found for the want-satisfying activities. Weber refers approvingly to Sombart's identification of the necessity of both profit-making as acquisition and want-satisfaction for historical explanation:

> Sombart in his discussion of the genesis of capitalism has distinguished between the satisfaction of needs and acquisition as *the two leading principles* in economic history. In the former case attainment of the goods necessary to meet personal needs, in the latter a *struggle for profit free from the limits set by needs*, have been the controlling form and direction of economic activity.(Weber, 1930, pp. 63–4; emphasis added)

This telling passage, whose substance can be found in less direct forms elsewhere in Weber (cf., e.g., 1968, p. 339), clearly indicates the basis for Weber's conception of capitalism's structure. There are two basic orientations to human economic action, the satisfaction of needs and the urge to acquisition. In the capitalist instance, acquisition, as the struggle for profit, becomes separated from the 'limits set by needs'. Profit oriented to capitalist calculation is institutionally separated from those ends of human actions oriented to the satisfaction of needs. It is ultimately this philosophical anthropology which stands behind the separation of *individuals* from their capitalist functions in enterprises, and the separation in the market-place of their needs from the calculation and pursuit of gains as profits. I want to argue that, despite Weber's critical attitude towards the inequalities and inhumanities of capitalism for which he is specifically lauded by several commentators,[10] the notion that capitalism can be defined by a separation of the ends of certain eternal forms of human activity reduces these criticisms to a simple *moral* attack with no convincing theoretical basis.

The critique of capitalism boils down to three substantial charges:

(1) that capitalist rational bureaucratic employment of human actions is impersonal and dehumanising;

(2) that at the level of industrial organisations this dehumanisation results from the subjection of workers to the managerial authority of the enterprise;

(3) that despite capitalism's formally rational organisation of production and exchange, the actual distribution of its goods can be clearly seen as substantively *irrational* from the point of view of many of its members.

The basis for subjection and dehumanisation is considered below. Consider first of all the inequality of capitalism's distribution system. It may be remembered that the market mechanism of 'provisioning wants' which Weber associates with modern capitalism is not one that he was able to demonstrate had any *necessary* articulation to the organisation of production of utilities by capitalist enterprises.

Because Weber's definition of capitalism hinges upon a simple distancing of production as capitalist profit-making from consumption, he is completely unable to offer any explanation of unequal distribution other than a vacuous reassertion of the difference of profit-making requirements from consumption requirements.

The discussion of this issue in *Economy and Society* is littered with remarks about the limitations of marginalist economic theory for explaining substantive inequalities under capitalism, such as:

> For purposes of economic theory it is the marginal consumer who determines the direction of production. In actual fact, given the actual distribution of power this is only true in a very limited sense in the modern situation. (1968, p. 92)

As sociologists, what we really have to consider, however, is 'the optimum conditions for the *formal* rationality of economic activity and its relation to the various types of *substantive* demands which may be made on the economic system' (1968, p. 118; emphasis in original).

However, Weber cannot conceptualise these 'demands' in a distinctively sociological fashion since despite his references to the importance of incomes (1968, p. 108), money (p. 93) and its distinctive power, all differences in the relative chances of demands are only variations in a universal category of action. This is simple human acquisitiveness which in *any* market economy means 'individuals acting to provide for their own ideal or material interests' (1968, p. 252). Whilst this takes the form of a 'striving for *income*' as 'necessarily the ultimate driving force', there is no principle which can give any differential weight to the forces which distribute economic rewards. For income, like any other resource, is 'in the last analysis . . . determined by consumers' demand' (1968, p. 205). It cannot therefore be accepted that Weber's emphasis upon the importance of various possessions between groups constitutes an explanation of unequal distribution.[11]

Marginalist theory does then remain the last resort of explanation for Weber's description of the mechanism of distribution under capitalism because it is the only form in which individual demands on the system can be structured. It is necessary for individual-consumption-oriented activities to persist under capitalism since Weber has no theoretical means of superseding them.

The supra-individual rationality of capitalism's organisation of production and exchange for profit is the only such force that organises 'profit-making'. Budgetary orientations as the antithesis of profit-making remain individual since the ends of budgeting are personal requirements which are necessarily definable only in terms of individual wants.

Since the separation of the two orientations, which are eternal and unalterable, is most clearly achieved by capitalism, it is hardly remarkable that Weber can consider capitalism as a relatively superior form of satisfying consumer claims – 'the experience of the last few decades would seem to show that formal and substantive rationality coincide to a relatively high degree' (1968, p. 109); while socialism is doubly inferior since, on the one hand, with a planned economy there would have to be an 'inevitable reduction in formal, calculating rationality which would result from the elimination of money and capital accounting'. On the other hand socialism would not overcome the universal self-seeking acquisitiveness of the individual:

> What is decisive is that in socialism, too, the individual will, under these conditions, ask first whether to him personally, the rations allotted, and the work assigned as compared with other possibilities, appear to conform with his own interests. This is the criterion by which he would orient his behaviour. . . . (1968, p. 203)

The reason for Weber's qualified critique of capitalism's distribution system is therefore the same as his rejection of socialism. He conceives of economies principally in terms of a host of individual actions which are defined by subjective calculations of shadowy external circumstances and conditions such as money sums, markets and means of production. Capitalism allows the clearest forms of calculation because it allows a one-sided transcendence of these personal conflicts by constituting enterprises which are oriented to supra-individual ends of sums of profit. However, since we have seen that the profit-making/budgetary distinction is a completely arbitrary pre-economic construction of Weber's and the internal structure of capitalism is a purely teleological conception, defined in terms of unconditioned subjective attitudes, the critique of both capitalism and socialism does not have any separate basis beyond a plea for the promotion of marginal utility calculations.

RATIONAL DOMINATION IN CAPITALIST ORGANISATIONS

When we turn to the issues of the ubiquity of the depersonalising effects of rational or bureaucratic organisation under capitalism, and its corollary, the imposition of the authority of the organisation upon its members, similar arguments can be used to reject these characterisations as effects of spurious formulations of social relations under capitalism.

While it is necessary to consider Weber's propositions about the modern ubiquity of rational organisation as the principal mechanism for creating the capitalist division of labour and the depersonalising nature of internal relations within bureaucratic organisations, because of their influence (both positive and negative) within much sociological discussion of 'industry' and 'capitalism', it can also be shown that these conceptions cannot form a basis for an adequate critique of capitalism. It would only be possible to assume there is any reasoned analysis behind such criticisms if it could be accepted that economies can be conceptualised *solely on the basis of the clarity of subjective calculations* that separate fundamental and pre-economic dispositions of end-oriented actions. It is these concepts which require so much emphasis upon the problem of the degrees of freedom of subjective meanings. It can be shown that the whole 'problem' of the ubiquity of formal rational organisation and the constraints of domination and authority upon capitalism's subjects is a fabrication stemming from the contradictory insistence upon discrete individual pursuit of ends and their supra-individual provisioning through the formalisation of economic calculation.

As with Weber's other institutional forms of economic activity, the manner of employment of labour services is decided by the dominance of either profit-making or want-satisfying ends.[12] According to Weber in a budgetary unit, for example a 'household', services will be employed almost exclusively for the satisfaction of wants. In the various forms in which profit-making activities are organised, services are utilised for income purposes or for profits as monetary sums irrespective of the objective uses of the results of these services. The economic reasons for the expropriation of workers in general and the purchase of their services in a formally free manner under capitalism are that such arrangements free management from the substantive 'rights' of labour (including technical and clerical workers), improve its market standing and (perhaps most significantly)

It is generally possible to achieve a higher level of economic rationality if the management has extensive control over the selection and the modes of use of workers as compared with the situation created by the appropriation of jobs or the existence of rights to participate in management. These latter conditions produce *technically* irrational

obstacles as well as economic irrationalities. In particular, considerations appropriate to small-scale budgetary administration and the
interests of workers in the maintenance of jobs ('livings') are often in
conflict with the rationality of the organisation. (1968, pp. 137–8)

Within the organisation that employs labour it is important that there be
no *rights* of workers to the way that they will orient their services. Their *ends*
must be displaced in the execution of tasks which can be redefined in terms
of an orientation to the ends of the enterprise. Their activity thus becomes a
technical form of action (application of technically most suitable means to
a given end). Where such a technical form of prescription of workers' tasks
is not employed, then there can of course be no calculation and assignment
of tasks to the changing ends of the enterprise.

It is only by displacing the other basic form of economic orientation,
that concerned with the satisfaction of wants – typified in the budgetary
forms of economic allocation of effort and resources – that the organisation
of labour services in the interests of another party's ends (that of the
enterprise) is achieved. Preferences can still be ranked by individuals to
satisfy their desires, but their individual pursuit of means to provision these
desires takes place by completely appropriating the task-performing
capacity of individuals as services whose ends are independently determined by enterprises.[13]

The striving for acquisition is thus problematised in the execution of
work tasks since these actions are not formed by the actors' *own* ends.
Weber recognises this distinction in terms of voluntary and involuntary
economic actions; where the orientations must involve

> a specific sense of incentive to execute one's *own* plans, or those of persons
> *executing one's work*, it must be determined either by a strong *self-interest*, in
> the outcome, or *by direct or indirect compulsion. The latter is particularly
> important in relation to work which executes the disposition of others.* (1968, p.
> 150)

Weber predates a whole tradition of industrial sociology (much of it
stemming from his concept of rational bureaucratic organisation[14]) with
the conception that an effective social division of labour by specialised
occupations and specification of occupational tasks within organisations,
entails a problem of meaningful commitment to such tasks by the human
subjects involved. For Weber in particular the specification of economic
tasks *for* the actor and not *by* him problematises his definitions of economic
action ('Economic action is a peaceful use of the actor's control over
resources which is rationally oriented, by deliberate planning to economic
ends' (1968, p. 63).) If the actor must in addition be constrained by some
form of external compulsion, then not only does the rational choice
element become eliminated from economic action in capitalist organ-

isations, but the autonomy of the individual becomes subsumed under external and possibly non-individual determinations.

It is here that we encounter again the theoretical dilemma mentioned in the introductory passages of this paper and also in the discussions of the market: how a *structure*, which must operate over and above any individual source of action or form of individual actions, can be harmonised with the pre-ordained *capacity* of the individual to constitute his actions for himself:[15]

> The primary meaning of work is as a means to an end, or ends, external to the work situation, that is, work is regarded as a means of acquiring the income necessary to support a valued way of life of which work itself is not an integral part. Work is therefore experienced as 'mere' labour in the sense of expenditure of effort which is made for extrinsic rather than intrinsic rewards. (Goldthorpe *et al.*, 1968, p. 37)

Here one set of actors, those employed as workers, act according to certain values external to 'work' but it is in work where they encounter the *means* to these valued ends. The work itself is something 'extrinsic' to the central meanings of their action. On the other hand, the work of these actors is also a means to the ends of another actor or actors, those who specify the work situation (in offices, factories, etc.) in their employment of workers' services. For this latter category of actors, be they entrepreneurs, managers or heads of bureaucracies, the worker is an intrinsic means to their ends: production, administration, profit, etc. Those who are employed cannot therefore be expected to orient their actions in the work situation in the same manner as those who 'see' the work as an essential and 'intrinsic' means to their ends.

The problems of the conflict of internal and imposed actions of subjects employed in rational economic organisations with the simultaneous inherent purposiveness of these actors' 'external' orientations to work, thus stems directly from Weber's assumption that meaningful economic activity involves the rational pursuit of means and ends for *all* individuals and the contradiction between this requirement and his attempt to base the supra-individual profit-making structures of 'capitalism' on this same rational basis. It is Weber's resolution of the contradiction between rational organisation as supra-individual uniformity, and actions as individually derived and located, that is responsible for the concept of rational bureaucratic organisation's internal conflicts, and for the problematisation of these as internal to actors' subjective states of mind. Contrasting rational regulation with substantive and personal interactions, Weber says:

> For every purely personal relationship of man to man of whatever sort, and even including complete enslavement, may be subjected to ethical requirements and ethically regulated. This is true because the structures

of these relationships *depend upon the individual wills of the participants* leaving room in such relationships for manifestations of the virtue of charity. But this is not the situation *in the realm of economically rationalised relationships, where personal control is exercised in inverse ratio to the degree of rational differentiation of the economic structure.* (1968, pp. 584–5; emphasis added)

The mechanism of rationalised depersonalisation can be seen at work in the case of the puritan entrepreneurs of capitalism's infancy. It was primarily the negative effects of the condemnation of *personal* utilisation of wealth which undermined the subordination of profit making to consumption, and the doctrines of methodical duty to one's (entrepreneurial) vocation of profit-making, for the sake of God, which removed traditionalistic standards of fair prices, profits and application of one's self to business (Weber, 1930, pp. 171–5).

In the expansion of such capitalist forms of economic action, the religious ethic having achieved its destructive work, falls into the background to be supplanted by the more general orientation to profit-making as a value in its own right and, more importantly for the problem of orienting the *individual* to such formal and soulless occupations, it leaves modern capitalism with the ethic of vocational *duty* to fulfil one's task in whatever way formal rationality requires (Weber, 1930, pp. 180–2). The complete establishment of rational capitalism depends therefore on a struggle between ideas.

In the non-economic but formally rational practices of other modes of employing human services, on the other hand, different ethics of duty may inhibit respect for profit-making but still adequately motivate the individual to fulfil his allotted tasks:

> The main difference between the utilitarianism of the officials and the specifically bourgeois ethics has always been the former's abhorrence of the acquisitive drive which is natural for a person who draws a fixed salary or takes fixed fees, who is ideally incorruptible, and whose performance finds its dignity precisely in the fact that it is not a source of numerical enrichment. (1968, p. 1108)

It is always, for Weber, a problem of changing or neutralising the evaluation of ends which may be antagonistic to the rationalised duties of office or occupation. In terms of Weber's economic categories the problem is one of eliminating the infiltration of the satisfaction of personal or household ends of private consumption from the strict observation of the task requirements laid down by the organisation.[16] The bureaucratic phenomenon comes to be seen as a universal principle of modern society. In the case of the establishment of enterprises:

This whole development is obviously a precise parallel to the separation of the bureaucratic office as a 'vocation' from private life, the 'bureau' from the private household, the official dealings from private dealings. . . . (1968, p. 379)

It is no wonder that bureaucracy appears as a universal form of organisation in modern capitalist society, for without such formally rational actions it would be impossible for him to conceptualise a society which could calculate economic and administrative operations in ways which did not swamp these by the intervention of atomised self-seeking actors, or collectivities oriented to economically irrational ends.

The limitations of the rationalisation thesis are firstly its vacuity (for all organisations can be subsumed under it) and secondly the paradoxical effect it has of reverting questions of emphasis on their internal structure back to variations in subjective attitudes.[17] The conception is vacuous since it can 'rationalise' practically all collective actions. There is little chance of distinguishing between rational organisations, and even between bureaucratic and certain actions which are not conducted in organisations. Weber tells us that in the practice of law as in the factory there are formalised abstract procedures to which individual actions are oriented as ends to the exclusion of other ultimate values and personal aims.[18] There is therefore little possibility in these cases of theoretically distinguishing between organisational structures in terms of the internal effects of their different social functions.[19] All that remains to distinguish them is the ideational relations they establish among their members and employees, whether these are administrative officials or factory workers.

It is pointless, therefore, to attack Weber's characterisation of bureaucratic forms of organisation because they do not correspond to the specific practices of economic or other organisations. Weber's humanist conception of action means that capitalist organisations are theorised not in terms of determinate economic, political, etc., relations, but rather in terms of the contradictory requirement that supra-individual personal values as abstract and impersonal mechanisms confront the potential autonomy of action of social actors.[20]

Of course, the only remaining way of differentiating between occupational types and economic functions (and therefore the second limitation of the thesis) is in terms of subjective meanings. It is in this sense that Weber remarks on the need for 'discipline' in the rationalised organisation of actions. Discipline for Weber is the achievement of a reorientation of subjective orientations to the non-personal norms of conduct of the organisation. While even here there have to be subjective capacities for such 'obedience':

their conduct to a socially relevant degree occurs as if the ruler had made the content of the command the maxim of their conduct for its own sake.

Looked upon from the other end, this situation will be called obedience. (1968, p. 946)

On the other hand, where the market situation prevails there are different sets of meanings required. Here it is necessary to orient action rationally to take account of a 'constellation of interests'. While consumers and others will calculate market utilities as means to personal ends, to the extent that entrepreneurs are primarily oriented to market situations as direct sources of money sums, as rationally calculable profits, their relative superiority stems from their 'relative immunity from subjection to the control of rational bureaucratic knowledge', the 'bureaucratic control' to which 'all others are inevitably subject' (1968, p. 225).

In other words, capitalism at its most formally rational does not totally depersonalise its subjects. Because of the emphasis on subjective meanings necessitated by the continuing presence of individual actors as consumers or income-chasing maximisers, subjective meanings have still to be formulated.[21] Actions have still be be subjectively recognised as bound by norms of 'duty' on methodical profit-making, and even where employees have to be disciplined they must subjectively internalise the norms that such discipline entails. Such normative subjection also allows Weber to celebrate the entrepreneur in terms of freedom of rational calculation.

CONCLUSION

Capitalism as an economic system does indeed pose a series of problems for Weberian sociology. These issues are presented as the depersonalising division of labour, the domination of individuals by rationalising organisations and the alleged inequalities of distribution in a capitalist market system of distribution. These problems are, however, specific to Weber and sociological theories which accept his position and make sense only in terms of the teleological construction of economic forms and idealist and individualist conceptions of the social relations which exist within these forms.

Intractable difficulties face any theory which attempts to speak, explicitly or not, of non-individual structures such as economic systems from the position of a consistent theoretical humanism. In Weber's case I have contrasted his attempt to demarcate capitalist and non-capitalist forms of economic organisation as structures, with his consistent employment of concepts of the individual economic and social subjects whose actions are constituted by certain ideal capacities for relating the ends of action to possible means. A brief recapitulation of the main points of this paper on Weber's theoretical humanism should demonstrate both its effects and limitations for a Weberian sociology of the economy.

It is not simply a case of Weber's characterisation of the economic basis of capitalism being inadequate. His teatment of any forms of economic organisation and economic system must be viewed with suspicion because of the effects of the concepts of individual economic subjects and the idealist constitution of their activities as meaningful actions. The instrumental rationality of action is purposive in terms of the particular subject's *own conscious* deliberation of what ends are to be achieved and through what means. 'Value-rational' action opens up the possibility of the added determination of the ends by absolute values; certain of these values may, however, be social in the sense of supra-individual. Whatever Weber may say about these values, if they are absolute then they are sets of criteria which are beyond the choice of the individual actor. Subjects cannot choose ultimate values.

On the basis of this distinction of rationality it is possible for Weber to conceptualise uniform social kinds of action which are still rational at the level of individual choice. It is the conjunction of *particular* values with 'profit-making' as an opposition to the self-defined ends of consumption typical of 'budgetary' forms of action, which makes it possible for Weber to construct distinct historical forms of economic action which are not arbitrary at the level of the individual and which form the basis of economic systems.

The calculation of the ends of economic action in money terms reaches its height with profit-making oriented to money sums through capital accounting. Here efficiency in terms of formal rationality is maximised while various substantive considerations traditionally associated with the satisfaction of wants take a back seat. A high degree of deliberation of what ends are to be achieved takes place through values which are not limited to any one individual. 'Value-rational' action (and especially where the values are those of the systematic pursuit of profit through capital accounting) makes it possible for absolute values to define selection of ends without detracting from the mechanism of their individual choice.

I have argued that Weber's is only a limited and theoretically unsustainable critique of capitalism. The forms of action governing modern rational capitalism represent the essence of economic action. Monetary calculation of ends links the pursuit of profit by entrepreneurs and the satisfaction of wants for consumers. For the capitalist entrepreneur his ends are defined in terms of money sums as a value in their own right. For consumers the pursuit of incomes as money sums is a means or utility towards the satisfaction of wants as a substantive end. Because the entrepreneur orients his activities to the demand of the consumer expressed in monetary terms, profit-making and budgetary forms of action are related via different rational calculations of their respective ends.

Similarly, Weber conceptualises the division of labour under capitalism as an accommodation between action governed by different forms of subjective meaning. Entrepreneurs rationally calculate their ends in terms of profits subject only to the extra-individual effects of other market forces, while the economic actions of other actors are conceptualised in terms of the definition of ends for them by employers or employing organisations – ends which have to be subjectively accepted by the actors, whether through other values such as 'duty' or through signification in terms of their own interests (incentives such as incomes).

Weber denies his own protocols about the source of social actions being located solely in the meanings generated by individuals, since the ends of capitalist firms or other rational organisations and the forms of calculation imposed by the uniformities of the market are not necessarily reducible to the meanings of any particular actor. Rather, with the postulated dominance of formal rational orientations under capitalism they can only be seen as impersonal impositions upon any and every actor.

Denying his own definition of the nature of social relations does not, however, allow Weber to construct a convincing concept of economic organisation under capitalism. His basic conception of action only allows these supra-individual constraints upon actors to be conceived as various ideational influences manifested as subjective meanings. Superficially it appears that Weber has constructed a collective organisation of economic actions as rational profit-making to complement the individualistic want-satisfying (budgetary) forms of action, already established by economic theory.

It must be recognised, however, that these forms of organisations are, and can, only be postulated as ideational and cultural forces. This specification of the organisation of individual actions is completely teleological. Because instrumentally rational action may be subject to a choice of ends peculiar to the actor's own desires and to the economic detriment of others, it is necessary for Weber to postulate the capacity for choice between ends as a formally rational process. The ends themselves are determined by some supra-individual influence which will permit of common orientations to uniformly rational behaviour, as in the market situation. Since for Weber only differences in subjective meanings can constitute such different actions, it is inevitable that capitalism's economically rational action as a distinct historical form will be an ideal essence of particular values. Different social and historical forms of economic activity thus become so many different influences of distinct values, which may be distanced in a hierarchical manner, in terms of their different reductions of, or interference with, the rationality of choosing ends and calculating means to these ends. Since for Weber different actions are the constituents of different economic systems, this also entails a teleological characterisation of different *economies* and opens up his position to the charge of historicism and linear evolutionism vis-à-vis 'capitalism's' relation to previous systems.[22]

This explanation is also idealist since the decisive essence is the possession of the correct cultural values. We have seen how the objective conditions that Weber refers to – money sums, fixed capital, the correct supply of labour and a market system – are not necessarily determinants of the appearance of capitalism. In the last analysis it is only the correct subjective interpretations as formed by cultural values of the *already existent* phonemena which produce the distinctive formal rationality of modern capitalism. The *source* of these values is, moreover, only specifiable as an autonomous product of (religious) culture. The self-seeking, preference-ranking subject postulated by marginalist economic theory still remains as a kind of mass substratum of individual actors. Unlike the values that influence them under other economic systems, under capitalism these consuming individuals have *their* desires subordinated to a higher rationality sanctified by a rational culture: the fruits of the spirit of capitalism.

Several writers have maintained that for Weber modern capitalism represents a kind of reified structure for which human individuals are merely oppressed tools, since this capitalism reproduces itself autonomously as a rational system, with ends that are indifferent to the specific objectives of individual subjects.[23] It has been argued in the latter part of this paper that such a conception cannot be consistently presented as Weber's own. Social and economic action are the constitution, through subjective meanings, of *individual* ends. These mechanisms require that even where these actors do act according to supra-individual formal criteria, they still remain individual, end-seeking subjects without whom rational capitalism could not be conceptualised.

Because Weber's differentiation of forms of economic organisation merely represents an idealist addition to the standard economic individual, there can be no question of accepting his characterisation of capitalism. The principal trait of Weberian capitalism is a kind of organisation in which rational calculation of potential ends has to be raised to a guiding principle of the actions of stategic groups in society. The conception of the bureaucratic principle as depersonalising the actions of 'office' holders and displacing the ends of its workers through the *domination* of their subjective beliefs by authority, is only tenable as a conclusion if we accept its premise. It is this assumption, shared with post-classical economics (that the starting-point for social analysis is the natural requirements and psychological abilities of a universal human subject), which Weber only *modifies* by adding an idealist dimension of subjectively acceptable and realisable meanings. Weber's concept of rationalised capitalism is only possible because of these idealist and individualist assumptions. Rationalised capitalism is only an acceptable construction if we also accept that there is a standard and invariant human subject which is differentiated by ideal variations in the definition of his pursuit of ends.

In this paper I have tried to show that the concepts producing Weberian capitalism involve major theoretical inadequacies: a teleology of economic forms based upon an idealist reductionism. Weber's notions of the market, formally rational economic and administrative organisation, and authority resting upon the separation of personal ends from abstract duties are direct effects of these inadequacies. The use of these notions should therefore, at the very least, be critically re-assessed by those who consider such concepts of the economy as a theoretical basis for sociological projects.

NOTES

1. Parsons (1949a) pp. 473–696.
2. Possibly the most accurate presentation of Weber's characterisation of capitalism available in English is Mommsen (1974). This work does not, however, question the basic assumptions of the 'action' conception, nor its efforts on Weber's substantive treatment of capitalist society.
3. Principally the so-called 'Austrian School', taking their lead from Menger. See his *Principles of Economics* (1950), also Böhm-Bawerk, *'Value and Price* (1973).
4. Of production, Weber says:

> Where action is rational, this type of action will take place, so far as according to the actor's estimate the urgency of *his* demand for the expected result of his action exceeds the necessary expenditure, which may consist in (a) the irksomeness of the requisite labour services, (b) the other potential uses to which the requisite goods could be put, including that is the utility of potential alternative products and their uses. This is production in the broadest sense which includes transportation. (1968, p. 72)

> Here production can take place only in and through definite subjective capacities of the individual 'producer'. In this familiar Robinson Crusoe situation only the 'irksomeness' of his Man Friday appears as a non-subjective benefit or sacrifice.

5. Where exchange is involved, what determines the outcome of the *different* ends of the parties is not the structure of objective circumstances from each side (quantities required or costs of production) but the very act by which the parties negotiate. This is 'compromise of interests on the part of the parties, in the course of which goods and advantages are passed as *reciprocal compensation'* (1968, p. 72; emphasis added). The resulting allocation of goods, etc., from an exchange is therefore *compensation* to the parties for *not* being able to realise their subjective aims. There are no external economic requirements which are met by exchange. The principal social constraints on exchange situations appear to be the possibility of their regulation by norms of *tradition* or *convention. Rational* economic exchanges, however, preclude regulations, since each exchange is an individual act of self-regulation; it is 'a resolution of previously open or latent conflict of interests by means of compromise' (1968, p. 72).
6. Parsons' translation of this terminology makes it clear that *erwerben* is a broad outgoing acquisition for gains and is translated as 'profit-making' to show its opposition to *haushalten* as allocation of what is given. The source of these activities is implicit in the rational choice of ends and means. Profit-making emphasises the pursuit of the means and choice between ends as outcomes; householding, the choice between means to given wants.
7. 'Where the *individuality* of a phenomenon is concerned the question of causality

is not a question of *laws* but of concrete causal relationships; it is not a question of the subsumption of the event under some general rubric as a representative case but of its imputation as a consequence of some constellation' (Weber, 1949, pp. 78–9; emphasis added).

8. The unspecificity of market relations for the characterisation of capitalism means that the effects of these cannot be accepted as constituting a critique of capitalism. This has been suggested by, *inter alios*, Giddens (1973, p. 101) and Mommsen (1974, pp. 66–7).

9. (1968) pp. 128, 136, 137–8, 149, 162, 199; (1930) p. 21.

10. cf. Mommsen (1974) chaps 3 and 5; Gerth & Mills (1970) pp. 70–4.

11. This is a common and incorrect assessment of the effectivity of possessions in Weber's version of market capitalism. cf Giddens, op. cit; Rex (1969) pp. 137–8; Rex & Moore (1971) p. 36.

12. The greater effectivity of the concepts of profit-making and budgetary orientations in the characterisation of forms of labour services is clear from (1968) pp. 114–21. Similarly, the technical aspects of the division of labour under capitalism, for example, are constituted by the level of *economic* rationality: 'rational technology could not have come into existence . . . had not rational calculation formed the basis of economic activity'.

13. It should be noted, however, that actors whose own economic ends are displaced because they must initially work for the ends of others do not thereby lose their personal qualities. They do not, for example, become differentiated into 'roles' in the manner suggested by some functionalist theories. Their essential nature as self-seeking, need-fulfilling *persons* is still located, together with their relevant technical capacities as workers, etc., in their conception as meaning-endowing subjects.

14. This area of problems is typically associated with theories of organisation authority and draws heavily upon Weber's legal-rational (i.e. modern) form of bureaucracy. Whether these debates recognise the historical rather than the internal-situational context of this concept, as with Bendix (1960) and Albrow (1970), or criticise Weber (wrongly) for not accounting for the generation of informal normative patterns within organisations, as with Gouldner (1955, pp. 18–29) and Blau & Scott (1963, chap. 2), none of these debates considers the underlying assumption that the imposition of duties upon an innate capacity for personal substantive ends is in any way problematic.

15. The consequences for such a conception of capitalism as an organisational imposition on otherwise free subjects is illustrated in much of the literature on organisations and industry. cf., *inter alios*, Bendix: ' . . . the industrial entrepreneurs and the workers in their enterprises, and the ruling social groups are engaged in social and political interaction in their respective efforts *to come to terms with* the industrial way of life. Each group seeks to do so in a manner that *it regards* as advantageous, or less disadvantageous to itself' (Bendix, 1956, p. 6; emphasis added).

An objective structure which 'reorganises' individual orientations (for Bendix, 'industry') has to be freely translated by the actor into meanings, irrespective of the objective forces at work in this structure. In this way the reconstituted meanings can constitute 'interests', or claims on the objective structure. Bendix, who is quite faithful to Weber's position here, is representative of many such writers on the development of industry.

16. The distinction between personally derived and externally and impersonally imposed meanings is illustrated even more clearly in the discussion of the distinctiveness of charismatic abilities:

> The decisive difference – and this is important for understanding the meaning of 'rationalism' – is not inherent in the *creator* of ideas or of works or of his inner experience, rather the difference is rooted in the manner in which the ruled and led experience and internalise these ideas . . . rationalisation proceeds in such a fashion that broad masses of the led merely accept or adapt themselves to the external resultants which are of practical significance for their interests (as we 'learn' the multiplication table and as too many jurists 'learn' the techniques of law) whereas the substance of the creator's ideas remains irrelevant to them. This is meant when we say that rationalisation and rational organisation revolutionise from the outside. Whereas charisma . . . manifests its revolutionary power from within, from a central *metanoia* (change) of its followers' attitudes. (1968, p. 1116–17).

17. It is only by this manner of problematising the individual-structure relationship as one of subjective states of mind that the investigation of workers' beliefs and values becomes possible; as an example, consider Caplow (1962) chap. 6.

18. It must be stressed that the exclusion of personal ends from official function as means to wider impersonal ends cannot in any sense be regarded as a similar notion to Marx's concept of the separation of proletarians from their means of production under conditions of industrial capitalism, as some authors have suggested.

On the contrary, what is being separated for Marx are certain instruments and materials of production which are specifiable in terms of corresponding levels of technology, as commodities, from the category of one economy agent, the direct producer, to another, the capitalist. This is not a case of the separation of personal ends but of economic appurtenances from one mode of economic direction to another.

The bifurcation is one of distinct economic categories having a determinate place in a system of production and circulation generating use values and exchange values. For Weber, on the other hand, what is being separated is not any material economic appurtenances at all but only subjectively meaningful orientations which are self-defined from the subjective capacities for executing technically rational operations.

It is absurd for Weber to suggest, as he does, that bureaucratisation, as the separation of *person* from *function*, is responsible for the same separation of university researchers from their scientific apparatus as that separation of factory workers from their means of production (cf. 1968, p. 983).

19. Once the autonomous human subjects surrender their own definition of ends on the labour market, then as employees in formally rational situations there is no basis for differentially analysing them, from the point of view of Weber's sociology:

> other gradations lead to the position of the secretary, the engineer, or the worker in the office or in the plant, who is subject to a discipline no longer different in its nature from that of the civil service or the army, although it has

been *created* by a contract concluded in the labour market by formally 'equal' parties through the 'voluntary' acceptance of the terms of the employer. (1968, pp. 944—5)

20. Organisations are conceived as formal systems of discipline. This conception necessarily precludes the consideration of the effects of the purposes of different organisations or their interrelations. As subjugators of human essences they are all, formally, alike.

    The deliberate, and for Weber, necessary, retention of the *capacity* subjectively to accept duties and authority norms through meanings thus gives the lie to those such as Gouldner (1955) who claim to have 'discovered' a sphere of meaningful actions within, and in opposition to, the norms of the organisation. All that has been 'discovered' is the space for such alternative meanings already created by Weber himself.

21. It is not, therefore, the case, as Levine & Levine (1975) have suggested, that Weber intuits the objective requirements of *capital* as an entity having its own impersonal system of reproduction which entails the destruction of the ends of individual human participants. Individuals surrender their own personal ends in Weber's scheme (a) through a consciously rational compromise (exchange) of interests and (b) so that a system of rational supra-individual procurement can provide goods for their *individual* powers of consumption.

22. Kolko (1959) is a notable example of the kind of critique which recognises the resultant evolutionism in the delineation of capitalism, but fails to reveal its conceptual source.

23. Some approval of Weber's construction of capitalism as a formally rational structure has been voiced by quite disparate commentators, who have criticised other aspects of the thesis. Cf Levine & Levine (1975) who interpret this conception as equivalent to a self-reproducing system, beyond the control of individuals.

    Similar interpretations, may be found in Marcuse (1968; also published in Stammer, 1971) and Habermas (1971, pp. 81—121). These authors differ in their precise *evaluation* of the significance of formally rationalised structures in capitalism's administrative and technical spheres, yet they accept the relative *dominance* of 'instrumental rationality' and 'technique' (their usage, not Weber's) as effects of Weber's system of formal rationality. Rather than criticise such a conception itself, it is necessary in their view to search out possible countervailing substantive values — Eros, youth culture, sociology. etc. That is to say, they fully accept Weber's erroneous concept of capitalism. Their solutions are therefore non-solutions to a non-problem.

3 'Substantivism' as a Comparative Theory of Economic Forms

ALAN JENKINS

INTRODUCTION

The general aim and purpose of this paper is to discuss and criticise the dominant elements of what has become known as the 'substantivist' conception of the economy which, by and large, now appears to constitute an important element of accepted orthodox discussions of the relation of economy to society in much economic history, comparative sociology and economic anthropology. Now it cannot be said that 'substantivism', as a position within the social sciences attempting to pose and answer the problems arising from the varied place of the economic within the social whole, constitutes a really rigorous theoretical system supported by a body of work of advanced theoretical sophistication. Its true inauguration began in the 1950s as the fruit of a collaboration between economists and economic historians, anthropologists and sociologists, and since this initial effort[1] the substantivist torch has been carried primarily by anthropologists – chiefly Bohannan, Dalton and Sahlins in the United States. It cannot be said, however, that their subsequent work has produced substantial advancement in the theoretical rigour of substantivism since that time; it has sought rather to refine certain of Polanyi's theses and to extend the domain of their application. Accordingly, the paper which follows may be said to possess a character quite different in some ways from the others here, in terms of the theoretical sophistication of the system of concepts examined.

Nevertheless, the critique presented will, however, be a *wholly theoretical one*: I hope to show that because of specific conceptual deficiencies central to the position, substantivism cannot possibly achieve the objectives it sets itself and that it thus cannot be considered as constituting an adequate basis for a satisfactory discussion of comparative economies. None of the discussion will refer to *empirical* deficiencies of substantivist studies which may, for instance, be imputed to a failure to take into account observable and pre-theoretical details of a current or historical social situation. Those 'failures' which are highlighted are all dependent upon the level of conceptual rigour of the substantive position, a rigour moreover which can only be ascertained by a close examination of those most basic theoretical principles which are common to substantivist studies and upon which the many and varied discussions of different types of empirical economic formations and institutions (which my exposition must, for reasons of brevity, neglect somewhat) implicitly rely.

This 'reliance' is central to the task of all comparative theories of economic formations, a task which has two fundamental elements:

1. On the one hand, provision of specifications of the mechanisms internal to economic processes *qua* economic.
2. On the other hand, provision of specifications of the reasons for, and the mechanisms governing, the varying modes of articulation between constituent economic processes and types of non-economic social relations present and determinate in pre-capitalist societies.

The theoretical value of any theory of comparative economies must be judged by the coherence and rigour of the concepts used in the attempt to fulfil the requirements of this task.

For substantivism, two theoretical elements are important in its attempt to confront the above task, and it is upon these, above all, that the paper which follows concentrates. First and foremost, there are the concepts associated with the idea of the economy as '*embedded*' or '*instituted*' *in social relations*, and secondly, those used to specify *the '*mechanisms*', '*patterns*' or '*forms*' of integration of economies*. The whole purpose of this paper is to show the central theoretical inadequacy of these elements and how this necessarily implies a failure at the level of a comparative theory of economic formations.

After this general introduction to the extension and nature of substantivism and its position with respect to existing disciplines, in a second section I shall outline what I conceive to be the dominant substantial elements of the position to which all substantivist authors must adhere and subscribe. This general exposition of the position is followed by my main critique which *firstly* establishes the central points of internal theoretical inadequacy in the position, and *secondly* briefly traces the specific effects of these deficiencies in the context of the concrete discussion of specific historical institutions, types of economy and their inter-levels, etc. A concluding statement gauges the implications of the critique within the context of what is theoretically necessary for any discussion of different modes of economic organisation – their reciprocal and social articulations, and their change and transformation.

THE FORMAL/SUBSTANTIVE DEBATE

Before going on to the main content of the paper, however, it is necessary to outline the terms of the polemical debate which the development of substantivism precipitated in the discussion of pre-capitalist economies.[2] The importance of the debate stems from the crucial nature of the central question upon which it is ultimately focused – that of the actual theoretical definition of what one conceives to be the economy in society and of the 'space' occupied by economic phenomena themselves. The 'substantivist revolution', as it has been called,[3] initiated the debate at two levels.

On the one hand, in its central polemical thrust it offered:

(a) a critique of what it conceived to be the dominant orthodox prevailing conception of the economic, and of the consequent conceptualisation of pre-capitalist economies (called by substantivists the 'formal' conception);

and on the other it propossed:

(b) the formulation of what was claimed to be a positive alternative 'substantive' conception avoiding the failures of the former and supplying a fully adequate conceptual basis for theorising different types of economies.

In practice, both elements (a) and (b) are fused in programmatic substantivist statements.[4]

With respect to (a), very schematically it may be said that the central target of the substantivist polemic was the conception of the necessary mode of treatment of pre-capitalist economies (whether 'primitive' or 'archaic') embodied in the major economic/anthropological texts of the 1930s and 1940s which attempted to 'fuse' anthropological data with economic theory, i.e. to apply, with varying degrees of manipulation and adjustment, the categories of 'orthodox economic theory' to pre-capitalist socio-economic conditions. Dominant within this tendency were the texts of Herskovits, Goodfellow, Tax, Nash and Firth.[5] In conjunction with the main part of this paper – a critique of the substantivist 'alternative' – I must make a number of points with reference to this negative and essentially critical element of the position. Substantivism intends to supply a fully adequate critique of hitherto existing modes of theorising the relation of economy to society, of the economic and its social conditions; this critique must itself be examined.

It consists of a number of elements and theses:

1. The dominant prevailing conceptions of the economy in society have a central common theoretical core which unifies them as what

Polanyi calls 'formal' conceptions of the economy. Substantivism provides a wide categorisation of the nature of these positions.

2. All 'formal' conceptions of the economy are deemed inadequate for basic reasons stemming from the failure to realise the historical relativity (and of course non-universality) of the elements hitherto regarded as essential to all economic forms. If these elements are in fact dependent upon determinate social and historical conditions for their existence (as it is argued), then it becomes obvious that a prospectively comprehensive definition of the economy-in-general which relies upon them is inadequate for tackling economic forms where these conditions do not obtain. 'Formal' conceptions are inapplicable to such economic forms and thus unable to provide a comparative theory of different economic formations because, for instance, rational maximisation on the part of economic actors is not an essential features of all economies.

In more detail we can say that (with reference to (1) above), for substantivism, all formal conceptions of the economic have the following elements:[6]

(a) The domain of the economic is inscribed as that of 'economising action' involving the rational maximal achievement by the human subject (endowed with consciousness, will, motivation, etc.) of some end via the minimal expenditure of some means.

(b) 'Economising calculation' derives from the 'general logic' of rational action which 'is appropriate to a large number of theoretical and empirical situations; these have in common implicit ends, delimited means and definite rules of alternative choice for the achievement of ends with the stated means' (Dalton, 1971, pp. 149–50).

(c) Choice made by human subjects is induced by a 'scarcity situation' with respect to an insufficiency of means. Broadly speaking, factual conditions of action consist in the existence of more than one use to a means and the grading of ends in terms of preference according to some social standard.

These points sketch out the basis of what Polanyi, with some vagueness, calls 'economic theory' (as he conceives it to be operative in the texts of Robbins, Samuelson, Burling and von Mises) which constitutes the theoretical basis of the operational 'economic analysis' of the capitalist economy.[7] The nature of the specifications of the economic entailed in 'formal' conceptions denotes the universal nature of that which may be analysed as economic *per se*: it follows that the categories so derived are held to be applicable to all economic forms because they derive their substantial content from the form which 'economising' behaviour takes. Economic theory so understood is thus universally applicable; with some 'qualification' it may be extended with success to even the most 'primitive' economic processes.[8]

I have noted (returning now to (2) above) that substantivism disputes this assertion vehemently on the grounds that 'rational economising', as a historical product governed by determinate historical conditions for its appearance, cannot be conceived as an essential and universal element of all economies and cannot accordingly be used as an element of a definition of the 'economy-in-general'.[9] As, for the substantivists, rational economising activity appears as a dominant element of economies only under the conditions of dominance of a 'system of price-making markets', two things may be stated by substantivism.

On the one hand, reference to 'economising' is futile for an understanding of 'primitive' and 'archaic' economies where such action plays a limited economic role. On the other hand, economic theory which analyses the conditions of such action in capitalist economies retains its validity provided the limitation of its scope is acknowledged. It occupies its rightful place as a discipline which analyses sequences of actions of a maximising nature which are central to capitalist economy.

Thus the substantive 'critique' of economic theory (as understood in the above terms), in focusing on the question of its domain of applicability, is a limited and restricted one and does not challenge the basis of orthodox economic analyses provided by leading twentieth-century exponents (e.g. Samuelson). It merely seeks to relativise the elements of the theory and thus 'find a place' for economic analysis; the central theoretical analyses by economic theory of the 'market economy' are upheld and retained.

However, this 'retention' is only possible on the basis of a recognition that the rational choice and maximisation of economic subjects is always accompanied by definitive 'substantive' economic conditions (through which basic human needs are satisfied) whose structure must be delineated – that is, only possible on the basis of the positive construction of a 'wider' conception of the economy within which such action retains relevance. Accordingly, Polanyi *et al.* aim to supply just such a conception by displacing the dominance of 'rational maximisation' in the conception of the economic and economic action *per se*. For substantivism, economic action will always be 'mediated' by determinate institutional arrangements which facilitate the satisfaction of needs.

This 'partial' critique of economic theory and the retention of its analysis of the structure of market economies generates a central *ambiguity* within substantivism which manifests itself most acutely in the substantivist characterisation of the market economy as a unique type of economic formation of which *both formal and substantive criteria* for that which is economic must be used. In effect, a demarcation between 'market' and 'non-market' economies is erected (which parallels the traditional classifications of *Gemeinschaft/Gesellaschaft, status/contractus* as modes of social organisation) in the form of the contrast between 'embedded' and 'relatively disembedded' economies. Later the symptomatic nature of this 'central ambiguity' will be discussed; for the moment, the essentially *limited* nature of the substantivist critique of the basis of formal economic theory is the thing to notice. As Godelier notes correctly:

> this dispute about the definition of what is economic has only a limited significance, since, as soon as they have left behind them the discussion about this definition, both substantivists and formalists can find themselves in agreement on the essential definitions of non-marxist political economy, concerning the concepts of value, wages, profit, price etc. (Godelier, 1970, pp. xv—xvi)

THE SUBSTANTIVE POSITION

I must now turn to the main exposition of the major positive contribution of 'substantivism' to the comparative study of economies, before setting out, in the third section, my critique of its dominant elements.

Firstly, however, what is claimed for the substantive concepts – that is, what is the theoretical objective which substantivism sets itself? Basically the substantivist 'programme' envisages the construction of a set of concepts adequate for providing a coherent and systematic knowledge of the internal structures and mechanisms of different types of economy and of the conditions governing transition between different types. Thus, according to Polanyi, 'Only the substantive meaning of "economic" is capable of yielding the concepts that are required by the social sciences for an investigation of all the empirical economies of the past and of the present' ('The Economy as Instituted Process', p. 244 in Polanyi *et al*, 1957; hereafter cited as Polanyi (1957a)). As we shall see, it is suggested that these concepts shall be constructed out of the traditional substantive idea of the economy as the mode of interaction between man and his environment producing 'want-satisfying provisions'.

We begin with the modification of this encyclopedic (and somewhat theoretically vacuous) designation in the initial definition of the economy as 'an instituted process of interaction between man and environment resulting in a continuous supply of want-satisfying material means'. It is Polanyi and Hopkins who have provided the substance of the foundation of this conception in their 1957 papers.

It is necessary to emphasise that while a proliferation of substantivist studies have been essayed, the theoretical basis of the position – its most basic tenets – has remained static since these early contributions. Twenty-two years later, in a discussion of 'what is an economic system?', the leading protagonist of substantivism, George Dalton, is unable to achieve a higher degree of theoretical rigour in conceptualising the economy.[10]

THE ECONOMY AS 'INSTITUTED PROCESS'

The concept of the economy as an 'instituted process' (and derivative distinctions shortly to be mentioned) composes the mode in which substantivism attempts to theorise two interlinked problems: on the one hand the internal unity and structure of processes and types of action which are distinctly economic, and on the other that of the necessary 'external' relations of the economic with the non-economic (that is, of the economy with its social environments). In order to show how substantivism deals with certain aspects of these problems I shall follow Polanyi's discussion of the connotation of the component terms 'process' and 'institutedness', but by welding the conjoint propositions of Polanyi and Hopkins.[11]

The economic process. The specification of the internal structure of the *economic process per se*[12] depends on the recognition of two types of 'movement of material elements' which compose it and which 'may be said to exhaust the possibilities comprised in the economic process as a natural and a social phenomenon'[13] These types of action/movements produce an interaction of ecological, technological and societal elements through their operation and their 'continuous flow'. On the one hand are *locational* movements and on the other movements called *appropriational*. From the joint testimony of Polanyi and Hopkins the following can be gleaned with respect to these movements which constitute the invariants of all empirical economies.

Locational movements are supposed to correspond to what Hopkins calls 'changes in an object's relation to other objects' within the economic process. These movements fuse natural processes with determinate 'social arrangements' and in this sense are indicative of the traditional essential constitutive features of economies: the production and transportation of objects. By contrast, *appropriational movements* are designated as internal economic processes which entail changes of objects' relations with respect to distinctively social units (such as roles) of the economic system so that social relations of rights and obligations are implicitly involved. These actions, correspondingly, 'comprise almost all appropriational movements, whether these are one-sided dispositions or two-sided transactions, whether of "things", "rights" or what Max Weber called "opportunities"' (Hopkins, in Polanyi *et al.*, 1957, p. 300). Expansive definitions indeed. It seems that locational movements refer vaguely to the bare bones of what is usually called production and (in a purely mechanically transportive sense) distribution mechanisms and modes of organisation. Hopkins notes that 'in mixing particles or masses of matter in Locke's phrase "men mix their labour with their produce"' (ibid., p. 301). In conformity with their specification as having direct reference to existing social structures of rights and obligations, appropriational movements refer more directly (although unfortunately equally vaguely) to the allocation, circulation and administration of goods between and by socially defined classes of personnel or producing units of economies.

While locational economic actions constitute the specific interchanges linking the social and the non-social aspects of the economic process, the appropriational in turn are those which link the economy as a social process to other social processes (and incidentally other economic systems). The internal economic movements thus characterised accordingly are held to maintain *boundary relations* with the social and the non-social environments.

The 'institutedness/embeddedness' of the economic process. Importantly, both Polanyi and Hopkins (and later Dalton, Bohannan and Sahlins) are strongly emphatic that it is impossible to have an adequate theory of the economy without some conception of the necessary social conditions of existence of the economic process. That is to say, substantivists stress the absolute necessity of an understanding of the relation between all economies and their existent supporting social environments. Substantivism tries to articulate this by the famous contention that economic processes are 'instituted' in society or relatively 'embedded' in social relations. For Polanyi, then,

> the instituting of the economic process vests that process with unity and stability; it produces a structure with a definite function in society; it shifts the place of the process in society, thus adding significance to its history; it centres interest on values, motives and policy. Unity and stability, structure and function, history and policy spell out operationally the extent of our assertion that the human economy is an instituted process. (Polanyi, 1957a, pp. 249–50)

What then does substantivism have to say about the nature of *the mechanism* of the instituting/embedding of the economy with specific social conditions? This after all is the really determinate theoretical issue.

Hopkins' contentions must be taken as the *most rigorous* formulations on this question and even these provide only the elements of a 'quasi-functionalist' conception of the relation of economy to society in attempting to clarify the 'embedding' thesis (formulated somewhat vaguely, usually, by Polanyi).[14] His account has three features which are worth noting.

(i) Hopkins makes some attempt at specifying the mechanism which orders economic actions. This is the mechanism of 'institutionalisation' which is responsible for the order which all social activity manifests. 'Thus, what goals are pursued either in regard to the economic process or otherwise, and how material objects are defined (i.e. the meanings imputed to them) can be viewed as patterned by social role definitions' (Hopkins, in Polanyi, *et al.*, 1957, pp. 295–6).

(ii) Secondly, with respect to the overall function of this set of actions (i.e. the economic) as a sub-set of a total social system, he suggests that it provides societal mechanisms through which tendencies towards instability and disequilibrium which are inherent in the social system might be kept to a minimum or neutralised. These tendencies derive from the fact that situational disturbances in the physical environment to the social system must be rendered more manageable. The economy provides an appropriate specialised functional mechanism by acting as a 'reduction gear' in changing large variations in the non-social part of the economic process into 'smaller rhythmic variations to which role-expectations can be attuned'. Tentatively, then, for Hopkins,

> as a boundary process it [the economy] functions to maintain the line separating the social processes which are internal to the society and compose it, from the natural processes which, while external to society, are causally related to the social processes. It performs this function by keeping the fluctuations in the natural environment from impinging on social processes in forms not taken into account by the instituted set of role-expectations. (Ibid., p. 297)

Accordingly, in brief, the economy is the core of the social system which achieves *adaptation* to these external physical disturbances.

(iii) Thirdly, and most importantly, attention is given to the specifically variable nature of the internal functional relationship which may obtain between the economic process *per se* and the different social relations external to it — those, that is, with which it forms a unity by the process of 'embedding' or 'instituting'. There are two features of Hopkins' attempted elaboration of the mechanisms behind this process which must be noted.

(a) In the first instance, 'embedding' and the 'degrees of embedding' of the economic in social institutions derive from the fact that

> the social arrangements that give to sets of economic actions their stability and recurrence are social units of more or less exclusiveness existing at different 'levels' within society. They may be, for example, the roles of which economic action patterns are a part; or the organisations of which economic roles are a part; or the broader structures of which economic organisations themselves are a part. One result of this complication is that *we must expect to see considerable variation from society to society in the 'level' at which economic action patterns are integrated with non-economic action patterns*. (Ibid., p. 298; emphasis added)

In what follows, Hopkins mentions 'the four most evident levels', but it must be noted that he provides little justification for his selection of the 'levels' which correspond to role, organisation and structure as those at which the economic and non-economic (itself really unspecified[15]) must be integrated. However, his conception of the four levels at which articulation may take place is worth noting for its attempt to throw light on Polanyi's theses in trying to *specify* fully the mode of articulation of the economic and non-economic. These are as follows.

Firstly, and at the level of the 'maximum embeddedness',

> economic actions are carried out in roles that are constituted pre-dominantly by actions having negligible effects on the economic process. The basic values defining activity in such roles . . . are not likely to be primarily oriented to the economic process, so that economic actions are closely integrated with non-economic considerations. (Ibid., p. 298)

Here the 'non-economic' intervenes in the organisation of economic actions through the criterion of role-membership. The carrying out of actual economic activities by subjects is organised according to the type of role occupied. The specification that production of a certain article, say, be carried on only by those occupants of specific religious roles, is an example.

Secondly, at a slightly lower level of 'embeddedness', economic roles may be units of non-economic structures of roles. In this case, the non-economic intervenes at the level of the structural organisation of economic roles themselves. An example may be the organisation of the production function according to political role so that only certain modes of organisation of production (i.e. those specified by the overall political structure) may prevail.

Thirdly, the non-economic intervenes at the level of economic organisation (factory production unit, plant, etc.) units. All Hopkins can specify here is that the non-economic makes its determination felt by its existence as a structural context modifying the behaviour of the economic organisation-units (he cites the example of an Israeli commune – a productive (purely economic) organisational unit within a non-economic structural unit).

Finally, we have the level of 'relative disembeddedness' at which the economic is more or less independent of non-economic determination. Here the dominant mode of organisation of the activity of economic units or organisations is itself economic in orientation; intervention of the non-economic takes place minimally and only in so far as economic and non-economic are integrated by participation in a system of common values which define elements of the roles entailed at both levels. The classic example, of course, is the 'market economy'. Hopkins concludes that

as the above description of system levels suggests, 'embeddedness' is a matter of more or less, at one end being economies whose constituent actions are patterned through their occurrence in non-economic roles, at the other end, those economies organised through such economic institutions as fluctuating prices and centralised planning. (Ibid., p. 299)

(b) However, a second specification of 'embedding' must be noted. While the economic process as a whole may be instituted at different levels from society to society, each representing a different degree of 'embedding', it is also possible that within *one* society the two component processes which substantivism specifies as forming the unity of the economic sub-system (that is, the locational and appropriational movements referred to above) may *each* be instituted at different societal levels accordingly. This raises significantly the complexity of the designation of 'embedding' by confounding the simplistic thesis that it is possible to specify with relative ease the overall nature of the instituting of the economic in the non-economic by using simple indices. If the economic process is characterised as structured into distinct types of actions and movements, then a concept of the integration of economic and non-economic (if it is to be rigorous) must be able to specify the conditions and modes of articulation of each sub-set of movements/actions (locational and appropriational) with a determinate sphere of the non-economic. Unfortunately, Hopkins *et al.* are unable to provide such a specification; the former suggests an empirical exemplification of his thesis,[16] but little theoretically.

INSTITUTING/EMBEDDING AND 'MECHANISMS OF INTEGRATION'

If the 'embedding thesis' is central to substantivist work, then no less substantially important is the conception of 'mechanisms of integration' which in practice express empirically specific aspects of the institutedness of the economy within the content of existing social conditions. Thus

> a study of how empirical economies are instituted should start from the way in which the economy acquires unity and stability, that is the interdependence and recurrence of its parts. In practice this is achieved through a combination of a very few patterns which may be called 'forms of integration'. Since they occur side by side on different levels and in different sectors of the economy it may often be impossible to select one of them as dominant so that they could be employed for a classification of empirical economies as a whole. Yet by differentiating between sectors and levels of the economy these forms offer a means of *describing* the economy in comparatively simple terms thereby introducing order into endless variation.
>
> Empirically we find the *main* patterns to be *reciprocity, redistribution and*

exchange. . . . (Polanyi, 1957a, p. 250; emphasis added)

Substantivism posits these three main mechanisms, along with a fourth called 'householding' (which seems to be less important than the others in substantivist texts), as the 'patterns which integrated sets of economic movements manifest' – they are the given empirical realisations of the modes in which the economic and the non-economic are integrated. It follows then that (consistent with what has just been said about 'embedding') these mechanisms *ought* to be the products of complex articulations between the two types of movement/levels of the economic process and a spectrum of non-economic conditions – articulations, more-over, which vary as described above.

Hopkins' *merit* is caution in realising the dangers of the absence of any substantial theorisation of these articulations. Accordingly he states that

> *the theoretical underpinnings of the 'forms of integration' have not been clearly stated* – so that at times the 'forms' are used to refer to locational changes of objects, at other times appropriational changes and occasionally to both – and need to be developed if the concepts are to be basic tools as well as *pragmatically useful designations*. (Hopkins, in Polanyi *et al.*, 1957 p. 302; emphasis added)

In the twenty-two years since these lines were written it cannot be said that this advice has been taken. Substantivist economic anthropology has in this time failed to develop theoretically in this direction. But what of the patterns themselves? They are conceived as 'socio-economic transactional modes', 'patterns' or 'forms' (a variety of names are used in substantivist texts) and vaguely held to operate in the following fashion.

Firstly, *reciprocity*. Here the integration of the economic takes place through the organisation of its constituent processes on the basis of a transactional connection between symmetrically placed social groups which constitute its institutional preconditions. Economic movements may take place between the 'correlative points' of symmetrically placed social units and it is possible for reciprocal linkage to effect a complex interconnection by acting in accordance with two or more axes of organisation. The descriptive accounts of Malinowski, Thurnwald and Mauss[17] are usually cited for exemplifications of the scope of the effectivity of the mechanism within certain types of primitive society (where kinship, ritual gift-exchange, etc., impinge upon the organisation of economic activities). Marshall Sahlins' later discussion of *types* of reciprocity is an attempt to expand and develop substantivist conceptions of the different modes of operation of this mechanism drawing on the support of further and more detailed ethnographic accounts.[18] Some mention is also made of the second mechanism, *redistribution* (Sahlins calls it 'pooling', cf. Sahlins, 1974, p. 188).

In this case it is the social precondition of *centricity* and not symmetry which the mechanism utilises as a means to the effective organisation of the internal movements of the economic process. Given a modicum of variation in types of centricity in social organisation, it follows that there will be corresponding variation at the level of realisation of the mechanism, albeit the same principle of action being manifested. Thus in examples discussed by Sahlins:

> the everyday variety of redistribution is familial pooling of food. The principle suggested by it is that products of collective effort in provisioning are pooled: and especially should the cooperation entail division of labour. Stated so, the rule applies not only to *householding* but to higher-level cooperation as well as to groups larger than households that develop for some task of procurement . . . say buffalo impounding in the North plains or netting fish in Polynesian society. With qualifications . . . the principle remains at the higher as well as at the lower level: goods collectively procured are distributed through the collectivity. (Sahlins, 1974, p. 189)

For Polanyi it is possible to assert that this principle occurs 'for many reasons on all institutional levels from the primitive hunting tribe to the vast storage systems of Egypt, Babylonia and Peru'. It is possible for the mechanism, given the requisite social condition of centricity, to 'integrate groups at all levels and at all degrees of permanence' from the state to smaller units in so far as the allocation of goods is collected and is distributed according to custom, law or central decision in a redistributive flow.

Exchange is the *third* mechanism. In this case the definite institutional requirements are described as a 'system of price-making markets' which entail a regulated flow of economic elements and of commodities between economic units. Polanyi schematically suggests three variants: 'operational' exchange, 'decisional' exchange and 'integrative' exchange. The operational variant corresponds to the locational movements entailed in the economy while both decisional and integrative variants correspond to the appropriational. For the decisional variant the rate of exchange is described as 'set', for the integrative it is 'bargained'.

Where exchange 'integrates' an economy (as, it is held, in the case of modern capitalism) it is integrated in 'a strictly economic sense' and 'Labour and natural resources are brought together, moved and allocated to specific lines of production in response to profitability as measured by money cost and money-price' (Dalton, 1971, p. 26).

Finally, we have the mechanism called *householding* (which seems to be less important than the previous three). Polanyi notes that 'An historically important fourth pattern might be seen in householding, that is, the manner in which a peasant economy or a manorial estate is run, though formally this is actually redistribution on a smaller scale' (Dalton (ed.) 1968, pp. 307–8). The brief characterisations available of this mechanism reveal the following. Householding is in operation when locational and appropriational movements are organised to the end of 'production for one's own use' ('catering for the needs of the household'). Empirically manifest only with the appearance of advanced levels of agriculture, the principle requires minimally the existence of an institutional pattern which Polanyi calls 'the closed group' (be it family, settlement or manor). Given this institutional nucleus, production and storing is geared to the satisfaction of the wants of the internal members of the nucleus, as is the redistributive flow of provisions which is logically necessitated if the group is to reproduce itself.[19] The principle can be effectively realised in many forms. On the one hand the nature of the focus of the institutional nucleus may vary between sex (patriarchal family organisation), locality (village settlement) or political power (seigneurial manor), and on the other hand the internal organisation of the group itself may vary between despotism (Roman *familia*) and democracy (South Slav *zadruga*) and be either large (Carolingian magnates) or small (peasant household). After this brief categorisation of the mechanisms of integration, the following important points should be noted.

Firstly, each is a *manifestation* of one or more aspects of the mode of interrelation of the economic with the non-economic in society or of the mode in which the economy is 'instituted/embedded'. Accordingly, each exemplifies a certain manner of structuring of either locational or appropriational movements, or it seems both, in conjunction with certain definite social preconditions which each requires. Only if these institutional conditions (e.g. symmetrical social units, group centricity, etc.) are satisfied can the mechanisms be realised and integrative effect be achieved.

Secondly, empirically *any number* of the mechanisms may exist simultaneously *in combination* within a particular social system, each contributing in a distinct fashion to the overall total unity of economy and society. However, it is suggested that in the last analysis one mechanism in particular will tend to exert a dominant integrative effect. Thus, while Western capitalism, for example, may be conceived as structured by all three mechanisms simultaneously, 'market exchange' tends to assert overall hegemony within economic organisation, in so far as it dominates the organisation of locational and appropriational movements. In the same way, for other economies, other combinations of mechanisms exist in which one in particular exerts a dominant influence while others play a subordinate role. It follows that it is possible for substantivism to elaborate a *typology of economic systems* on the basis of the different types of combination and articulation of mechanisms present and exerting different modes of structuration.[20]

The concepts of these mechanisms occupy an extremely important position within virtually all substantivist studies, this must be made plain, for it is only on the basis of the recognition of the presence or absence of specific mechanisms that it becomes possible to supply *primarily* (as I have just mentioned) a typology and classification of different economic systems, but also *secondly* a formulation of the overall significance of the isolated economic institutions conventionally studied by economic anthropology, economic history and comparative sociology (such as forms of commerce and trade, the development of different types of market and currencies etc.), with respect to the different systems. Thus as Dalton notes with respect to institutions such as the Kula gift trade, silent trade, slave trade, bridewealth and bloodwealth, types of markets, etc., substantivism holds that 'Polanyi's schema attempts to make analytical sense of these by suggesting that trade, money and markets take only a few organisational forms in traditional economies, *depending upon which of the transactional modes ("patterns of integration") dominates'* (Dalton, 1971, p. 29; emphasis added). Parenthetically, it must always be stressed that the representation of this or that empirical economic institution is *always* contingent upon the concepts and theoretical means which attempt to delineate the space, structure and elements of the economic, its social conditions of existence, and so on and so forth. Accordingly the double emphasis of substantivist studies – on the one hand a conception of the types of economic system under consideration, and on the other a conception of the significance of isolated institutions within these systems – is directly dependent for its value upon the central concepts to which I have referred, and can be judged on the basis of the theoretical rigour of these concepts, as we shall see. If the concepts are theoretically inadequate, then this must have crucial effects on the worth of specific 'empirical' discussions which are determined by them. Later on it will be demonstrated that this is indeed the case in a large proportion of substantivist work.

For the moment, however, something must be said about the relation between the transactional modes/patterns of integration and

(a) the typology of economic systems;
(b) the consequent discussion (with respect to these systems) of trade, types of money and markets;
(c) the treatment of 'development' and 'transition' of economic systems and forms.

ECONOMIC SYSTEMS, MECHANISMS AND ELEMENTS, TRANSITION

Polanyi states that

Traditional groupings of economies which roughly approximate a classification *according to the dominant forms of integration* are illuminating.

What historians are wont to call economic systems seem to fall fairly into
this pattern. Dominance of a form of integration is here identified with
the degree to which it comprises land and labour in society. . . .
(Polanyi, 1957a, p. 255)

Now while empirical economies are held to receive their form from the
conjoint effect of the operation of a combination of patterns of integration
(one exerting dominance), Polanyi stresses that *no temporal order* exists
between patterns. The conditions of their appearance are not goverened
by a 'theory of stages of development'; ultimately the patterns or
mechanisms may be realised and operate alongside other mechanisms in
any order of succession and dominance, provided that requisite institutional conditions obtain.

In general, most substantivist discussions are *dominated* by the conception of the mechanisms of integration in the sense that, as well as the fact
that (a) any empirical economy and elements relevant to it (such as trade,
markets, money) are defined by reference to a specific combination of
mechanisms, also (b) transition of any economy is conceived as a change
in the order of articulation and dominance of the mechanisms or as the
instantiation of a new dominant mechanism.

(a) The first point is easily illustrated if one considers Dalton's
classification of the types of 'traditional economy' (in the paper Theoretical Issues in Economic Anthropology') and by Bohannan and Dalton's
joint discussion of the different types of economy in African societies (in
Bohannan and Dalton's introduction to *Markets in Africa* and in Dalton's
paper 'Traditional Production in African Economies').[21] Various empirical economies manifest different modes of combination and orders of
dominance of the mechanisms. In the first paper a classification is
presented which differentiates:

1. Primitive bands and some tribes all without a centralised polity (e.g.
   the Tiv).
2. Primitive tribes with centralised polities: chiefdoms, kingdoms,
   empires (Nupe, Bantu, Inca, Dahomey).
3. Peasant economies (Malay fisherman, Latin American Peasantries).

In each case one of the mechanisms is integrative with respect to
locational and appropriational movements while others may be present on
a subordinate footing. For example, the difference between types 1 and 2
consists in the displacement of reciprocity by redistribution as the
'dominant' mechanism using a centralised authority structure as the
'institutional centricity' necessary for its realisation. Similarly, type 3 is
distinguished by the importance which the mechanism of market exchange
constitutes within this economic form: 'It is the relative importance of
markets for resources and products and for cash transactions which is the

principal difference between peasant and primitive economies' (Dalton, 1971, p. 95). In the discussions of primitive African economies, once more the mechanisms assume a determinate importance: the point is again reiterated that absence of the mechanism of market exchange as the dominant mode of economic organisation (and hegemony of reciprocity or redistribution) is crucial.[22] In most of these societies the market exchange mechanism is never dominant and integrative although markets may function at the periphery of substantial economic organisation.[23]

Polanyi's monograph on the archaic kingdom of Dahomey[24] provides a second illustration. Here again the respective spheres of operation of the different mechanisms are located, and some attempt made to establish their relative degrees of importance in the overall economic organisation. Here we are told that

> In the state sphere *redistribution* was the main pattern. That is the movement of goods, actual or dispositional, was toward a centre and out of it again. In the non-state sphere, the familial and local orbit, *reciprocity* and *householding* were the dominant patterns. In the absence of a market system *exchange* was only secondary since it did not comprise labour and land and even commodity markets were isolated and did not form a system. (Polanyi, 1966, p. 32; emphasis added)

In a similar way the many considerations of the nature and degrees of development of types of trade, money and markets considered as 'elements' of economies, pose their problems in terms relative to the existence and dominance of the mechanisms in particular economies. Generally the prescriptions contained in Polanyi's essay 'The Economy as Instituted Process' have been adhered to, if expanded in content slightly, by others after him.

Polanyi differentiates 'trade', 'money uses' and 'market elements' into categories which correspond to reciprocative, redistributive and 'catallactic' modes of organisation of economies. Therefore, types of trade thus differentiated correspond to the modes of integration which link partners to transaction: gift trade, administered trade, market trade. Similarly, different types of money are defined as different types of 'operational' devices within 'sociologically determinant situations[25] whose reality is moulded by the specificity of the mechanisms: different types of 'money use' correlate with different substantive economic structures – the 'payment' use to an economy dominantly integrated by reciprocity, the 'standard' or 'accounting' use to one integrated by redistributive organisation, and the 'exchange/equivalency' use, of course, to the one suffused by market exchange.[26] This can be seen in more detail in Polanyi's 'The Semantics of Money Uses' (Dalton (ed.), 1968) and Dalton's 'Primitive Money' (Dalton, 1971).

My exposition must be necessarily brief at this point – the whole aim is to demonstrate the determinacy of the 'mechanisms of integration' within the substantivist definition of types of economic institution. While substantivism is not *reducible* to the concepts of the mechanisms, without them many subsequent definitions would be devoid of substantial theoretical support – this is the essential point. Substantivists are furthermore at great pains to assert that a diversity in types of substantive economic organisation may generate a diversity of market institutions: the occurrence of types of market is not tied restrictively to a situation (e.g. modern capitalism) where only one particular type of exchange (called by Polanyi *et al.* 'integrative') is dominant. The latter type of exchange 'is typically limited to a definite type of market institution, namely *price-making markets*' (Polanyi, 1957b, p. 267; emphasis added). In so far as other modes of exchange are isolatable, other and quite distinct types of market institution are possible economic configurations provided that the requisite 'elements' (apart from certain modes of 'exchange relation') are socially in evidence.[27] In the last analysis, the *variant forms* of exchange are absolutely central to the characterisation of the forms that market institutions may assume.

(b) The determinacy of the 'mechanisms of integration' within substantivism is no less in evidence in the places where discussion turns to the problem of explaining the transition between, and change of, economic forms. Polanyi's text *The Great Transformation* (Polanyi, 1944) analyses aspects of the transition between feudalism and capitalism and its mode of discussion may be regarded as illustrative of the way substantivism is conceptually constrained in its attempts to tackle the mechanisms which govern transition.

All that can be provided at the moment is an indication of the way Polanyi is forced by his conceptual apparatus to think the transition from feudalism to capitalism in a certain specific manner. (A detailed analysis of *The Great Transformation* cannot be attempted here.) Polanyi's particular problem is to explain the conditions which governed the 'emergence' of a quite unprecedented form of economic organisation (the 'market economy') – one, that is, which is dominated by the integrative variant of exchange discussed above, linked to a system of price-making markets. This 'emergence' is also of course the site of transition from a situation in which the economy is 'embedded' in social relations, to one where the 'economy' is relatively independent of the latter and more or less 'disembedded'. For my purposes, only the following key points can be made with respect to the discussion:

(i) Its main theoretical problem is *a change in the functional relationship of economy to society* (and measuring the effects of this change). Transition is from an 'embedded' economy to one which constitutes a more or less autonomous and self-regulating system through a new mode of instituting and organising the economic process.

(ii) the empirical indices of this *transformation in the mode of instituting of the economic process* are discerned in the change in the relations of combination and dominance of the types of forms (or mechanism) of integration; the focus of the emergence of capitalism out of feudalism is the *accession to dominance* of the mechanism of 'exchange' and its subordination of the other mechanisms (which may remain marginally operative within limited areas of the economy, viz. tax as redistributive payment, for example) to its rule. Whilst most of Polanyi's text gives a descriptive account of the societal effects of the economic transformation, it cannot be doubted that its central theoretical problem consists in explaining how and why this 'accession to dominance' takes place. Above all, the theoretical value of the account of transition is contingent upon the extent to which this problem is solved.

All substantive discussions of transition and change in fact face similar theoretical constraints imposed by the conception of the mechanisms (and their interrelation) which are so central to the problematic. Once again we find that substantivism depends directly upon *a central theoretical core*, and it is this main theoretical platform which ought to be the focus of an adequate critique. Such a mode of criticism is set out in the following section.

CRITIQUE

From the tenor of what has already been said, the main lines of criticism will be evident. If, above, I have stressed at some length the importance for substantivism of the conception of the 'institutedness' or 'embeddedness' of the economy in social relationships, this is because in it we have the strategic core of the way substantivism must conceptualise the relation of economy to society. If substantivism is inadequate and even impossible for a comparative theory of economic systems, it is because of the *particular* inadequacy of this conception along with associated ones which are in some way its derivatives.

The so-called 'alternative' set of concepts which Polanyi, Hopkins, Dalton *et al*. provide for the analysis of pre-capitalist economies furnishes us with only the most basic elements of a 'quasi-functionalist' conception of the relation of economy to society which cannot possibly fulfil the claims advanced for it and the objectives which early substantivism envisaged. There are a number of levels of theoretical inadequacy which must be stressed. Three levels are focused upon in what follows:

1. The specifications of the nature of internal economic processes.
2. The crucial conception of the 'embedding' or 'instituting' of the economy in social conditions.
3. The theoretical status of the 'mechanisms of integration' and the effects of this status of the concepts of the mechanisms within substantivism.

1. If, for substantivism, what differentiates different types of economy are the different ways in which certain *substantive* invariant economic processes are instituted and organised in accordance with specific social conditions, then there ought to be a specification of these substantive processes *prior* to the question of their 'embedding/instituting'. The concepts of 'locational and appropriational movements' are supposed to provide just such a specification of the internal processes which are essential to all substantive economic organisation and which constitute the economy as a substantive *sub-system* of the social whole which interacts with other societal forms as its 'environments'. Now the various propositions on the locational and appropriational movements conceal more than they specify in their degree of broad generality. Nowhere in the substantivist discussions is there a really full elaboration of what each of these types of movements exactly entails; while each, it appears, must bring into contact and combination certain elements which are regarded as necessary for the functioning of all economies, nowhere are these elements rigorously defined (indeed they are usually given a more or less arbitrary specification).

The kind of problem involved here can be exemplified by considering substantivist discussions of *production*. Dalton's comments on production processes and their mode of organisation in primitive African economies may be taken as indicative in this respect.[28] Here we are provided with no *conceptual* specification of the nature of internal economic production processes themselves; we are merely told without justification that production always consists of three invariant elements. Thus

> for either the US or tribal Africa it is convenient to regard production of any kind as consisting of three component sub-processes: the allocation of labour and other factors; the work process of arranging and transforming resources into products; the disposition of what is produced. (Dalton, 1971, p. 124)

Here the way in which 'production' is characterised makes impossible any specification of what is or is not a possible 'factor' or 'means' in its technical processes other than one achieved through an empirical examination of the non-economic social relations within which production is embedded. These empirical social conditions decree what is or is not possible at the level of production and the latter has no 'law of organisation' beyond this. Accordingly, no theoretical indication is provided by Dalton which is capable of specifying how and why (if at all) his three component 'subprocesses of production' are related.

2. The way in which substantivism attempts to think the necessary social conditions of existence of the economy brings us to the *second* level of the critique and also to the most important. It is now necessary to show that this attempt to theorise the articulation economy ↔ society (posed as it is

in terms of 'embedding' and 'instituting' as referred to above) is quite simply hopelessly theoretically inadequate.

If 'embedding' or 'instituting' is to be more than a mere platitutde, then the substantivist problematic *must* be able to establish *the mechanisms* which generate different types of embedding or the different levels at which instituting is realised. We have already suggested that Hopkins is exceptional in the sense that he realises the necessity of providing a fuller elaboration of the functional relationship between the economy and its social environments which 'embedding' is supposed to represent, and of raising the level of theory underlying this conception in opposition to the relative simplism of Polanyi. Accordingly, and consistently with the terms of the problematic, Hopkins provides the elements of a 'functionalist' conception[29] and attempts to clarify the mechanisms and levels of embedding. His attempt, and those of others after him, to achieve what is theoretically necessary are, however, no more successful than Polanyi's simple formulations. The logical outcome of this substantivist position is an elaborated 'functionalism' and two points should be noted with respect to this: on the one hand, only the elements of this have been hazarded so that the full implications of the embedding theses have not been drawn, while on the other, it is possible to assert that even the *most theoretically rigorous* 'functionalist' conception of the relation of economy to society[30] must contain crucial theoretical inadequacies (as S. Savage demonstrates in his paper above). However, the elements established by Hopkins, despite the fact that they attempt to formulate 'embedding' as a *complex articulation* of economic with non-economic, remain quite inadequate in the following senses.

Firstly, and quite simply, Hopkins is unable to specify quite crucial aspects of the interchange economic $\leftrightarrow$ non-economic: we are given no indication of *which* extra-economic elements will be integrated with which particular inter-level of the economic process itself. All that is suggested are four levels at which the contingent and arbitrarily specified 'non-economic' might intervene in the organisation of economic activities and movements, etc. The citing of 'existent empirical examples' as evidence (Neale's analysis for example) merely produces a rationalisation for a relationship which is not *theorised*. Neither Hopkins, Neale, Polanyi, Dalton nor any of the other authors is able to furnish arguments for the limits of intervention of the non-economic in the economic or for the reasons for the intervention of any specific non-economic element. In the last analysis, the conception of the economy as an 'instituted process' or an 'embedded' system remains undeveloped even at the level of what is consistently required for a rigorous 'functionalism'. Substantivism has no elaborated conceptions of the detailed boundary interchanges between a complex specified economic sub-system and other equally complex non-economic sub-systems in the social whole and no conception of the structural differentiation of the economy comparable to those operative in the sophisticated theory of Talcott Parsons. Where the latter – containing the ultimate inadequacies demonstrated by Savage – produces highly specific concepts for the theorisation of the functional economy ↔ society interaction, substantivism satisfies itself with a minimum of theory and a recourse to contingent and arbitrarily selected empirical factors. The position is doubly inadequate.

3. Having laboured the point of the strategic centrality of 'embedding' for substantivism in my exposition, the *third* point follows directly from what I have just said and again concerns the *effects* of the lack of rigour in this concept. It was suggested above that the 'mechanisms of integration' are consistently represented as empirical manifestations of particular modes of the 'embedding' of the economy within society. This is certainly correct, but now one must go one step further and, following up what has just been said, state that substantivism cannot possibly provide any theoretical basis or necessity for these 'mechanisms'. They *ought* to be the products of different complex articulations between specified levels of the economy and certain elements at certain levels of the society which are non-economic. We have just shown, however, that this functional articulation is not thought in detail within the substantivist problematic and cannot be adequately. The basis of the complex articulation which is supposed to be at the root of the operation of each of the mechanisms will not be provided. Accordingly, the mechanisms themselves cannot be deduced (as they ought to be) from the conception of 'embedding' in substantivist terms and they must remain purely *descriptive indices* with scant theoretical basis.[31]

As 'principles' they are supposed to represent a certain form of the instituting of the economy, but they merely carry over and continue the arbitrariness and inadequacy of the functional conception of the latter in so far as they propose an integration of economic movements with 'in-stitutional preconditions' whose nature, in fact, beyond an initial specification ('symmetry' and 'centricity' of the social group in the cases of reciprocity and redistribution respectively, for example), must be left to a *contingent* and *arbitrary variation*. Thus, in discussing the principle or mechanism which Polanyi calls 'householding'[32] the latter notes that

> The principle is as broad in its application as either reciprocity or redistribution. *The nature of the institutional nucleus is indifferent:* it may be sex as with the patriarchal family, locality as with the village settlement, or political power with the seigneurial manor. Nor does the internal organisation of the group matter. (Polanyi, 1944, p. 53; emphasis added)

It seems that the principles can be 'realised' in any number of guises; unfortunately substantivism cannot ever supply any theoretical for-mulation on the *mechanisms which govern such realisations*. In effect, the historical incidence of the operation of the mechanisms is conceived as the empirical realisation of 'essences' in diverse form in the manner of certain idealist philosophies of history.

Two points are important here with respect to substantivist failures over the theory of *change and transition*. Firstly, the underdeveloped nature of the 'functionalist' basis to 'embedding' is accompanied by a failure to provide a rigorous concept (like Parsons' structural differentiation') of the mechanism through which 'disembedding' is achieved (and the modern 'market economy' born). Secondly, transition, change (and 'disembedding') are as a consequence thought in terms of the incidence of, and emergence of, certain mechanisms and *combinations* of the mechanisms. The failure to provide what is necessary for a rigorous functionalist theory of transition at the level of the economy is in the last analysis accompanied by teleological formulations on the realisation of the mechanisms of integration which are proposed to explain economic and social change.[33]

Thus the implications of the inadequate theoretical basis behind substantivism's 'mechanisms' are easy to grasp. If they have, as I have suggested, really the character of mere descriptive indices, then any typology of economic systems which classifies on the basis of their relations of combination and/or dominance must be inadequate, for its central element remains *untheorised*. In like fashion, there can be no consistent theoretical justification for the dominance of one over others operating conjointly with it; this would have to explain how such a particular combination *was produced* by an articulation of certain specified levels of the economic with other non-economic elements in a certain manner, and this, as I have suggested, is impossible given the terms of the substantivist problematic.

The problems of the substantivist position are amply illustrated by its characterisation of the *market* or *capitalist economy* which occupies a highly singular and ambiguous place within the classification of economic systems. The singularity of this economy derives from the fact that its economic processes are organised according to *economic* criteria and are not subject to the intervention of non-economic social relations as are all pre-capitalist economies (as stated above). Accordingly, the economy is characterised as 'relatively disembedded' from social relations.

Now because, as we have just seen, substantivism is unable to provide a detailed formulation of 'embedding' (and *ipso facto* of 'relative disembedding'), this generates distinct problems for an adequate detailed theory of the structures and processes of all types of economy, and in the last analysis all that substantivism can provide is the conception of mechanisms of integration of economies as the empirical manifestations of modes of embedding. For the 'relatively disembedded' economy the problem is particularly acute, and symptomatically, substantivism falls back upon the 'formal' theoretical formulae of economic theory to fill the gap, so that this economy is represented by two conflicting concepts of the economic, *the formal and the substantive at the same time.* The ambiguity of the market economy, subject to this *double determination*, is an effect of the retention of the formulations of orthodox economic (cf. my introduction) which in itself is symptomatic of the failure to elaborate independent concepts consistent with the terms of the substantivist problematic. Ultimately the return to the concepts of 'economic theory' for the analysis of the market economy signals the restricted nature of the 'substantivist revolution' and epitomises the general failure of the substantive concept of the economic.

CONCLUSION

If the assertions contained in the preceding sections are accepted as valid, then the central tenets of substantivism are prey to definite theoretical inadequacies which eliminate the possibility that substantivism might provide an adequate comparative theory of economic forms. Given this, all 'empirical' studies of this or that economy or economic institution which rely upon derived substantivist categories and classifications must be judged accordingly.

The initial promise of substantivism, contained in its *correct* realisation that conventional conceptions of the economic in pre-capitalist societies were faulty in failing to grasp the importance of the complex intervention of non-economic spheres of social life in the organisation of economic activities, bore little fruit primarily because of *a failure to provide adequate conceptualisation of this intervention*. This failure of its basic concepts left the position open to reliance upon often simplistic formulations and crucially teleological forms of explanation which are definite obstacles to an adequate theory of social forms.[34]

There are signs, however, that such obstacles are being overcome by the development of Marxist concepts to tackle problems within anthropology and sociology. Recent work,[35] following the theoretical interventions of Godelier, Althusser and Balibar, represents a decisive phase in anthropology confronting many problems from a quite distinct and new perspective. Yet it is at the theoretical level that problems persist and must be tackled so that the content of existing empirical studies may be given an adequately theoretically founded interpretation. While 'substantivism' cannot realise the probject of providing a foundation for a comparative theory of economic forms, the rigorous development of Marxist theory[36] presents engaging possibilities.

NOTES

1. Embodied of course in the programmatic *Trade and Markets in the Early Empires* (Polanyi *et al.*, 1957).

2. This is well documented in Firth (1967) and LeClair & Schneider (1968).
3. Cf. LeClair & Schneider (1968) sections III–V.
4. See Polanyi *et al.* (1957); Hopkins (1957); Dalton (1971).
5. See Herskovits (1952); Goodfellow (1939); Tax (1963); Nash (1966); Firth (1951).
6. This is a schematic condensation of the widely scattered assertions by substantivists on what is usually very *vaguely* described as the 'formal' position. This vagueness with respect to economic theory has occasioned criticism from authors such as Cook; see his paper in LeClair & Schneider (1968).
7. The latter having achieved much 'formalistic' success in contemporary economics in terms of accurate quantification, statistical prediction, etc.
8. This is the position taken more often than not by Herskovits, Goodfellow and, in some of his works, Firth.
9. Lange (1963) in his *Political Economy* has a similar position; cf. pp. 169, 172–3.
10. See the paper 'Theoretical Issues in Economic Anthropology' (1969) in Dalton (1971) for the basic position.
11. The relevant papers are in Polanyi *et al.* (1957): Polanyi's 'The Economy as Instituted Process' and Hopkins' only contribution to the selection.
12. Or of the composite 'economic action'.
13. Polanyi (1957a) p. 248.
14. See Polanyi (1944, 1966); Polanyi *et al.* (1957).
15. This lack of specification of the 'non-economic' will be elaborated upon later.
16. Namely, W. Neale's analysis of the different levels of integration and embedding of *locational* and *appropriational* actions in a traditional village economy. On the one hand, *locational* actions (viz. labour) are instituted via roles which are different ('community' roles). (In both cases, of course, it is at the level of the role (for this level of 'embeddedness' of the economy) that economic actions are organised.) Cf. Neale's paper in Polanyi *et al.* (1957).
17. For these accounts see, respectively, Malinowski (1922); Thurnwald (1932); Mauss (1954).
18. See Sahlins (1974) chap. 5, 'The Sociology of Primitive Exchange'.
19. It is Sahlins who, with the conception of a 'domestic mode of production' (DMP), has devoted most attention to this pattern of integration (cf. Sahlins, chap 2 and 3). This concept of the DMP is an attempt to link substantivist ideas with the formulations of A. V. Chayanov on the economic characteristics of households as productive units, but because of the inherent inadequacies of Chayanov's work itself (established in Littlejohn's paper below) the whole enterprise must be regarded as theoretically unfounded (cf. Hirst, 1976, for other general criticisms of Sahlins' form of substantivism).
20. Dalton elaborates such a typology in the paper 'Theoretical Issues in Economic Anthropology' in Dalton (1971).
21. All these papers are in Dalton's collection of essays (Dalton, 1971).
22. Cf. Dalton, 'Traditional Production in African Economies', p. 126 in Dalton (1971).
23. This subordinate role of markets in 'primitive' economies is the central concern of the joint paper by Bohannan and Dalton introducing *Markets in Africa*. Here, the two authors discuss some primitive systems where markets are 'peripheral' in economic organisation and function under the aegis of the dominant integrative mechanisms of *reciprocity* and *redistribution*. The principle

of *market exchange*, it is suggested, is in these systems only 'embryonic' (see later remarks on this in the third section of the paper).

24. Cf. Polanyi (1966).
25. See Polanyi (1957b) pp. 264–6, for a concise statement.
26. See above. 'Integrative' exchange is exchange at a bargained rate.
27. Polanyi, discussing these 'elements' of market institutions, locates them as 'supply crowds, demand crowds, physical site, goods presents, custom and law, equivalencies'.
28. Cf. Dalton's paper 'Traditional Production in Primitive African Economies', one of the essays in Dalton (1971).
29. Whose main 'inspiration' seems to be R. Merton. Cf. Hopkins in Polanyi *et al.* pp. 297–8 and p. 306, n. 28.
30. In the sense of a more or less differentiated *functional sub-system* of the wider social system.
31. Hence Polanyi's constant recourse to the descriptive accounts of Malinowski, Thurnwald and others.
32. This is the fourth 'mechanism' which Polanyi identifies apart from reciprocity, redistribution and exchange, upon which my exposition has concentrated (these are more *central* to substantivist studies). See above, pp. 76–80.

33. G. Dupré and P.P. Rey, 'Reflections on the Pertinence of a theory of the History of Exchange, *Economy and Society*, vol., II no. 2 (1973), demonstrate teleology with respect to a number of Polanyi's formulations on the existence of the 'seed' of the market economy within the economic institutions of the Ancient World. For a more general discussion of teleology, see Barry Hindess' paper (below) and the relevant chapters of Hindess & Hirst (1975) which discuss the problem of conceptualising the *transition* of economic forms.
34. See Barry Hindess' remarks on the central place of teleological formulations within sociological theory (in his paper in this volume) and his critique of the basis of teleology.
35. In France the Marxist anthropologists Meillassoux, Terray, Rey and Dupré and in England, for example, the contributions to the ASA monograph *Marxist Analyses and Social Anthropology*, ed. M. Bloch, and the journal *Critique of Anthropology*, provide representative authors. Of course, their positions are by no means homogeneous.
36. For basic concepts of Marxism (considered as the theory of modes of production) cf. Hindess & Hirst (1975).

4 Economic Development in Neo-Marxist Theory

LORRAINE CULLEY

INTRODUCTION

Much of the recent discussion of the question of 'underdevelopment' has been conducted by authors referring to a process not strictly of under-development' but of 'dependency'. The so-called 'dependency theorists' include allegedly Marxist and non-Marxist economists and sociologists, among them Dos Santos, Cardoso, Sunkel and Furtado. The work of certain 'neo-Marxist' writers, most notably Paul Baran, Paul Sweezy and André Gunder Frank, has undoubtedly been very influential in these recent theoretical developments. 'Dependency theory' accepts certain 'neo-Marxist' conceptions of the nature of development and under-development, in particular the conception of the interdependence of the capitalist world economy and the proposition that development and underdevelopment are partial, interdependent aspects of one global system.[1] The criticism of the Baran/Frank conception of 'underdevelop-ment' is largely confined to its alleged 'Eurocentricity'. It is argued that insufficient attention is paid to the effects of international interdependence on the internal structures of, for example, the Latin American economies. The dependency theorists are particularly concerned with the effects on the 'class structure' of these societies.[2] These writers do not, however, offer a rigorous theoretical critique of the Baran/Frank thesis. This has serious effects for the work of those authors who claim to be working within Marxist theory. The failure adequately to conceptualise the conditions of the class struggle in 'underdeveloped' societies is conceived largely as an oversight on the part of Baran and Frank, rather than a theoretical consequence of their discourse. While it is generally accepted that the Baran/Frank thesis is a correct starting-point for a Marxist analysis of 'economic development', it is demonstrated below that this is not the case.

In this discussion the texts concentrated on will be *The Political Economy of Growth* (Baran, 1973) and *Monopoly Capital* (Baran & Sweezy, 1970).

Reference will also be made to the work of André Gunder Frank, one of the best known of the allegedly Marxist writers on 'economic development' and 'underdevelopment'. In *The Political Economy of Growth*, Baran is concerned with three sets of problems: firstly, to indicate the inability of orthodox economics to explain the nature of the economy of the 'advanced' countries of the world; secondly, to put forward an alternative, Marxist conception of the 'monopoly capitalist' economy; and thirdly, to conceptualise the nature and origin of the 'underdeveloped' countries of the world. *Monopoly Capital* is intended as a more adequate Marxist explanation of the current structure of the capitalist system.

Baran and Sweezy see their task as countering the sterility of modern bourgeois economics. They argue that whereas classical economics was able to criticise the economic, political and social relations of the feudalist order, neo-classical economics has turned on its own past and become a mere attempt at an explanation and justification of the capitalist *status quo*, suppressing attempts to judge the existing economic order by standards of reason or to comprehend the origins of existing conditions and the potentialities they contain. Neo-classical economics and the New Economics of Keynes and his followers is bourgeois ideology. As such, they argue, it is unable to identify the irrationality, the limitations and the transitory nature of the capitalist order. In the nineteenth century, the analysis of economic and social change was largely left to Marx and Engels. There have, however, been significant developments since the days of Marx. The existing Marxist analysis of capitalism still rests in the final analysis on the assumption of a competitive economy; the question of monopoly, although not ignored by Marx, was never fully investigated. Baran and Sweezy's objective then is to remedy this situation – to develop a Marxist theory of the present-day capitalist economy and, particularly in the case of Baran, a Marxist explanation of 'underdevelopment'.

In general, Baran, Sweezy and Frank have been taken at their word in this respect. Their work has been interpreted and criticised as contributions to Marxist theory.[3] For example, Nicholas Kaldor, in his review of *The Political Economy of Growth*, introduces it as 'a bold attempt to analyse the state of the world on orthodox Marxian lines', and as such, Kaldor argues, it exhibits both the merits and the shortcomings of the Marxian technique of 'socio-economic' analysis (Kaldor, 1958, p. 164).

This paper proposes to discuss the issues of the conceptualisation of 'monopoly capitalism' and the origins and nature of 'underdevelopment' on the grounds that both these conceptions represent an evolutionist, idealist and fundamentally incoherent philosophy of history in which the concept of 'economic surplus' is a dominant element. In the course of demonstrating the contradictions and incoherence of Baran and Sweezy's discourse it will be shown, in addition, that such a theory bears little theoretical relation to Marxism.[4]

This paper has the following structure. The first section contains a summary of Baran and Sweezy's arguments on the specificity of contemporary capitalism and its reproduction. The second section will involve a discussion of, firstly, the conception of contemporary capitalism as monopolistic as opposed to competitive. It is argued here that Baran and Sweezy fail adequately to establish the conditions of existence of 'monopoly capitalism'. Secondly, the paper will discuss in more detail the concepts of 'economic surplus' and the proposed 'tendency of the surplus to rise', the concepts of 'unproductive labour' and 'capitalism'. The discussion will consider these concepts as they appear in Baran and Sweezy's discourse and in relation to the Marxist concepts of 'surplus labour' and 'surplus value', 'unproductive labour' and 'capitalism'. This is necessary given the terminological similarity of these concepts and bearing in mind the claims of Baran, Sweezy and Frank to be contributing to Marxist theory. While these authors indicate that the concept of surplus is not the same as that of surplus value, the full theoretical implications of this difference are not made clear. In the case of the concept of unproductive labour, no reference is given to the Marxist concept, but Baran quotes Marx in such a way as to suggest a direct correspondence of the concepts.[5] The effect of the concept of 'surplus' is the formulation of a conception of determinate societies differentiated in terms of their degree of 'rationality'. There is no basis for the conceptualisation of 'feudalism', 'capitalism', 'socialism', etc., as determinate modes of production with distinct forms of articulation of relations and forces of production, which is basic to Marx's theory. The concept of class struggle, dominant in Marxism, cannot be derived from Baran's conception of societies defined by the 'rationality' or otherwise of the *use* of their surplus.

The third section of the paper will consider at a more general level Baran and Sweezy's conceptualisation of 'economic development' and 'underdevelopment' and will briefly discuss the work of André Gunder Frank. It will be argued that Baran and Sweezy's theory involves a fundamentally incoherent teleology of history.[6]

'MONOPOLY CAPITALISM'

For Baran and Sweezy, the advanced capitalist economies of the modern world are defined as 'monopoly capitalist'. Monopoly capitalism is a system made up of 'giant corporations':

> the giant corporation of today is an engine for maximising profits and accumulating capital to at least as great an extent as the individual entreprise of an earlier period. But it is not merely an enlarged an institutionalised version of the personal capitalist. (Baran & Sweezy, 1970, p. 58)

The major differences between competitive and monopoly capitalism, which Baran and Sweezy argue are of key importance for a general theory of monopoly capitalism, are that the corporation has a longer time-horizon that the individual capitalist and that it is a more rational calculator, both of which are related to the larger scale of the corporation's operations. These two key features generate certain 'characteristic attitudes and modes of behaviour', the most important being a systematic avoidance of risk-taking and an attitude of 'live and let live' towards other members of the corporate world. The advanced capitalist economy is dominated by the giant corporations. The equalisation of the rates of profit operates only in the compressed competitive sector of the economy. In the monopolistic sphere rates of profit are unequal and, most importantly, very high, and the mass of profit available for investment is prodigiously large. There is, however, a continuous and growing inadequacy of private investment in relation to the volume of economic surplus (i.e. the difference between output and consumption) under conditions of full employment. While there is at the same time a plethora of technically possible and socially urgent undertakings that could readily absorb the surplus and more, this is impossible under conditions of monopoly. The transformations in the capitalist system in the first half of the twentieth century represent the natural result of capitalist development and indeed are necessitated by this development's intrinsic logic, that is, the growth of large-scale enterprise, monopoly and oligopoly.

In *The Political Economy of Growth* Baran argues that the growth of monopolies slows down the rate of economic growth, not principally on account of excessive prices or profit margins but on account of the reduction in the speed of technological change and adaptation. Under competitive capitalism the widespread introduction of new technologically improved methods is an inbuilt necessity. Only at the peril of its extinction can the competitive firm disregard the available possibilities of cost reduction. The competitive economy, however, was able to provide sufficient outlets to absorb the economic surplus under conditions of full employment, though full employment was not a 'normal' or necessary outcome. This is not to argue that capitalism was rational. Indeed, the result of competition was 'a wasteful utilisation of the economic surplus, premature destruction of capital assets, with both investment decisions and capital losses caused by the vagaries of technological developments, by fortuitous emerging of extra-profits' (Baran, 1973, p. 195).

Capitalism was able to absorb the economic surplus but it did not do so rationally; much of the investment constituted a loss to society which in turn depressed the rates of growth markedly below their *potential* magnitude. Under conditions of monopoly and oligopoly there may be a strong tendency to wait with outlays on new equipment until the technological conditions have become settled or to suppress technological change until existing equipment is written off. In any given situation an expansion of output is likely to be contrary to the monopolists' profit-maximisation policy. Whereas the competitive capitalist is compelled to introduce any available new machine regardless of the concomitant capital losses or be driven out of business, the monopolist is exposed to no such pressure. Consequently, 'under conditions of monopoly, outlays on technological improvements as well as capital losses – both important forms of utilisation of the economic surplus under capitalism – are significantly reduced' (ibid., p. 200).

A crucial feature of monopoly capitalism is the absence of price competition. The typical giant corporation is not a monopolist in the sense that it is the only seller of a commodity for which there are no substitutes. Rather it is one of several corporations producing commodities which are more or less adequate substitutes for each other. Price competition among these producers would have serious effects on the profit-maximisation policy, as this would create unstable market situations. This is avoided 'by the simple expedient of banning price cutting as a legitimate weapon of economic warfare' (Baran & Sweezy, 1970, p. 68). A price war to the finish would call for large amounts of capital and would involve such great risks that accommodation is preferred to ruinous warfare: 'price competition under conditions of oligopoly has a tendency to become increasingly odious to the businessmen involved' (Baran, 1973, p. 202).

Oligopolists adhere to a principle of 'live and let live' which exercises a significant influence on the structure of oligopolistic industry. High-cost firms are allowed to carry on beside more productive enterprises. Consequently, excess capacity that has developed either as the result of earlier economies of scale or in order to meet fluctuating demand does not have a tendency to be squeezed out of the industry. Excess capacity in turn discourages new investment. 'Thus the monopolist and oligopolist grows necessarily more cautious and circumspect in his investment decisions and finds *in any given situation* little inducement to plough back his profits into his own enterprise' (ibid., pp. 203–4; emphasis in original). The monopolistic or oligopolistic firm therefore, suffocating in its profits, seeks to employ them in competitive industries and as a result monopoly spreads. The competitive sector is reduced to a technically determined rock-bottom and the investment outlet for overflowing profits is closed. There is a possible outlet for surplus in the founding of new industries. With adherence to the principle of 'live and let live', however, such operations, it is argued, are rarely undertaken because of the possibility of a new industry competing with already established businesses.

In *Monopoly Capital*, Baran and Sweezy adopt a new position with regard to the question of cost reduction. Whereas in *The Political Economy of Growth*, Baran argued that the necessity to introduce innovatory techniques was reduced under monopolistic or oligopolistic conditions, in their later book Baran and Sweezy argue that a tendency for costs of production to fall is 'endemic to the entire monopoly capitalist economy' (p. 78). This formulation is central in their argument concerning the inherent instability and inevitable decay of monopoly capitalism. They argue that the system of oliogopolies generates pressures which force corporate managers to cut costs and improve efficiency, i.e. 'certain modes of behaviour are imposed upon them by the workings of the system itself' (p. 77). The firm with lower costs and higher profits enjoys a variety of advantages over higher-cost rivals in the struggle for market shares. In addition, the lower-cost, higher-profit company acquires a special reputation which enables it to attract and hold customers, recruit the ablest graduates, etc. So, under oligopolistic conditions price competition is at a minimum but firms still strive incessantly to reduce costs. The inevitable result is a strong and persistent tendency for the economic surplus to increase both absolutely and relatively as the system develops. Thus Marx's law of the falling rate of profit must be replaced by a new characteristic of monopoly capitalism – the tendency of the economic surplus to rise. Thus, they argue, 'What is most essential about the structural change from competitive to monopoly capitalism finds its theoretical expression in this substitution' (Baran & Sweezy, 1970, p. 81). This tendency, they argue, if unchecked, would necessarily culminate in permanent economic depression. Monopoly capitalism is a self-contradictory system. It tends to generate ever more surplus, yet it fails to provide the consumption and investment outlets required for the absorption of a rising surplus and hence for the smooth working of the system. 'Since surplus which cannot be absorbed will not be produced, it follows that the *normal* state of the monopoly capitalist economy is stagnation' (ibid., p. 113; emphasis in original).

However, 'Counteracting forces do exist. If they did not, the system would indeed long since have fallen of its own weight.' In order to survive, monopoly capitalism must stimulate demand. It is precisely the mechanisms which are employed to achieve the creation of markets, i.e. the 'sales effort', 'militarism' and 'imperialism', which constitute the irrationality of monopoly capitalism. It is these forms which constitute the inhumane and morally bankrupt effects monopoly capitalism has on the 'quality of life', producing a society 'without faith and without morals' (ibid., p. 341). The *decay* of monopoly capitalism is essentially a moral, social process brought about by the necessities of the functioning of the economic order.

Before discussing these mechanisms, it is necessary to demonstrate Baran and Sweezy's reasons for rejecting apparently obvious ways of absorbing surplus. Firstly, surplus cannot be absorbed by investment in new production methods and products. Considering the enormous depreciation allowances of corporate capitalism, 'it is quite possible that businesses can finance from this source alone all the investment it considers profitable to make in innovations . . . leaving no "innovational" outlets to help absorb investment-seeking surplus' (ibid., p. 108). Nor is foreign investment likely to help matters: 'foreign investment, far from being an outlet for domestically generated surplus, is a most efficient device for transferring surplus generated abroad to the investing country' (ibid., p. 113).

Given the limitations to the capitalist's consumption and investment, the two major sources of surplus absorption are the 'sales effort' and, most importantly, government spending ('militarism' and 'imperialism'). The 'sales effort' includes a large part of all distribution costs, advertising, model and style changes, finance, insurance, real estate and legal services, all regarded as unproductive and wasteful use of surplus. Even such unproductive expenses can not come near providing a sufficient outlet for the overflowing surplus. More deliberate 'outside impulses' are needed and these can only be provided by the state. However, several of what might appear obvious outlets for surplus or adequate methods of obtaining equilibrium between aggregate demand and supply are not possible largely because of the objection of the leaders of big business. For example, a reduction of output by a general shortening of the number of working hours, or government spending on additional consumption by disbursement of funds to people unable to satisfy their consumption requirements, which could not fail to increase effective ·demand! Such subsidies are, however, 'altogether inconsistent with the spirit of capitalism and most unattractive to dominant interests . . . such unearned receipts would be wholly alien to the fundamental system of ethics and values associated with the capitalist system' (Baran, 1973, p. 231).

While there is not such widespread objection to 'collective consumption' spending by government, e.g. construction, etc., the amount of money that the government can spend for such purposes is somewhat limited. Government could invest in productive facilities, yet this is completely taboo under the regime of monopoly capital – any kind of productive investment by government is intolerable to the dominant interests. With all these avenues closed, government expenditure is forced into 'unproductive' areas. The most significant of these is the government's 'foreign economic relations', subsumed under the headings 'militarism' and 'imperialism', which provide a vast outlet for the overflowing surplus. Such expenditures encompass loans and grants to foreign governments, outlays on military establishment needed to 'protect' certain territories or enforce certain policies abroad, the nuclear arms race, etc. However, even such expenditures cannot solve the basic problem of monopoly capitalism. Demand and investment is stimulated, productivity increases (although the increases are nothing like what could have been achieved if the wasted economic surplus had been turned into rationally allocated investment). The system eventually adapts itself to the new level of income and employment. Demand becomes stabilised and monopolistic firms again reach their optimal positions with regard to output and price. The problem for monopoly capitalism arises, however, from the possibility of a 'mood of optimism' among not only adventurous small businessmen but habitually prudent and cautious corporate mangements. 'In this state of exhilaration, the increase of capacity is driven further than what would be warranted by the new level of aggregate demand' (ibid., pp. 251–2).

The result is that excess capacity becomes ever more pronounced. Thus what confronted the system before appears in a more acute form. The result of government spending is not merely an increase of total output but also a rise of the share of the economic surplus in national income. This in turn necessitates an increase in investment. Nothing resembling the required increase can be expected from private investment because there is already excess capacity. Thus we reach the conclusion that the stability of monopoly capitalism is highly precarious. Its preservation depends on the systematic 'ideological processing' of the population to ensure its loyalty to the system (p. 259). The result is that 'A spider-web of corruption is spun over the entire political and cultural life of the imperialist country and drives principles, honesty, humanity and courage from political life' (ibid., p. 259). It is this aspect, the moral crisis of monopoly capitalist society which Baran and Sweezy elaborate in the second half of *Monopoly Capital*. It is a crisis which effects 'everyman's everyday existence': 'A heavy, strangulating sense of the emptiness and futility of life permeates the country's moral and intellectual climate' (Baran & Sweezy, 1970, p. 274).

For Baran and Sweezy, then, the United States economy is 'inherently' stagnationist and there is an endemic crisis in the system based on this tendency to stagnation. Monopoly capitalists are drowning in their profits and lack adequate investment outlets. The 'irrational' activities of corporations and government which attempt to counteract these tendencies are not sufficient to offset them. The weakness of surplus absorption cannot be adequately dealt with because of the restraints on government action in any sphere which is contrary to the desires of the monopoly capitalists. These 'massive private interests' are not opposed to spending and taxation as such, but they are concerned with its composition. 'The big question, therefore, is not whether there will be more and more government spending, but on what. And here private interests come into their own as the controlling factor' (ibid., p. 153).

Unfortunately, the mechanisms whereby this 'controlling factor' operates are not revealed. However, the narrow circumscription of the government's use of the surplus has two aspects. Firstly, governments are not allowed to invest in 'productive' areas, which may conflict with private interests, or in 'socially desirable' fields such as housing, education, health, etc., beyond the level of bare necessity. The government thus uses the surplus for all kinds of 'irrational' spending on defence and 'imperialist' activities. Secondly, there are inbuilt limits to the effectivity of such expenditures to stimulate the economy. 'The fateful question "on what?" to which monopoly capitalism can find no answer in the realm of civilian spending has crept subversively into the military establishment itself. From all present indications there is no answer there either' (ibid., p. 214).

MONOPOLY AND COMPETITION

Why do Baran and Sweezy regard contemporary capitalism as *monopoly* capitalism? They insist on the absence of price-cutting as a weapon of economic warfare, at least under the 'normal' functioning of the corporations, but they do not deny that such warfare exists. Firms do not compete on price terms for fear of reducing the profits of the group as a whole. But, we are told, 'The abandonment of price competition does not mean the end of all competition; it takes new forms and rages on with ever-increasing intensity' (Baran & Sweezy, 1970, p. 76). New forms of competition are at the level of introducing cost-reducing innovations and 'excessive' advertising to fight for larger market shares. The 'monopoly' aspect of contemporary capitalism, therefore, would appear even in their own terms to be a somewhat limited one. It is based on the assumption that alliances and agreements between giant corporations will result in the price of output being fixed at the theoretical monopoly price, which management agrees will maximise profit for the group as a whole. At every other level it appears that competition and struggle continue.

What is the basis of Baran and Sweezy's periodisation of capitalism? It is clear that for Baran and Sweezy the transition from competition to monopoly is conceived as the maturation of the relations always already present at the inception of capitalism. The pertinent differences between the variations of capitalism are an effect of the increase in the size of firms. In this conception the conditions of existence of monopoly are reduced to a change in the subjective orientation of the controllers of the production unit, arising out of a change in the scale of production. The determinant difference between competitive and monopoly capitalism is located at the level of the personalities of the individual capitalist entrepreneur and the corporate management. Competitive capitalism is a system made up of individual capitalists while monopoly capitalism is a system of giant corporations, that is, there are fewer firms and they are bigger. 'The replacement of the individual capitalist by the corporate capitalist constitutes an institutionalisation of the capitalist function' (ibid., p. 55).

. Baran and Sweezy criticise formal economic theory for continuing to operate with the assumption of the profit-maximising individual entrepreneur. They do not, however, argue against the subjectivism of neoclassical economics, but merely argue that economics should operate with the assumption of a collective capitalist subject in the form of the corporate management of large corporations, whose motivational and behavioural patterns are quite different from the nineteenth century entrepreneur or the 'robber baron' tycoon of the early twentieth century.

It is clear from the summary of Baran and Sweezy's argument in the first section of this paper that it is precisely the subjective attitudes and values of the monopoly capitalists which are determinant for monopoly capitalism. It is the 'live and let live' mentality which determines the lack of price competition. It is the monopoly capitalists' 'mood of optimism' which results in overproduction. It is monopoly capitalists' attitudes which prevent surplus being absorbed in productive outlets, thus simultaneously producing 'irrational' expenditure, 'waste', 'moral decay' and, ultimately, their own destruction.

Baran and Sweezy's position represents a voluntaristic conception of the reproduction of the capitalist economy. It assumes that corporate management, like the capitalist entrepreneur of vulgar economics criticised by Marx, is essentially an agent of free will, rather than 'bearer' the of social relations assigned functions to perform by social forces. In Marxist theory the reproduction of the capitalist economy cannot be reduced to the subjectivity of capitalist agents.[7]

For Baran and Sweezy, whether the capitalist economy reproduces itself or not is entirely dependent on the subjectivity of corporate management. We are given no real indication of the political conditions of existence of monopoly capitalism. The authors ignore any effectivity of the economic class struggle, and at the level of politics Baran and Sweezy's characterisation of the state consists in the simplistic and vulgarised conception which sees in the state simply the tool or instrument of the dominant class, the monopoly capitalists. For Baran and Sweezy, the function of the state is to act always in the direct interest of the dominanat class. In Marxist theory, the state is a condition of existence of class society, and is by no means simply reducible to its function as an instrument in the hands of the ruling class.[8]

THE 'ECONOMIC SURPLUS' AND ITS 'TENDENCY TO RISE'

The concept of 'economic surplus' is a dominant concept both for Baran and Sweezy and in the work of André Gunder Frank. Frank's central proposition is that it was world capitalism which created the condition of 'underdevelopment' and which maintains it in existence at the present time. In establishing this proposition, the concept of the economic surplus plays a central role. For Frank, the causes of 'underdevelopment' can be traced to what he regards as the 'contradictions' of capitalism. A major contradiction is the expropriation/appropriation of economic surplus. Surplus expropriation/appropriation is

> the exploitation link which in chain-like fashion extends the capitalist link between the capitalist world and national metropolises to the regional centres (part of whose surplus they appropriate), and from these to local centres, and so on to large landowners or merchants who expropriate surplus from small peasants or tenants, and sometimes even from these latter to landless labourers exploited by them in turn. (Frank, 1971, pp. 31–2)

At each point the capitalist system generates economic development for the few and underdevelopment for the many. We shall return later to the implications of this conception for Frank's argument.

It is evident from the summary of their argument presented earlier that the concept of surplus is dominant in the work of Baran and Sweezy. For these writers, the understanding of the factors responsible for the size and mode of utilisation of the economic surplus is one of the foremost tasks of a theory of economic development. In explaining the concept of the economic surplus, both Frank (1971) and Baran and Sweezy (1970) refer to the definition given by Paul Baran in *The Political Economy of Growth*. Here Baran distinguishes three variants of the concept of the economic surplus: the actual economic surplus, the potential economic surplus and the planned economic surplus. These concepts are decisive in Baran's formulation of the concepts of capitalism and socialism and the conceptualisation of the transition from one type of society to another. The concepts of surplus determine the theoretical nature of Baran and Sweezy's critique of capitalism and their arguments for the necessity of its supersession. They also determine the conceptualisation of the origin and continued existence of 'underdevelopment'.

Actual economic surplus is

> the difference between society's *actual* current output and its *actual* current consumption. It is thus identical with current saving or accumulation, and finds its embodiment in assets of various kinds added to society's wealth during the period in question: productive facilities and equipment, inventories, foreign balances, and gold hoards. (Baran, 1973, p. 132; emphasis in original)

As such, actual economic surplus has been generated in all societies. The second variant of the concept of surplus, i.e. the *potential* economic surplus, is a most important one in Baran's discourse. It is primarily by an analysis of their *potentialities* that types of society – feudalism, capitalism, monopoly capitalism – are assessed. Potential economic surplus is 'the difference between the output that *could* be produced in a given natural and technological environment with the help of employable productive resources, and what might be regarded as essential consumption' (ibid., p. 133; emphasis in original).

The potential surplus appears under four headings. One is society's excess consumption, the second is output lost to society through the existence of 'unproductive' workers, the third is output lost because of the 'irrational and wasteful organisation of the existing productive apparatus', and the fourth is the output lost by the existence of unemployment caused 'primarily by the anarchy of capitalist production and the deficiency of effective demand' (ibid., p. 134). While the actual surplus is relatively easy to calculate in any given case, the identification of the potential surplus runs into problems largely arising from the fact that 'the category of the potential economic surplus itself transcends the horizon of the existing social order' (ibid., p. 134). Indeed, it relates to 'the less readily visualised image of a more rationally ordered society' (ibid., p. 134). The Utopian nature of this conception is quite clear. It allows Baran and his followers to launch an attack on capitalism as an irrational phenomenon with respect to his own ethical position.

There has been considerable criticism of the surplus concept used in *Monopoly Capital*, in particular from 'orthodox' economists. Raymond Lubitz, for example, points out several of the ambiguities involved in the concept. There are, as we have seen, three different meanings of 'the surplus', and in the case of *Monopoly Capital* it is not always clear which, if any, of these meanings is being referred to at any particular time. It will be argued here, in fact, that the surplus concept used to establish the major theoretical conclusions of *Monopoly Capital* is the idealist 'potential surplus'.

Equating surplus with profits, which Baran and Sweezy maintain is an adequate provisional definition, Lubitz argues that it is possible to compute a surplus in either income or product terms (the two measures being equivalent). However, Baran and Sweezy argue that the 'expanded concept' of surplus includes profits and 'other forms' of the surplus, which assume 'decisive importance' (Baran & Sweezy, 1970, p. 80). Lubitz, however, points out that

> What the rest of the text presents as other forms of *income* surplus are in fact *expenditures*, i.e. government expenditure and 'waste'. In effect the authors have taken expenditures from the *product* side of the national income equation and added them on to the 'surplus' on the *income* side. (Lubitz, 1971, p. 169; emphasis in original)

Critics have also pointed out the contradictions involved in treating all government expenditures as part of the surplus. Lubitz argues: 'To equate *all* government spending with surplus assumes that no government taxes come out of wages. This, as all of us who look at our paychecks know, is absurd' (ibid., p. 170). Ron Stanfield, in attempting to 'empirically evaluate' Baran and Sweezy's hypotheses, finds it necessary substantially to revise the concept of surplus to take account of the fact that certain government expenditures must be seen as essential costs of production.[9]

We have seen that the tendency of surplus to rise *as a proportion of national income* is a fundamental conception in Baran and Sweezy's discourse. If, in Baran and Sweezy's terms, national income equals wages plus surplus (provisionally equated with profits), a rise in the share of surplus must mean that real wages rise less fast than labour productivity. If real wages and productivity rise at the same rate, the division of national income between wages and profits will be constant. As Lubitz points out, Baran and Sweezy provide no explanation at all of the determination of real wages. The assumption appears to be that, as Baran argues in *The Political Economy of Growth*, the share of real wages in income remains constant. As Nicholas Kaldor points out, this involves an inescapable contradiction: 'In the first place, since the growth of monopolies necessarily involves "vaster and vaster profits" – not just absolutely of course, but in proportion to turnover – how can it fail to depress the share of wages in total income?' (Kaldor, 1958, p. 165).

Baran and Sweezy's attempts to deal with this type of criticism, however, are wholly unacceptable, while at the same time giving us a clearer understanding of their position. Their defence consists of two elements. Firstly, in answer to Kaldor, they argue that 'the tendency of the surplus to rise' may in fact refer not to a rise in the share of profit but to something else: 'Under certain conditions surplus will be equal to aggregate profits; but as already noted, in the actual economy of monopoly capitalism only part of the difference between output and costs of production appears as profits' (Baran & Sweezy, 1970, p. 84). We are not, however, offered an explanation of a tendency of 'other parts' of the surplus to rise.

The second element is a recourse to the 'potential surplus' concept as constituting the real definition of surplus. They argue that a rising share of profits, going beyond the point where it covers investment needs and consumption of capitalists, is a self-limiting process, 'and cannot appear in the statistics as an actual continuing increase of profits in the share of total income' (ibid., p. 84). They point out, quite correctly, that profits which are neither invested nor consumed are no profits at all. Thus,

> It may be legitimate to speak of the potential profits which would be reaped if there were more investment and capitalists' consumption, but such potential profits cannot be traced in the statistical record – or rather they leave their traces in the statistical record in the paradoxical form of unemployment and excess capacity. (ibid., p. 84)

Here we have it. The tendency of the surplus to rise is in effect the tendency of the potential surplus. The potential benefits to society from technological progress are very large indeed. This potential is not realised for the good of society as a whole but finds its expression in 'excessive consumption', 'unproductive expenditure' and all kinds of 'irrationalities' and 'waste':

> The contradiction between the increasing rationality of society's methods of production and the organisations which embody them on the one hand and the undiminished elementality and irrationality in the functioning and perception of the whole creates that ideological wasteland which is the hallmark of monopoly capitalism. (ibid., p. 328)

The giant corporation has proved to be an unprecedentedly effective instrument for promoting science and technology, but in direct proportion to the accelerated speed of technological change has grown man's alienation: 'Men are still being specialised and sorted, imprisoned in the narrow cells prepared for them by the division of labour, their faculties stunted and their minds diminished (ibid., p. 330). The moral, intellectual decay of monopoly capitalism is the real issue for Baran and Sweezy – the breakdown of family life, the increase in delinquency, psychological disorders, etc. The root cause of all the ills of monopoly capitalist life is to be found in the working of the economic order and provided by the concept of the potential economic surplus. Humanism and idealism are located not only in Baran and Sweezy's denunciation of alienation but in the analysis of the economic system which is its alleged origin.[10]

It is on the basis of the concept of potential economic surplus that Baran develops his concept of capitalism. The determinant element in the elaboration of any concept of feudalism or capitalism is the size and the *mode of utilisation* the of actual surplus produced and its relationship to what could be produced in a 'more rationally ordered society'. For Baran and Sweezy, a 'more rationally ordered society' represents an ethical ideal in which full human potentialities are realised. It can occur only when a rational, i.e. a planned, utilisation of economic surplus occurs. Rationality is arrived at when 'society' as a whole decides what the level and nature of output should be and what the level of consumption should be in a given technological environment; that is, when the surplus is planned and all production and consumption in excess of the 'needs' of society is correspondingly curtailed. Thus, for Baran and Sweezy, the planned economy represents the rational ideal against which all other economies must be judged. In this judgement, 'capitalism' is highly irrational. What is designated by the concept of capitalism is an irrational utilisation of economic surplus. All that is wrong with man's existence in the monopoly capitalist system is in the last instance a product of the basic contradiction of monopoly capitalism – the problem of surplus absorption.

It is primarily by its irrationality that we are to distinguish capitalism from socialism. Both appear as forms of *utilisation* of economic surplus. Capitalism is not socialism essentially because it does not realise its potentialities. There exists in capitalist society 'excess consumption', that is, consumption in excess of 'essential consumption', defined as a level of real income necessary for what is socially considered to be a 'decent livelihood'. As we have seen in Baran and Sweezy's analysis of monopoly capitalism, it is the lack of consumption rather than the excessive consumption of the masses which spells danger for the system. Underconsumption is indeed 'irrational', but in this case it is irrational from the point of view of the existence of the monopoly capitalist system, not from the point of view of socialism. This contradiction illustrates a major problem with the construction of an economic theory from the basis of a relativist and idealist notion of 'rationality'. While advertising, 'militarism' and 'imperialism' may well be irrational from the point of view of Baran and Sweezy's ideal society, they may appear as totally rational from the standpoint of monopoly capitalism.

A similar relativism is encountered with Baran's concepts of productive and unproductive labour. In deciding what is to be regarded as unproductive employment, once again, Baran argues, the decision has to be made from the standpoints of the requirements and potentialities of the historical process: 'Most generally speaking, it consists of all labour resulting in the output of goods and services the demand for which is attributable to the specific conditions and relationships of the capitalist system, and which would be absent in a rationally ordered society' (Baran, 1973, p. 144). It is clear, Baran admits, that considered in this way, a not insignificant part of the output of goods and services marketed and therefore accounted for in the national income statistics of capitalist countries represents unproductive labour. A good many of these unproductive workers are engaged in manufacturing armaments, luxury articles, marks of social distinction; others are government officials, members of military establishments, clergymen, lawyers, public relations men, merchants, speculators and so forth! Indeed, all labour that is not directly related to the process of essential production and is maintained by a part of society's economic surplus. This formulation may well give rise to some confusion, for essential consumption here cannot mean essential consumption defined by the needs of capitalist society. Unproductive workers in capitalist society are those who produce goods considered as inessential not in terms of capitalism's needs but in terms of the requirements of another, more rational society. The absurdity of this proposition becomes even more clear when we remember that Baran's category of 'essential consumption' was defined as a 'socially determined' magnitude and type of output.

There are in addition workers who are not directly concerned with essential production but who should not be regarded as unproductive. This category includes scientists, physicians, artists and teachers. The only justification why these people should not be included among capitalism's unproductive workers is that whereas other workers maintained by society's surplus would be eliminated in a rational society, the demand for these people would become intensified.

The difference between capitalism and socialism in Baran and Sweezy's discourse is reduced to the existence of the rationally planned economy. The irrationality of capitalism is contrasted to the ultimate rationality of socialism. 'Socialism' is when the economic surplus is planned. Planned economic surplus is 'the difference between society's "optimum" output attainable in a historically given natural and technological environment under conditions of planned "optimal" utilisation of all available productive resources, and some chosen "optimal" volume of consumption'

(Baran, 1973, p. 155). 'Optimum' in this sense represents a considered judgement of a socialist community guided by reason and science. We are given no theoretical means of distinguishing feudalism, capitalism and socialism, other than the degree of rationality they involve. In the conception of the mode of utilisation of economic surplus as the major factor distinguishing types of society, there is no systematic conception of the social and political conditions of existence of particular social formations. Any conception of the relations of *production* is totally obscured in favour of an analysis of the allocation of resources.

The above argument is significant in considering Baran and Sweezy's theory in relation to Marxist theory. Marxism has always rejected concepts of surplus derived from the postulate of irreducible needs or concepts in which surplus is presented as an excess over the basic consumption needs of a society. In *Capital* the concepts of necessary and surplus labour are strictly economic concepts and are not derived from any extra-economic concept of human needs. For Marx, surplus value is the specifically capitalist mode of appropriation of surplus labour. The concept of necessary labour is defined as that labour time necessary to secure the conditions of reproduction of the labourer. Surplus labour, that is, labour over and above necessary labour, exists in all modes of production, because the conditions of reproduction of the labourer are not equivalent to the conditions of reproduction of the economy. This is the case even in the concept of the communist mode of production, as Marx shows in *Critique of the Gotha Programme*. Necessary and surplus labour must always be defined in relation to a determinate mode of production. The precise form of surplus labour is determined by a definite mechanism of extraction. The mode of appropriation of surplus labour is a dominant element in the concept of any determinate mode of production:

> The essential difference between the various economic forms of society, between, for instance, a society based on slave labour, and one based on wage-labour, lies only in the mode in which this surplus-labour is in each case extracted from the actual producer, the labourer. (Marx, 1974, vol. I, p. 209)

For Marx, surplus value is the mode of appropriation of surplus labour specific to the capitalist mode of production. The concept of surplus value involves a mechanism requiring private property in the means of production and separation of labour power from the objective conditions of labour.

Baran points out that the concept of surplus does not correspond to that of surplus value, which it has been argued is a dominant concept in the Marxist concept of capitalism, i.e. the capitalist *mode of production*. In a revealing footnote, Baran notes the difference between surplus value and potential economic surplus. Potential economic surplus refers to a different quantity of output than what would represent surplus in Marx's sense. On the one hand, it *excludes* such elements of surplus value as what was called above *essential* consumption of capitalists, what could be considered *essential* outlays on government administration and the like; on the other hand, it comprises what is not covered by the concept of surplus value – the output lost in view of underemployment or misemployment of productive resources. (Baran, 1973, p. 134; emphasis in original)

In contrast to the concept of surplus value, the concept of potential surplus relies in its definition on an idealism. Potential surplus depends on 'what could be considered' essential or non-essential production or consumption. In *Capital*, Marx is not attempting an ethical critique of capitalism.[11] The object of *Capital* is the elaboration of the concept of the capitalist mode of production and the conditions of production and exchange corresponding to that mode.[12]

We have seen how Baran's conception of 'unproductive labour' is specified as such by its relationship to an image of an ideal society. The Marxist concept is quite different.

Productive labour, in its meaning for capitalist production, is wage-labour which, exchanged against the variable part of capital (the part of the capital that is spent on wages), reproduces not only this part of the capital (or the value of its own labour-power) but in addition produces surplus value for the capitalist. (Marx: 1972, part 1, p. 148)

Very schematically, productive labour is defined in terms of the relations of production. Thus in the capitalist mode of production, productive labour is that which (always on the basis of use-value) produces exchange value in the form of commodities and so surplus value. In this conception, productive labour does not rely in its definition on any ideal state of affairs; it is defined always in relation to a determinate mode of production.

There is little justification for attributing to Baran or Sweezy any conception of feudalism, capitalism or socialism as modes of production in the Marxist sense. The concept of surplus used by Baran denegates any conception of the mode of production of surplus. What is relevant for Baran and Sweezy is the mode of *utilisation*. This clearly must place Baran and those who accept the concept of surplus outside the terrain of Marxist theory, in which the concept of mode of production is central.

Without a clear conception of the mode of production Baran cannot develop a consistent concept of the relations of production and thus of the class struggle. Indeed, there is a striking absence of any conception of the conditions of the class struggle under 'monopoly capitalism' which would be of central concern in any Marxist analysis. It must be emphasised that this cannot be considered merely an omission on the part of Baran. It cannot be coherently argued that the Marxist concept of class struggle may be added on to the concept of capitalism that Baran and Sweezy present.[13] On the contrary, the Marxist concept of class struggle cannot be derived from Baran's conception of capitalism or any 'type of society'.

For Marxism, the general concept of mode of production designates an articulated combination of relations and forces of production, structured by the dominance of the relations of production. There can be no definition of the relations or forces of production independently of the mode of production. The concept of the class struggle cannot be divorced from the concept of a determinate mode of production. In the case of the capitalist mode of production, surplus labour is appropriated by a class of non-labourers (capitalists), in the form of surplus value, from a class of labourers (wage-labourers). This constitutes antagonistic relations of production and a social division of labour between a class of direct producers and a class of capitalists.

The problem of the conception of social relations between classes in relation to the concept of economic surplus is highlighted particularly in the work of Frank. For Frank, the appropriation of economic surplus is the 'exploitation relationship' employed with reference both to relations between spatial entities (metropolis – satellite, etc.) and to relations between social classes.[14] As Ernesto Laclau points out,[15] Frank totally dispenses with any concept of relations of production in his definitions of capitalism and feudalism. The process of 'capitalism' designates equally the appropriation of surplus by landowners from peasants, by capitalists from workers, by big capitalists from little capitalists and by one nation from another.

The conception of a relation of 'exploitation' between one nation and another cannot be a conception of Marxism. As Bettelheim demonstrates, the concept of exploitation expresses a production relation between the production of surplus labour and its appropriation by a social class. It necessarily relates to *class* relations and a relation between countries cannot be a relation between classes.[16] Bettelheim shows that the notion of 'exploitation' of one *country* by another *country* may give rise to the formulation that the proletarians of the rich countries appear as 'exploiters' of the workers of the backward countries. This is precisely what is alluded to by Baran and Sweezy when they argue that the militarist and imperialist operations of government in monopoly capitalist society are fully acceptable to the society as a whole: 'Under such circumstances there evolves a far-reaching harmony between the interests of monopolistic business on the one side and those of the underlying population on the other' (Baran, 1973, p. 247). It is largely on the basis of such a notion that Baran and Sweezy reject the possibility of revolutionary action on the part of any section of the American people, and look to the underdeveloped *countries* to begin the 'world revolution' and to show by example that it is possible to build 'a rational society satisfying the human needs of human beings',[17] whence it is hoped Americans will start to question their existence and the powerful supports of the irrational system will crumble.

Baran and Sweezy maintain also that it is just possible that the universal 'mental' decay of the whole population of monopoly capitalism may provide the conditions of a total breakdown. It has been argued that Baran and Sweezy's analysis of the 'advanced' capitalist economies represents an ethical critique of capitalism. The ethical and Utopian nature of their theory is exemplified in their discussion of the quality of life in monopoly capitalist society. The similarity of their discussion with the nineteenth century Utopian socialists criticised by Marx and Engels is striking. The capitalist system, once progressive, is now a formidable hurdle to human advancement. It is 'capitalism' which condemns untold multitudes to privation, degradation and premature death by preventing the mobilisation of the potential economic surplus. An essential aspect of the *decay* of monopoly capitalism is its effects on the moral and psychological decay of 'man'. Monopoly capitalist society is 'a society without faith and without morals – and without the ability to provide its members with ways of using their energies for humanly interesting and worthy purposes' (Baran & Sweezy, 1970, p. 341). While, as we have seen, it is unlikely that 'organised labour' will take a stand against monopoly capitalism in America, it is possible that the present process of decay will continue 'with the contradiction between the compulsions of the system and the elementary needs of human nature becoming ever more insupportable' (ibid., p. 350). The logical outcome would be 'the spread of increasingly severe psychic disorders leading to the impairment and eventual breakdown of the system's ability to function even on its own terms' (ibid., p. 350).

ECONOMIC DEVELOPMENT AND 'UNDERDEVELOPMENT'

The conceptualisation of the nature of 'underdevelopment' in the work particularly of Paul Baran has been very influential in the modern attack on what is termed 'traditional' development theory. This is particularly evident in the work of André Gunder Frank who, in arguing that underdevelopment is in large part the historical product of relations between the underdeveloped 'satellites' and the present 'developed' countries, acknowledges his theoretical debt to the work of Paul Baran.

As we have already mentioned, Frank's best-known thesis is that economic development and underdevelopment are opposite faces of the same coin. Here Frank is clearly foreshadowed by Paul Baran. In Frank's work the concept of economic surplus is a central aspect of the three 'contradictions of capitalism' which are intended by Frank to trace the causes of underdevelopment. The first contradiction, as we have seen, is the 'expropriation/appropriation' of economic surplus, the 'exploitation' link which extends from landless labourers and others in the under-

developed country to the metropolitan countries. The second contradiction Frank calls the 'metropolis – satellite polarisation'.

> Thus the metropolis expropriates economic surplus from its satellites
> and appropriates it for its own economic development. The satellites
> remain underdeveloped for lack of access to their own surplus and as a
> consequence of the same polarisation and exploitative contradictions
> which the metropolis introduces and maintains in the satellite's
> domestic economic structure. (Frank, 1971, p. 33)

The metropolis – satellite relation, rather than constituting a direct cause
of underdevelopment, appears here to be established as an effect of the
surplus appropriation mechanism.

The third contradiction is that of 'continuity in change', 'the continuity
and ubiquity of the structural essentials of economic development and
underdevelopment throughout the expansion and development of the
capitalist system at all times and places' (ibid., p. 36). This proposition,
despite the lack of elaboration, is a constant thread in Frank's arguments,
both in his earlier books and in the more recent work *Lumpenbourgeoisie and
Lumpendevelopment* (Frank, 1972). Here Frank attempts to answer his critics
and argue that an analysis of class structure in underdeveloped societies *is*
important, although he provides no rigorous concepts for such analysis.
However, Frank reasserts the simplistic notions that Latin American
societies are capitalist societies and have been since the Conquest, and that
'development' is impossible under capitalism. Frank, however, still
remains silent on what capitalism actually is.[18] With little specification of
the nature of the Latin American economy, we are still left with the
implication of capitalism defined by exchange/consumption relations
alone. 'Classes' are involved in that the 'lumpenbourgeoisie' produces a
policy of 'lumpendevelopment'. Thus 'contemporary underdevelopment is
simply a continuation of the same fundamental processes of dependence,
transformation of economic class structure, and lumpenbourgeois policies
of underdevelopment which have been in operation throughout our
history' (Frank, 1972, p. 92).

Franks's rhetorical phrase 'the development of underdevelopment'
defines a universal historical process for the underdeveloped countries. The
emphasis on 'continuity of capitalist contradictions', however, leaves us
with the problem of how to explain the variations, historical and
contemporary, between specific social formations. Frank's argument
obscures the growth in production and the change in economic structures
and class relations which have occurred since the Second World War in
particular. There is no specification of the economic, political and
ideological conditions of existence of specific social formations. Frank has
not gone uncriticised on this account. Bill Warren, for example, has argued
that, contrary to the view that characteristics of 'backwardness' and

underdevelopment are necessary results of imperialism, substantial progress in capitalist industrialisation has already been achieved in the Third
World.[19] Frank has not totally ignored such growth, as his own analysis of
Brazil suggests, but he refuses to call this 'development'. In his more recent
work, Frank introduces the term 'lumpendevelopment' as a description of
contemporary events. But a change in terminology in no way fills a
theoretical void. The notion of 'continuity in change', in so far as it is not
entirely vacuous, serves to denegate the determination of specific variations in the concrete situation in Latin America and elsewhere.

Frank's insistence on the impossibility of 'development' under capitalism clearly indicates a similar conception of capitalism to that of Baran.
If capitalism is by definition irrational, then any increase in its scale of
operation merely increases the amount of irrationality. *True* development
can only occur where economic growth involves the introduction of
'socialism'.

In *The Political Economy of Growth* Baran is concerned to explain both the
original cause of 'underdevelopment' and the conditions of its continued
existence. 'Underdeveloped' countries are characterised by the paucity of
their per capita output. The explanation for 'underdevelopment' is to be
found in an analysis of the development of European capitalism. Baran
argues that it was the development of capitalism in the West which
simultaneously produced 'underdevelopment' in Latin America, Asia and
Africa, and it is the very existence of the advanced countries today that
prevents the economic development of the 'backward' countries. In his
analysis of the 'evolution' of capitalism out of feudalism, Baran attaches
central importance to the accumulation of money in the form of merchant
capital. In Western Europe such mercantile accumulations were particularly large and provided a strong impulse to the development of capitalist
enterprise. However, it is precisely the nature of Western European
development which prevented economic development in the now underdeveloped countries of the world. Whereas the Western European
'entrance' into North America, Australia and New Zealand took the form
of emigration and the settlers developed from the outset a capitalist
structure, in other parts of the world Europeans came up against existing
societies which largely precluded the possibility of any mass settlement.
Consequently, 'the Western European visitors rapidly determined to
extract the largest possible gains from the host countries, and to take their
loot home' (Baran, 1973, p. 274).

Such overseas operations greatly increased the economic surplus of
Western Europe. The increase in surplus came into the hands of capitalists
who could use it for investment purposes. The effects of the extraction of
the surplus from the 'donor' countries provided the basis for underdevelopment. The decomposition of the pre-capitalist structures, which was
everywhere gradually occurring, was accelerated. Peasant-occupied land
was seized, creating a large pool of pauperised labour, improvements were

made in communications, etc., but while providing such favourable
conditions for capitalist development, the determinant element, the
economic surplus, was removed. The result was that capitalist development 'was forcibly shunted off its *normal course, distorted and crippled* to suit
the purposes of Western imperialism' (ibid., p. 276; emphasis added).

Examining the current situation of economic 'underdevelopment', the
concept of economic surplus is again the dominant element in explaining
this phenonmenon. While the surplus in absolute terms has been small in
the backward capitalist countries, it has accounted for a large share of total
output – as large as if not larger than in 'advanced' capitalist countries.
The main cause of continued underdevelopment is not simply the
'irrational' use of the actual surplus, but the way in which their potential
economic surplus is utilised. The potential surplus, that is, what would be
available for investment given a purposeful utilisation of the national
output, is sufficiently large in all underdeveloped countries to enable them
to attain very high rates of growth. The utilisation of this surplus is
considered the principal obstacle to rapid economic growth. It is absorbed
by various forms of excess consumption by the upper class, by maintenance
of 'unproductive' bureaucracies and redundant military establishment,
and a very large share of it is withdrawn by foreign capital. The conclusion
is that it is 'the economic and social system of capitalism and imperialism
that prevents the urgently needed full mobilisation of the potential
economic surplus and the attainment of rates of economic advancement
that can be secured with its help' (ibid., p. 396). This being the case, the
way to solve the problems of underdevelopment is to institute a more
rational utilisation of the economic surplus; that is, economic surplus must
be planned. Such a rationally planned economy is called a socialist
economy and 'socialism' becomes 'an essential, indeed indispensable,
condition for the attainment of economic and social progress in underdeveloped countries' (ibid., p. 416).

One of the most influential conclusions arising from Paul Baran's work
on 'underdevelopment' is the conceptualisation of a realationship between
capitalist development in the West and underdevelopment in Latin
America, Asia and Africa. Certainly it is this conception which has
received the greatest attention in the work of Frank and most of the
'dependency' theorists. As we have seen, Baran's argument is that
underdevelopment 'was actually determined by the nature of Western
European development itself' (ibid., p. 273).

For Baran, the determinant element in Western European capitalist
development was the accumulation of 'capital' by merchants. This greatly
added to the countries' economic surplus, which was then used for
investment purposes, thus giving capitalist development a 'boost'. However, at the same time this 'wealth' accumulated by European merchants
was gained by plundering the now underdeveloped countries, thus
reducing the economic surplus at their disposal and therefore preventing

their accumulation of capital. However, Western European development need not necessarily have prevented economic growth in other countries. While it is unlikely that they would have been able to eliminate the gap between themselves and the European pioneers, the underdeveloped countries 'could nevertheless have entered a growth process of their own, attaining more or less advanced levels of productivity and output' (ibid., p. 272). Baran's argument thus relies on two major propositions. Firstly, that the accumulation of merchant wealth was the determinant element in the development of European capitalism, and secondly, that 'independent' economic growth was possible for the now 'underdeveloped' countries.

We are told that in Western Europe merchant fortunes were very large and that this wealth had 'the usual tendency to snowball', the result being a mighty impulse to the development of *capitalist* enterprise in the form of shipbuilding, outfitting of overseas expeditions, etc. The West developed as accumulated merchant capital gradually turned to industrial pursuits.[20]

The process of the 'decomposition' of the 'feudal order', due to its own 'internal stresses and strains', was not just occuring in Europe; 'the pre-capitalist order, be it Europe or be it Asia, had entered at a certain stage of its development a period of disintegration and decay' (ibid., p. 268). Moreover, while 'in different countries this decomposition was more or less violent, the period of decline was shorter or longer – the general *direction* of movement was everywhere the same' (ibid., p. 268; emphasis in original). The reason why the development of capitalism was able to take its *normal course* in Western Europe was the existence of large sums of money created by trade.

The teleology of this argument is clear. It relies on a unilinear and evolutionist conception of historical development. Feudalism was everywhere declining of its own accord. Its natural form of succession was capitalism. 'Underdevelopment' occurs when the historical process is interrupted. The teleological nature of Baran's conception of 'economic development' becomes quite evident when he attempts to explain the non-essentiality of underdevelopment. Taking the example of India, Baran argues that the effect of British plundering of Indian wealth was to stunt the growth of indigenous capitalism: 'It would have been, however, an entirely different India . . . had she been allowed – as some more fortunate countries were – to *realise her destiny* in her own way, to employ her resources for her own benefit' (ibid., p. 285; emphasis added). However, while India was prevented from realising its destiny, Japan was not. The essential point of difference is that Western penetration of Japan was held back due to a 'felicitous confluence of a large number of more or less independent factors'. By the time the West began to make inroads into Japan, Japan had been left to its own devices for a longer period of time and therefore had been able to advance further along the line of progress to capitalist development. Feudalism had been allowed to decay of its own accord.[21]

If we look briefly at how Baran's argument relates to Marxist theory, we can see that while Baran does not take the view that 'capitalism' is synonymous with commodity exchange, the expansion of trade is seen as a major cause of the development of capitalism. In Marxist theory, the capitalist mode of production is not simply defined by the existence of commodity relations or the production of commodities on the basis of wage-labour. These forms may well develop within the ancient or feudal modes of production. Nor can the capitalist mode of production be defined simply in terms of a switch from agriculture to industrial production. What is crucial in the concept of the capitalist mode of production is that capital should function as an instrument of production of surplus value and its relisation for a class of capitlists. This functioning cannot be determined at the level of the labour process in individual units of production. Whether or not manufacturing is capitalist depends not on the form of organisation of the labour process but on its articulation within the system of social production as a whole.

If the period of transition from one mode of production to another is conceived as consisting of a number of transitional conjunctures and the transition as effected by means of a number of displacements in the movement from the conjuncture to another, no transition can be conceived as a unitary event, the singular effect of a single cause or sequence of causes. There can be no question of explaining the origins of European capitalism as the result of the expansion of maritime commerce. It is not argued here that extensive development of commodity production and trade and the consequent development of merchant's capital are not necessary conditions of the transition from feudalism to capitalism, but that there can be no reduction of the conditions to the simple basis Baran suggests.[22]

CONCLUSION

It has been argued that Baran's concept of 'underdevelopment' depends on an evolutionist conception of a process of economic development. It is clear from *The Political Economy of Growth* the feudalism is conceived as a transitory phenomenon whose natural form of succession is capitalism. 'Underdevelopment' occurs when there is an interruption of the 'normal' course of history. We have seen from Baran and Sweezy's discussion of contemporary capitalism that the conditions of existence of 'monopoly capitalism' are always already present in competitive capitalism and that 'monopoly capitalism' is in its conception a decaying system. The transitory nature of 'monopoly capitalism' is not determined by any analysis of the material conditions of a specific conjuncture, for example by the condition of the class struggle, but is established principally because of the 'inner essence' of capitalism., its irrationality.

While Baran's analysis of the origin of 'inderdevelopment' relies on an evolutionism, Baran and Sweezy's discourse as a whole is clearly teleological. The crucial feature of the teleological postulate is not the necessity of a temporal sequence but its essentialism, the conceptualisation of distinct forms (in this case types of society) as the realisation or expression of their position in a hierarchy of forms.[23] We have seen how Baran and Sweezy's societies are differentiated primarily in terms of their degree of potential rationality. Feudalism is irrational but the difference between its actual rationality and its potential rationality is not very great. Capitalism, and in particular monopoly capitalism, has a much higher potential because of the evolution of the techniques of production. Societies are ranked according to their divergence from a rational ideal society. This ranking constitutes the conception of the societies. The irrationality of capitalism is undoubtedly the major theme of Baran and Sweezy's work. The concepts of capitalism and feudalism consist primarily in their divergence from the ultimate rationality of the planned economy, or 'socialism'.[24]

In examining the conceptual structure of Baran and Sweezy's theory of contemporary capitalism and economy development, it has been argued that these authors do not achieve their objective of developing Marxist theory. In particular, the effect of the concept of 'economic surplus' precludes the development of a Marxist concept of mode of production and the class struggle. In addition, the paper has demonstrated that Baran and Sweezy's discourse contains several contradictions and incoherences, arising from the ambiguity of the concept of 'surplus' and its use, the relativism of the concept of 'rationality' and, most fundamentally, their teleological conception of the economy and economic development.

NOTES

1. 'Dependent' countries are conceived as those countries which lack an autonomous capacity for change and growth.
2. For a discussion of 'dependency theory' see O'Brien (1975).
3. A notable exception is Laclau (1971).
4. The object of this paper is not to say that Baran, Sweezy and Frank, the subjects, are not Marxists, but that the major concepts they employ are neither concepts which appear in the dominant works of Marx, nor could they be said to be elaborated from Marx's basic concepts.
5. Baran (1973) pp. 135–6.
6. It is not an object of this paper to discuss Baran and Sweezy's epistemology. Suffice to say that it is a crude epistemology of models.. 'Scientific understanding proceeds by way of constructing and analysing "models" of the segments or aspects of reality under study' (Baran & Sweezy, 1970, p. 27). According to Baran and Sweezy, Marx's theory is a model derived from the study of Britain. The error in this conception is made clear in Althusser & Balibar (1970). Baran and Sweezy regard their own work as a theoretical model based on a study of the United States. For a critique of this type of position see Hindess (1973).
7. Baran and Sweezy's position cannot be redeemed from its concentration on

subjective aims and values of corporate managers merely by saying that 'the character of the system determines the psychology of its members and not vice versa' (1970, p. 53), for we are given no conception of the 'system' independent of the psychology of its members.

8. See Poulantzas (1973, 1975).
9. Stanfield (1973).
10. In criticising Baran and Sweezy's arguments concerning a 'tendency of surplus to rise', I do not want to argue in favour of what they see as the alternative concept, i.e. the tendency of the rate of profit to fall. The conception of an inbuilt tendency for capitalism to stagnate or fall into crisis as a result of the falling rate of profit is open to serious objection. According to Marx's formulation, an increase in the productivity of labour results in a rise in the organic composition of capital. As the rate of profit is held to vary inversely with the organic composition of capital, this means that there must be a tendency for the rate of profit to fall. However, increases in productivity can affect both constant and variable capital. There are no theoretical grounds for postulating any increase or decrease affecting the organic composition of capital. There is also a more general problem here, that of the inadequacy of Marx's explanation of the relationship between prices and values, which it is not possible to discuss here. The point here is, however, that while Marx's formulation of the falling rate of profit is inadequate, Baran and Sweezy's replacement is not a coherent alternative.
11. This is not to argue that one cannot find humanist passages in *Capital*. They are not, however, dominant elements in conceptualising the capitalist mode of production.
12. We have no ground for considering that Baran and Sweezy's rejection of the concept of surplus value in favour of a concept of 'surplus' is an attempt to deal with the problem of the relationship between values and prices.
13. As Baran and Sweezy suggest (1970, p. 22)
14. See Booth (1975).
15. Laclau (1971) p. 25.
16. Bettelheim (1972)
17. Baran & Sweezy (1970) p. 352.
18. The absence of any precise definition of capitalism in Frank's previous work was pointed out by Laclau (1971, p. 24).
19. Warren (1973).
20. Baran appears here to suggest a correspondence between 'capitalism' and the growth of industry. If the growth of trade and ancillary activities is to be called capitalism, it has clearly been around for centuries.
21. For a critique of teleological theories of the transition from one mode of production to another see Hindess & Hirst (1975) esp. chap. 6.
22. It is not maintained here that there are no teleological or essentialist passages to be found in *Capital*, or in the work of Lenin and other Marxist writers. However, the fundamental concepts are anti-teleological and anti-essentialist.
23. For an examination of the conceptual structure of teleology, see the paper by Hindess in this volume.
24. It is not argued here that the concept of socialism does not involve a concept of economic planning, but that the conditions of existence of socialism cannot be reduced to or deduced from the concept of a planned economy.

5 Peasant Economy and Society

GARY LITTLEJOHN

INTRODUCTION

The considerable body of literature devoted to the peasantry, with its variety of definitions of the concept, has induced various writers (for example, Thorner, 1971) to attempt a definition of the peasantry based on a fairly comprehensive review of the relevant literature. Rather than 'duplicate' this work to provide yet another wide-ranging discussion, it is proposed to deal primarily with the work of a major theorist in this field, A. V. Chayanov,[1] indicating where appropriate similarities in the work of other theorisits. While Chayanov's work was an important weapon against the agrarian policies of the Bolsheviks (and for that reason was criticised by Stalin[2]), the main contemporary reason why his work deserves serious consideration is not simply that it has had a continuing influence on present-day sociologists who study the peasantry, notably Thorner (1962, 1966, 1971) and Shanin (1972),[3] but primarily because his theory is a particularly clear example of the type of position which sets up the 'peasant economy' and 'peasant society' as distinctive forms of economy and society. Hence an analysis of the theoretical implications of his position is likely to be more illuminating than a discussion of a variety of positions, which runs the risk of concentrating on superficial differences between these positions.

It will be argued that Chayanov's theory has certain inherent difficulties which cannot be solved in terms of his concepts. After an exposition of the basic concepts, the analysis will concentrate on the effects of the opposition which this theory sets up between subject and structure, an opposition which is of central importance in defining the relations between its concepts. It will be argued that the opposition betweeen an economic subject whose consciousness constitutes the structure of a sector of the economy on the one hand, and a 'wider' economic and social structure in which 'objective' factors are thought to have causal effectivity on the other hand, creates serious problems for this theory. The counterposing of two distinct kinds of causality within a single theory inevitably leads to inconsistency. In this case the inconsistency is effectively resolved in favour of the subjective determination of the peasant economy. The peasant economy is therefore conceived as the phenomenon of a human essence, located not at the level of the individual but at the level of the peasant family, a collective subject. The difficulties encountered in the attempt to reconcile the conception of the peasant economy as structured by the constitutive collective subject with the acknowledgement of the effects of the 'wider' economic and social structure (which includes the peasant economy as a part) on the peasant economy itself are illustrated (a) by an examination of Chayanov's use of the labour – consumer balance to analyse peasant farm organisation, (b) by an examination both of the posited effects of the family farm on demographic and social differentiation, and of the supposed future development of the peasant economy in the Soviet Union, and (c) by an analysis of his theory of rent. Rent in this theory provides a crucial link between the peasant economy and the national economy, but in addition to its intrinsic importance in the theory, his analysis of rent is of interest as the site of a claim that this theory is similar to that of Marx on peasant proprietorship of land parcels. For this reason, the analysis of Chayanov's theory of rent is conducted in terms of a comparison with the relevant section of Marx's *Capital*. The main purpose of this paper, however, is not to delineate the differences between this type of theory and Marxism (although this is necessary at times), but rather to provide a critique of this type of theory itself.

BASIC CONCEPTS

The fundamental concepts of this theory 'devoted to the composition of the individual agricultural labour farm' (p. 223) are the family labour farm, the single labour income and the labour – consumer balance. It is these concepts which fundamentally determine the conclusions Chayanov draws, such as the view that the differentiation of the peasantry was primarily due to demographic factors, rather than factors causing farms to become capitalist and proletarianised. The family labour farm is conceived of as the unit of production, and therefore as the basis on which the theory is constructed around the '*organisational* problems of agricultural *production*' (p. 37 – hence the name of the Organisation and Production School). 'On the family labour farm, the family, equipped with means of production, uses its labour power to cultivate the soil and receives as the result of a year's work a certain amount of goods. A single glance at the inner structure of the family labour unit is enough to realise that it is impossible without the category of wages to impose on this structure net profit, rent, and interest on capital as real economic categories in the capitalist meaning of the word' (p. 5). After a deduction from the gross product to cover material expenditure during the year, we are left with the family labour product. 'This family labour product is the only possible category of income for a peasant or artisan family labour unit, for there is no way of decomposing it analytically or objectively. Since there is no social phenomenon of wages, the social phenomenon of net profit is also absent. Thus it is impossible to apply the capitalist profit calculation' (p. 5). Because of its *conceptual indivisibility*, Chayanov usually refers to the family labour product as a single labour income, as when he expounds his main hypothesis: ' . . . to explain theoretically the organisational peculiarities that have been observed – a hypothesis based on the concept of the peasant farm as a family labour farm in which the family as a result of its year's labour receives a single labour income and weighs its efforts against the material results obtained' (p. 41). The motivation of the peasant's economic activity is thus not that of an entrepreneur, but of a 'worker on a peculiar piece-rate system which allows him alone to determine the time and intensity of his work. The whole originality of our theory of peasant farm organisation is, in essence, included in this modest prerequisite, since all other conclusions and constructions follow *in strict logic* from this basic premise and bind all the empirical material into a fairly harmonious system' (p. 42; emphasis in the original).

The labour – consumer balance is the main regulator of the economic activity of the farm. An equilibrium level of income has to be established which is determined by two main elements: (a) the consumption needs of the family, and (b) the degree of labour effort ('drudgery') through which the working members effect a certain quantity of labour units in the course of the year, that is, the amount of labour expended to produce the labour product for that year. However, the amount of the labour product is not only determined by the degree of labour effort. It as also determined by the size and composition of the working family, in particular by the proportion of its members able to work (called the 'consumer – worker ratio'), by the quality of the soil and the relation of the farm to the markets (which Chayanov considers are rent-forming factors, even if this is not capitalist rent), and by the availability of means of production (which at times he calls 'capital'). Since these must all be taken into account in addition to the degree of drudgery in the analysis of the labour – consumer balance, it is clear that the equilibrium point is potentially very variable. However, there is a minimum below which the single labour income cannot be allowed to fall – the family subsistence level. While the amount of the single labour income is determined by the demographic structure of the family, by the productivity of the labour unit (determined by the rent-forming factors and the availability of 'capital') and by the degree of labour effort, it is mainly through adjusting the latter that the family brings its income into equilibrium with its consumption needs. It is in this sense that Chayanov considers that the peasant farm has a work motivation analogous to a piece – rate system, which determines the volume of the farm's economic activity and thereby its income. The capacity to establish an equilibrium between consumption needs and income in widely varying circumstances is the justification for treating the peasant farm as 'one of the organisational forms of private economic undertakings' (p. 43), a form which is relatively independent of the structure of the national economy.

There are two immediate implications of this position which Chayanov tried to deal with. Firstly, what is the nature of the equilibrium, the single labour income, established by the labour – consumer balance? Secondly, what is the relation of the unit of production, the family labour farm, to the wider economic system? Chayanov appears at times to describe the labour – consumer balance in terms of purely subjective evaluation. Thus on p. 46 he says: 'I use the hypothesis of the subjective labour – consumer balance to analyse the on-farm processes and to establish the nature of the motivation of the peasant family's economic activity.' This apparently subjective approach, combined with his use of marginalist economic concepts, led critics to suppose that he was an adherent of the Austrian marginal utility school of economics. Chayanov differentiated himself from this school of thought, correctly criticising it for attempting 'to derive from subjective evaluations of the utility of objects *an entire* system of the national economy' (p. 220; emphasis in the original). His subjective analysis is restricted to on-farm processes and even there the labour – consumer balance is not merely an effect of the consciousness of the actors; he claims (on p. 48) that a Rothschild in the same situation would behave in the same way for all his acquisitive capitalist psychology. Rather the nature of the subjective evaluation is tied to the absence on the farm of the traditional categories used to analyse modern capitalist society. Externally, the farm can only appear through its objective actions. 'It is from the mass interrelations of these actions with those of others composing the system of the national economy that the objective social phenomena of price, rent, and so on are formed' (p. 46). Yet given the admission (p. 73) that the conditions determining the level of labour productivity depend not so much on on-farm factors as on general economic factors affecting the farm's existence, one is forced to question how 'insulated' the labour – consumer balance is from the national economy. For the structural integrity of the organisational form is crucial in this theory. If one argues that 'the organisational shape of the basic cell, the peasant family labour farm, will remain the same, always changing in particular features and adapting to the circumstances surrounding the national economy, so long as the peasant farm exists as such, of course, and has not begun to be reconstructed into other organisational forms' (p. 42 – 3), then clearly it is of major importance to determine whether the national economy merely affects the level of the labour – consumer balance or whether it is generating the very economic categories[4] which destroy the labour – consumer balance and change the organisation of the unit of production.

This problem is suppressed in this theory because of the way in which the concepts for the internal analysis of the family farm are produced, and because of the relation in this theory between the unit of production and the dominant economic system. The clearest exposition of the relation between the subjective labour – consumer balance and the absence of capitalist economic categories is contained in the essay 'On the Theory of Non-Capitalist Economic Systems' (pp. 1 – 28 of *The Theory of Peasant Economy*). The economic theory of modern society is regarded as 'a complicated system of economic categories which are *inseparably* connected with one another – price, capital, wages, interest, rent, which determine one another and are functionally interdependent. If one brick drops out of this system, the whole building collapses. In the absence of *any one* of these economic categories, all others lose their specific character and conceptual content; and cannot even be defined quantitatively' (pp. 3 – 4; emphasis added). This kind of theory is contrasted with a 'natural economy', where the price category (commodity exchange) is absent, but the remarks about the inseparability of the categories are immediately modified. One cannot apply, in *their usual meanings*, any one of the categories. Instead of the whole building collapsing, parts of it can still be used. None of it need be used for a completely 'natural economy', but clearly this leaves open the possibility of using some of the concepts where there is a certain degree of development of commodity production. With the concept of a 'natural economy', where the general structure of the economy is not specified because it is mythical,[5] there is no problem in introducing the concepts of family consumer needs, unit of production and conceptually indivisible product in only two sentences (p. 4; emphasis in original): 'In a natural economy, human economic activity is dominated by the requirement of satisfying the needs of each single production unit, which is, at the same time, a consumer unit. Therefore, budgeting here is to a high degree *qualitative*; for each family need, there has to be provided in each economic unit the qualitatively corresponding product *in natura*.' Only on the basis of this 'natural economy' without commodity production can one argue more or less convincingly for the conceptual indivisibility of the labour product, and for the need to balance labour effort and consumption needs. The subjective evaluation of the equilibrium is in this case an effect of the absence of prices and wages and of the production and consumption units being united in the family labour farm. So Chayanov seems initially to be unlike the Austrian marginalists, in that he is not apparently deducing the structure of the economic system from the actors' perceptions, but rather the reverse, since the economic structure generates the categories which the actors use. Even when Chayanov moves away from the 'natural economy' to other non-capitalist economic systems where money plays some part, and some of the capitalist economic categories are applicable, as summarised in Table 1 on 'Economic Systems' reproduced here, he only claims that there is a single indivisible family labour product *where the product is not sold as a commodity*. On this basis, the organisational form of the

TABLE 1 Economic Systems

		Family economy				Feudal system*		
Economic categories	Capitalism	Commodity economy	Natural economy	Slave economy	Qui-rent serf economy	Landlord economy	Peasant economy	Communism
Commodity price	+	+	−	+	+	+	−	−
Single indivisible family labour product	−	+	+	−	+	−	+	−
Technical process of production or reproduction of the means of production	+	+	+	+	+	−	+	+
Capital advanced by the entrepreneur and circulating in production according to the formula $M-C-M+m$	+	−	−					
Interest on capital in the form of rentier's income	+	+	−	+	+	+	−	−
Wages	+	−	−	−	−	−	−	−
Slave rent or serf rent	−	−	−	+	+	+	+	−
Slave price or serf price	−	−	−	+	+†	+‡	−	−
Differential rent	++	++	−	+	+‡	++	−	+
Land price	+	−	−	+	+	+	−	−
State production plan	−	−	−	−	−	−	−	+
Regulation by non-economic constraint necessary to maintain the regime	−	−	+	+	+	+	+	+

* The feudal economy is a symbiosis of the natural labour economy of tribute-paying peasants and the monetary and exchange economic orientation of the commodity-trading feudal lords. Therefore, it has two economic objects of a different kind and two systems of economic categories, the elements of which do not coincide. This circumstance made us allocate two different columns in this table.

† Rent does not occur here as a special independent income category; nevertheless, rent-generating factors affect the amount of the single indivisible labour product of the family.

‡ Rent is present here as an economic income category, but its genesis is different from that in the capitalist system.

family labour farm can be considered independent of the wider economic and social structure, although the latter affects the level of the labour – consumer balance by means of a variety of measures of non-economic constraint. The only exception to this rule is where Chayanov introduces commodity prices of the product as an acceptable variation of the family labour farm,[6] a move which is necessary to maintain his position that the theory is applicable to twentieth-century Russia, where the majority of the peasant farms engaged in some commodity production.[7]

The mechanism by which commodity-producing family labour farms are introduced as having a single labour income is interesting. It is accomplished by a shift in the discussion away from the 'natural economy', that is, away from the absence of the price category (p. 4) to the absence of the wage category (p. 5), followed by a declaration that even with the categories of price and capital present, the structure of an economy lacking the wage category lies outside the conceptual systems of an economics adapted to capitalist society. This is acceptable in the sense that one can have commodity production and (say, merchants') capital without the labour process itself being organised on capitalist lines with wage labour, but it diverts attention from what ought to be provided at this point, namely a demonstration that the concepts of family labour farm, labour – consumer balance and single labour income are the appropriate means for dealing with such an economic structure. Clearly, such an economy is one which *could* become a fully developed capitalist economy, and it could therefore be designated a transitional economy (without implying any necessary outcome to that transition). Yet while this is recognised to a certain extent in the final chapter of the book, the implications are not fully thought through. The reason for this is that Chayanov considers that the family labour farm can exist until it hires wage labour, thereby becoming capitalist, but even with the existence of simple commodity production, the concept of a single labour income is hard to sustain. If even *part* of the product is sold, the single labour income is no longer conceptually indivisible. It can be 'decomposed analytically' as well as separated materially. In other words, the effect of the market is not merely to determine the *level* of the labour – consumer balance, but if one were consistent to preclude the existence of the labour – consumer balance by splitting the single labour income into commodities and products in kind. If each economic unit does·not have to supply all the products it needs (or wants), the way is open for the quantitative determination through prices of what products are substitutable for those actually provided on the farm. The products no longer produced on the farm can be bought by producing and selling other products which require a lower degree of 'labour effort' than it would take to produce the products now being bought, as Chayanov implicitly recognises in his discussion of the development of exchange from the 'natural economy' (p. 4). With prices, the way is open for calculation of 'comparative advantages'. There is a quantitative basis for the evaluation of the labour-time necessary to produce a product within any given farm. Specialisation in those products requiring least labour-time is possible on the basis that they can be exchanged for other products necessary for the continuation of production. The production of commodities thus allows the division of labour to take place *between* units of production, not just within them as in the supposed 'natural economy' self-sufficiency of the non-commodity family labour farms. Hence if capitalism is dominant in the rest of the economy, the way is open for the increasing penetration of commodity relations to transform the rural units of production. Yet when Chayanov says (p. 48) that he expects trading and finance capital to dominate considerable sectors of agriculture, which as regards production will remain as before, composed of small-scale family labour peasant undertakings subject in their internal organisation to the laws of the labour—consumer balance, it is clear that his concepts preclude an examination of the development of capitalism in agriculture as it affects the forms of organisation of the production unit.[8]

SUBJECT AND STRUCTURE

The major difficulties raised by such a position should by now be fairly clear. The division between the sector of the peasant family farms subject in their internal organisation to the labour—consumer balance on the one hand and the rest of the economy on the other hand amounts to a separation of the economy into a sector determined primarily by the subjective perceptions of the actors and the 'residual' sector defined simply by the non-effectivity of the economic actor's perceptions. In this case the economic subject is a collective one (the family), which is counterposed to 'general economic conditions' or the 'national economy', where 'objective factors' are recognised to have effectivity. Thus the 'national economy' is a structure whose determination is not reducible to the constitutive action of economic subjects. This leads to an ambiguity in the theory since the structure is conceived of as affecting the peasant sector which is in a sense part of it, yet the peasant sector is also conceived of as a relatively homogeneous aggregation of peasant family farms, each determined by its own economic subject. The theoretical contradiction between these two forms of determination is resolved in favour of the economic subjects since the structure is effectively ignored. At times the effects of the structure are acknowledged within the peasant sector, as when the individual peasant farm is counterposed to 'local general economic conditions', but basically the peasant sector is seen as the realm of subjective determination. The main effect of the structure, which Chayanov admits cannot be explained in terms of subjective assessments,[9] is thought to be the generation of the categories available for economic calculation. Yet this point is not elaborated explicitly, and the theory concentrates on the sector determined by the economic subjects (after all, it is a theory of peasant economy).

The procedure of defining a sector or region of society and concentrating attention on it in constructing a theory seems to be justified by the view (still common in present-day sociology) that one can construct regional theories of a society in virtual isolation from other regional theories or theories of the whole society, then add these theories together to get a 'complete picture'. Chayanov's adherence to this view can be seen from his assertion that the peasant farm can exist in various economic systems with various modifications, coupled with a recognition of the need 'to give the theoretical tie-up of our organisational concept with the principal views on the national economy and its development' (p. 4). However, this 'recognition' amounts to treating the structure in virtually *ad hoc* descriptive terms,[10] as a result of the concentration on the area determined by economic actors. The dichotomy subject/structure thus involves the creation of a regional theory referring to an area determined by subjects, coupled with an 'external' structure which is inadequately theorised and which bears a loosely specified relation to the area determined by subjects. The trouble with this view of theory construction is that without an overall theory to define and locate the regional theory one finds oneself in the position of attempting to integrate theories based on incommensurable concepts, or else a theoretically arbitrary description of the structure is necessarily coupled with a speculative account of its effects on the area determined by the actors. This account has to conclude that, whatever the nature of the structure and its effects may be (unless it is defined as a structure incompatible with the peasant economy, for example slavery or capitalism), within the peasant economy determination by economic subjects is dominant.[11]

The arbitrary nature of such a conclusion is usually concealed by reference to empirical material which 'verifies' it. This is especially true of Chayanov, who relied on the extensive statistical work which had been carried out in Russia from the 1880s as a fund of empirical material on which to draw in elaborating his theory. However, such 'verification' assumes that the empirical material is theoretically innocent, whereas it is frequently the product of the broadly similar conceptual framework of those who collected it. Where the material is open to other possible interpretations, Chayanov's attempts to consider such interpretations are unsatisfactory. These points will be illustrated during the discussion of his detailed examination of the factors affecting the labour – consumer balance and the volume of economic activity.

THE LABOUR – CONSUMER BALANCE AND PEASANT FARM ORGANISATION

At the end of Chapter 1 (on the influence of the peasant family on the development of economic activity), Chayanov takes the view (p. 69) that only when all the elements affecting the volume of economic activity have been examined in terms of their 'interrelationships and the specific weight of each one in determining the structure and volume of the peasant farm's economic activity, can we also approach a knowledge of the nature of the peasant farm'. However, it is clear from the beginning of the next chapter (p. 71) that the idea is already firmly entrenched that the main determinants are in the on-farm processes. The crucial chapters in establishing this are Chapter 3, 'The Basic Principles of Peasant Farm Organisation', and Chapter 4, 'The Organisational Plan of the Peasant Farm', for it is there that the elements are evaluated, although this evaluation anticipates the results of later chapters, particularly Chapter 5, 'Capital on the Labour Farm'.

The analysis of the principles of peasant farm organisation is based on an assumption that earnings are proportional to the expenditure of physical effort, so that it is possible to talk of 'labour units' on which the peasant family can effectively base its evaluation of the labour – consumer balance. This assumption is only tenable if there is some rough equivalence of labour units from year to year, allowing the peasant to estimate the work required to produce a given annual income. Clearly there are problems with this position, since harvest yields can vary with the weather and, in so far as the peasant farm produces commodities, market fluctuations can influence the level of the single labour income in ways which cannot be forecast. Yet the concept of labour units is necessary if the family is to balance its expenditure of labour with its consumption needs, since otherwise the balance is not determined by the family. The labour units established on the basis of experience form the basis for the marginal analysis of the labour – consumer balance. The rough equivalence of labour units does not imply any assumption of constant returns. On the contrary, the marginal analysis referred to here presupposes changes in the proportions of factors of production. If they change, the labour unit will ostensibly change, in that the productivity of labour will change, but the family is thought to be capable of adjusting factor proportions by altering land and capital as well as labour. While the peasant family may not be explicitly aware of the concepts of this kind of marginal analysis,[12] the clear implication is that in so far as this analysis 'fits the facts', the subject is both implicitly rational and in control of the unit of production. The marginal analysis of the labour – consumer balance is thus the basis for establishing the implicit rationality of the economic subject.

The evaluation of the elements of peasant farm organisation is couched in terms of the combination of the traditional three factors of production of political economy – land, labour and capital (p. 90). If there is a shortage of one factor of production, technical necessity forces a proportionate drop in the other factors from the optimal level of combination and induces a reduction in the size of the farm. However, the reduction in productivity resulting from the violation of the optimal factor proportions can be offset by an increase in labour intensity. Apart from offsetting a shortage of, say, land by increased intensity of work, Chayanov sees the farm hands turning to *non-agricultural* earnings to attain the economic equilibrium with family demands if the latter are not fully met by farm income or by receipts from crafts and trades (p. 94).[13] If there is an excess of land or capital, the labour force is regarded by Chayanov as fixed, since it is limited to the family (p. 92), and the extra capital or land would not lead to an increase in the volume of economic activity. It would be a burden because of the increased intensity of labour necessary to exploit it. This problem could easily be overcome by hiring labourers or by co-operation between farms at crucial times of the year (both in fact resorted to in Russia at this time). Chayanov does not consider these possibilities because his analysis of the role of land and capital is already in terms of their effective subordination to the labour – consumer balance and the single labour income.

The main justification for the primacy of family size and composition in determining the on-farm equilibrium comes from the evidence that where there is a shortage of land and capital, the family farm tends to develop the factor proportions from the minimum to the optimum level. In the case of land, the existence of the repartitional commune plus the possibility of renting land make this sort of argument plausible initially, but Chayanov has already admitted (p. 107) that shortage of land and capital sometimes forces the family to move into crafts and trades as a source of income. In the case of capital, which will be used to illustrate his analysis of factor proportions, Chayanov argues in Chapter 3 (p. 113), on the basis of results to be established in Chapter 5, that the availability of the means of production tends to be adjusted to the optimal volume of activity, and says that where this is not possible, there has to be both an increase in the intensity of labour and a lower standard of living compared with a farm of optimal size and proportions. The analysis of capital on the labour farm in Chapter 5 must therefore be examined to see whether it supports Chayanov's conclusion that capital tends to be adjusted to the optimal proportion.

After reviewing some empirical material in Chapter 5, Chayanov concludes (p. 202) that 'while the farm's capital intensity has not yet reached its optimum, the growth rate of capital renewal in most cases exceeds that for personal budgets'. He immediately goes on to conclude that expenditures on capital renewal 'are included in our system of the basic economic equilibrium between the drudgery of labour and the farm family's demand satisfaction', and rejects the conclusion that in renewing itself the capital 'automatically gives for each unit a corresponding level of family well-being, and that there is no on-farm equilibrium at all'. He rejects the conclusion on the basis of a series of questions (p. 203), one of which is: why does the farm family not try to take the process of capital formation to the optimum that would ensure it the highest income? That is, he is here denying one of the conclusions that he claimed in Chapter 3 (p. 113) was derived from Chapter 5. The reason for this is that he is arguing here that the personal budget is not subordinate to, but rather dominates, the process of capital formation in determining the year's income level. He is at this point forgetting that he himself had earlier claimed (p. 119) not to have a consumption-determined theory of income level, but a theory based on the *equilibrium* between consumption and labour. In order to demonstrate that this balance is determined on the farm he ought to show, as he realised in Chapter 3, that the family size and composition (not necessarily the personal budget of each consumer) tends to raise the amount of capital to the optimum level of factor combinations. The change to the concern with personal consumption seems to be because an abstinence view of capital formation is held (p. 208): 'Any capital advanced means directing resources available to the cultivating peasant into production instead of into personal consumption, i.e. the reduction of consumption.'[14] However, if Chayanov were consistent, there is no reason for him to suppose this at all. Since the farm's concern is with total annual income, it can increase outlays of both capital and labour per unit area (p. 196), so that capital formation need not take place at the expense of consumption if the gross income is raised sufficiently.[15]

The discrepancy between the analysis of capital formation which would be required if the labour – consumer balance were the main determinant and the actual analysis in terms of abstinence from consumption means that the effectivity of the labour – consumer balance has not been demonstrated with respect to capital formation. The only reason why a failure to reach the optimal level of capital employed would entail *both* increased labour expenditure *and* reduced consumption is because the market would prevent the increased labour expenditure from raising gross income sufficiently. Moreover, the very admission that failure to reach optimal factor proportions is possible implies that the family farm is not in control of the elements determining its organisation and the level of its income.

Chayanov comes close to such a position in Chapter 4, 'The Organisational Plan of the Peasant Farm', where he is quite clear (pp. 120, 121) that the development of commodity production is the most basic determinant of the whole character of the farm's structure, and remarks on p. 125 that the subject of his analysis in earlier chapters is precisely a farm which has been drawn into commodity circulation. Yet here he clings to the position that commodity production affects the farm composition but does not directly affect the volume of its activity, and hence implicitly its income. On the other hand, Chayanov plainly takes the view that the market raises the total level of income of the farm (p. 126; emphasis in the original): 'Thanks to contact with the market, the farm is able to throw out of its organisational plan all production sectors which give little income and in which the product is obtained on the farm with greater effort than that required to obtain its market equivalent by other forms of economic activity which give greater income. Only that which *either gives a high labour payment or is an irreplaceable production element for technical reasons* remains in the organisational plan.' Such a view of the influence of the market can only obscure its role in generating class differentiation, but it must be interpreted as admitting that the market affects the *level* of the single labour income, as well as the farm's organisational structure. Yet despite this, Chayanov concludes the chapter on the organisation of the peasant farm with the supposition that the material analysed substantiates his theoretical conclusions, but it can hardly be said that the primacy of the family as work-force and consumer unit in determining the volume of economic activity and hence the level of income has been demonstrated. At almost every stage one is confronted with organisational elements which may be influenced by the market situation to some extent, but the actual extent of this influence is not weighed. This prevents Chayanov from seriously posing the problem of the extent to which the general economic situation (especially the growth of commodity relations) actually does influence the on-farm processes, and the notion of the primacy of the family in determining its level of income by adjusting the labour – consumer balance is retained by default.

THE FAMILY FARM AND THE NATIONAL ECONOMY

While it has been argued that a theory concentrating on the family farm precludes an adequate analysis of the relation between the unit of production and the structure of the national economy, Chayanov nevertheless attempts such an analysis in Chapter 7. His analysis indicates the difficulties of such an attempt.

The implications of the concept of demographic differentiation (defined in Chapter 1) are developed in relation to the effects of capitalism on the peasant sector of the economy. Demographic differentiation is related to the concept of the biological life-cycle, one of the chief factors in peasant farm organisation.

Variations in family size are taken to be almost a purely biological fact of the development of the family. Larger families are basically older families with more children. When the children marry they set up their own farm where possible, so the farm splits, yielding one small young family or more and a small old family. This biological life-cycle clearly has greatest impact in the repartitional commune where the land is periodically redivided among the families in the commune and the land area of each family farm is therefore not fixed (p. 68). Depending on the stage of the life-cycle at which the family finds itself, which determines the family size and composition in terms of proportion of adults to children, the labour – consumer balance will be affected by the consumer – worker ratio and by the possibility of applying the principles of complex co-operation among the work-force (which affects the levels of productivity). Hence the farm's size and thus the volume of economic activity is largely the result of family size and composition, rather than the reverse. Consequently much of the differentiation of the peasantry is demographic differentiation, as opposed to social differentiation. The existence of social differentiation is not denied (p. 68), but it must be studied by other methods than mere differences in sown area.

Even though changes in farm size are partly due to changes in the market situation, there is 'no doubt at all that demographic causes play the leading part in these movements' (p. 249). The evident implication of this is that it is the structure of the family farm which generates demographic differentiation, insulating the peasantry to a certain extent against the influences making for social (that is, class) differentiation. This restriction of the analysis to the family farm precludes any examination of social differentiation by the different methods which Chayanov rightly re-cognises are necessary.

Instead of such an examination, and despite the increasing domination of capitalism in agriculture (p. 257), Chayanov argues that capitalist farms (defined in terms of hired labour) are not very widespread among Russian peasants (p. 255), and social differentiation is still in its initial stages (p. 256). Chayanov rightly remarks (p. 257) that 'bringing agriculture into the capitalist system need by no means involve the creation of very large, capitalistically organised production units based on hired labour'.[16] He argues (p. 258) that trading links which convert the natural isolated family farm into one of a small commodity producer are always the first means of opening the way for the penetration of capitalist relations into the countryside. He then goes on to suggest that these links be strengthened by a system of wholesale and retail co-operatives which will ensure that the continued existence of the market will not develop oppressive forms of capitalist exploitation and that the rural market will be able to be subordinated to the state plan under what he sees as the existing state capitalist regime of the Soviet Union. This would only gradually transform the organisational basis of the family farm which he feels he has established (p. 269).

There are difficulties both with his views on differentiation and with his proposals concerning co-operatives. With demographic differentiation, if one takes seriously his recognition (p. 256) that the peasantry has provided the major source of recruitment for the urban proletariat, the question is immediately raised as to whether the young families remaining would have the land to set up a new farm if a large proportion of the population were not moving out of agriculture. It is clear from p. 246, for instance, that the highest proportion of farms disappearing are those with a small sown area, and it may be that the existence of 'demographic differentiation' among the surviving farms is possible only on the basis of the extinction of so many of the smaller farms. These smaller farms are probably more vulnerable to the impoverishment that is usually generated by the penetration of commodity relations into the countryside. Chayanov provides evidence on the existence of crafts and trades which indicates that they are frequently resorted to under very unfavourable economic conditions, and (p. 102) that the development of crafts and trades may be associated with class differentiation, although he does not interpret it as such. Yet there is no attempt to relate this evidence to the analysis of the single labour income (combining agriculture with crafts and trades) in terms suggesting not only that farms decide on the allocation of labour units as between agriculture and crafts and trades on the basis of the relative advantages of each, but that (p. 108) normally this means that crafts and trades are resorted to in favourable economic conditions, raising the absolute level of the single labour income. Chayanov is quite right that at times farms with a lot of crafts and trades activity have higher personal budgets (and higher capital formation, which means that capital formation is strongly affected by the market), but the fact that crafts and trades are *also* linked with impoverishment should lead him to a more serious consideration of the issue of class differentiation.[17]

The problem with the entire programme of 'vertical concentration' (use of wholesale and retail co-operatives to integrate the small peasant producers) is that it is an attempt to avoid large-scale capitalism and move gradually to socialism in agriculture without any sudden structural changes, a socialism that will leave the small peasant farms intact, since it will be (p. 269) 'a social co-operative economy, founded on socialised capital, that leaves in the private farms of its members the technical fulfilment of certain processes almost on the basis of a technical commission'. That this amounts to an idealisation of petty commodity production, despite his denial that he is idealising the petty bourgeois peasant farms, can be seen on p. 256 where he says 'we must hope that the labour farm, strengthened by co-operative bodies, will be able to defend its position against large-scale capitalist farms as it did in former times'. This is a view of socialism which seeks to abolish capitalist exploitation while retaining petty commodity production in the form of the small peasant farm. The separation of the analysis of the unit of production from the analysis of the wider economic system could not be clearer than in this attempt to theorise the transition to 'socialism' by way of 'state capitalism'. In effect, because of the conception of basically unchanged[18] units of production which are compatible with a wide variety of economic systems, there is no possibility in this theory of analysing transitional forms of the units of production as effects of the increasing dominance of new relations of production. By proceeding from the organisational unit of production to the wider system of the economy, Chayanov puts himself in the position of being unable to construct a theory of the wider economy, and resorts instead to the description of 'economic institutions' such as co-operatives. Both the wider economic system and the rural economy are conceived of as an aggregation of various types of institutions, which must first be described and analysed before the relations between them are theoretically established. This inevitably limits theory construction to the level of mere description of organisational forms. However, unless the structure of the economy as a whole is constructed first, it is impossible to determine what generates particular organisational forms rather than others, and what role a particular institution plays in the economy.

RENT

As has already been noted, Chayanov argues that while rent in the full capitalist sense does not exist in the family farm, since it is not a differentiated source of income, rent-forming factors do exist and raise the equilibrium point of the labour – consumer balance. Like new machinery, or a situation of more favourable market prices, rent-forming factors do not bring the farm any *unearned* source of income, but simply create better conditions for labour use (p. 230). The new equilibrium point established as a result of these better conditions for labour use will lead to one or more of the following, depending on the particular on-farm labour composition (p. 233): a higher consumption level, less labour intensity, a greater ability to form capital.

At various points throughout Chapter 6 (which is devoted to the analysis of rent and land prices), Chayanov draws attention to the similarities between his views on rent in the peasant economy and Marx's views on parcellated peasant farming. The three main points of similarity, in Chayanov's view, are:

1. (p. 228) Neither the origin nor the level of rents paid by parcellated farm peasants will correspond to the rents paid by farms organised on the basis of hired labour. Chayanov argued that Marx, noting this, wrote: '...this is rent only nominally, not rent as an independent category opposed to wages' (*Capital*, vol. 3, p. 810).
2. (pp. 235, 236) Marx in his time noted that in overpopulated areas, the poorest peasant families will pay the highest prices for land and rent. His views on land rent in the parcellated peasant farm and on the rents it pays are considered by Chayanov to be very close to his own theories.
3. (p. 240) Marx when analysing the origins of capitalist land rent

noted the considerable differences between parcelled peasant farming and capitalist agriculture. He asserted that in this parcellated farming 'production ...to a very great extent satisfies own needs (*sic*) and is completely independent of control by the general rate of profit'.[19] He came to a number of conclusions close to Chayanov's observations; however, neither he nor subsequent economists have developed these observations adequately.

In the light of the unspecified nature of the similar conclusions referred to in the last point, it is tempting to look for other similarities between Chayanov and the section on parcellated farming in the well-known Chapter 47 of Volume 3 of *Capital*. Where Marx discusses rent under the system of proprietorship of land parcels, he is explicit that no absolute rent exists there, yet not only does commodity production exist, but differential rent also exists (*Capital*, vol. 3, p. 805) 'much as under the capitalist mode of production. This differential rent exists, even where this form appears under social conditions, under which no general market-price has as yet been developed; it appears then in the excess surplus-product. Only then it flows into the pockets of the peasant whose labour is realised under more favourable conditions.' Such a passage is apparently similar to Chayanov's position referred to above that rent-forming factors create better conditions for labour use.

It is clear then that any consideration of the Chayanov's analysis of rent must evaluate these 'similarities' between his position and that of Marx, particularly in view of the important role which rent plays in Chayanov's theory. The analysis of rent is presented at the beginning of Chapter 6 as an important link between the internal organisation of the family farm and the wider system of the economy, and is thus implicitly seen as a vindication of the procedure of first analysing the organisation of the unit of production before dealing with the general economic consequences which follow from it. Furthermore, in his introductory article (1966, p. liii), Kerblay argues that rent was the central theme of both studies in *The Theory of Peasant Economy*.

Chayanov's position is best understood if one begins with his concept of capitalist rent. For Chayanov, capitalist rent is an obscure concept which, being primarily treated in terms of its non-applicability to the family labour farm, is not clearly theoretically differentiated from profit. Thus, on p. 8: 'Rent as an objective economic category obtained after deducting material costs of production, wages, and the usual interest on capital from gross income cannot exist in the family economic unit because the other factors are absent.' It is no mere slip that profit is not mentioned here as one of the absent factors, so that rent is effectively defined as the 'surplus' or net income retained by the capitalist. Chayanov is clearly operating with the 'cost-plus' theory of prices demolished by Marx in *Capital*, vol. 3. Chayanov's position is best illustrated in his formula for calculating economic profitability, a formula described (p. 3) as the key to understanding economic life in capitalist society: 'an enterprise is considered profitable if its gross income, *GI*, after the deduction of the circulating capital advanced (i.e. of the annual material expenditure, *ME*, and of the wage costs, *WC*), makes a sum *S*, which is as large or larger than the whole of the (constant and circulating) capital, *C*, of the enterprise at interest calculated according to the rate prevailing in that country at that time (*a*):

$$GI - (ME + WC) > C \cdot \frac{a}{100} \, . \, '$$

In short, net income is the surplus over the costs of production. Net income must equal or exceed the interest payable on the total capital. If there is any net income left after interest has been paid, the enterprise is considered profitable. It requires only a brief inspection to see that profit is here being defined in exactly the same terms as the definition of capitalist rent quoted above. Both are the net income after deducting material expenditures, wages and interest on capital. The only basis for distinguishing between profit and rent, then, must be that rent is the result of 'rent-forming factors' (better soil, better market location). Rent is thus conceived of as the return on the factor of production, land. If interest is the return on capital, then profit is a residual category, comprising whatever cannot be accounted for by the 'rent-forming factors', or else it is conveniently forgotten.[20] Thus if profit means anything at all in Chayanov's theory, it is simply the excess over the returns to the factors of production (land, labour and capital). Rent is simply the return to land, and consists solely of differential rent accruing to superior land. Hunger rent would not be paid, since presumably the capitalist would go out of business first.

This theory of capitalist rent stands in marked contrast to the Marxist concept of capitalist ground-rent, which not only distinguished between differential and absolute ground-rent, but treats both as an excess of surplus-value over the general rate of profit. The Marxist theory therefore presupposes the existence of a general rate of profit. However, the general rate of profit does not play a role analogous to 'the usual interest on capital' in the sense used by Chayanov in the passage on rent quoted above. The Marxist theory of capitalist rent does not treat it simply as a return to a factor of production that accrues only after production costs, plus a socially defined part of the surplus over production costs, e.g. rate of interest, have been set aside. Capitalist ground-rent is a relation of distribution. The intervention of capitalist ground-rent in the distribution of surplus-value means that ground-rent plays a role in the *formation* of the general rate of profit by determining the prices of production in agriculture. In the case of differential rent the price of production is determined by the costs prevailing on the least fertile land, whereas in the case of absolute rent the price of production is determined partly by the ability of the landowner to withhold land from cultivation, and partly by the political intervention of the state. Both kinds of capitalist rent thus contribute to the formation of the general rate of profit, even though capitalist rent presupposes a general rate of profit, so the Marxist concept of a general rate of profit does not bear the same relation to capitalist rent as Chayanov's concept of rate of interest bears to his concept of capitalist rent.

The difference between the respective theories of capitalist rent make it easier to evaluate the similarities in the theories of rent among the independent peasantry. It will be argued that Chayanov's specific claims, noted above, to have a similar analysis to Marx, are somewhat misleading, but that nevertheless there are similarities between Chayanov's analysis and Marx's text on parcellated land rent. However, it will be argued that such similarities as do exist are due to the fact that in analysing rent on parcellated land, Marx was not entirely consistent with the main body of his own theory.

A striking feature of Chayanov's theory of rent on the family farm is its similarity to his analysis of capitalist rent, in that rent is differential rent, treated as a return to the factor of production, land. Rent-forming factors (better soil and favourable market location) are effectively treated as intrinsic features of the land giving it value. Land is thus conceived of as a factor of production passing on its value to the product. Rent is not a differentiated revenue, it is embodied in the product. When Chayanov argues that rent-forming factors produce one or more of three effects on the labour – consumer balance (increasing consumption, lowering the labour intensity, increasing the power to form capital), he obviously regards the higher value of land with rent-forming factors as creating a surplus over the subsistence level,[21] a surplus that enters the price of production if the product is a commodity, or is passed on *in kind* (increased consumption, reduced labour intensity). Thus Chayanov views differential rent on the family farm as not being a differentiated unearned income, because the peasant is still working. Yet since it is an income from land *per se*, it might be considered unearned, were it not for the fact that Chayanov sees it as an economic return to the capital 'invested' in purchasing the farm. Differential rent, then, is an addition to the gross income of the farm, a revenue derived from the factor land[22] which is passed on to the product in money or in kind. The surplus is embodied in both the commodity and 'natural' components of the single labour income. An important difference between the peasant economy and capitalism, however, is in the formation of land prices. Whereas under capitalism the land price is the differential rent capitalised at the going rate of interest, and is thus limited by the size of the differential rent, the land price in the peasant economy is not determined by the amount of differential rent which accrues to the land. Rather, it is paid by the peasant if it enables him to reach an optimum level of the labour – consumer balance; in other words, if the utilisation of the additional land will raise the level of prosperity sufficiently to pay the lease or mortgage and still increase consumption and/or reduce labour intensity. While recognising (p. 9) that expenditure on land decreases the family's resources, he clearly considers it as capital invested in land, which, although having a value determined by intrinsic features (better soil, better geographical location), has a price which is determined by supply and demand.[23]

Hence, Chayanov argues (p. 9) that 'the land price level does not depend only on the market situation for agricultural produce and on the profitability of land cultivation resulting from it, but to a greater extent depends on the increase in local rural population density'. The greater the population density, the greater the demand for land, since no family can survive without a certain technically necessary minimum area of land which would require a high degree of labour intensity. There is thus a considerable incentive to acquire more land, so that the farm more closely approximates to an optimum level of land utilisation. Hence the poorer farms owning less land will pay more rent (p. 9). This rent could be far higher than capitalist rent, even at the cost of a labour payment below capitalist wages (p. 235), in which case the farm is paying what Maslov called 'a hunger rent'. Although Chayanov considers this analysis similar to Marx's position on parcellated land, it will be seen that Marx makes no reference to overpopulation, but associates high land prices with high interest rates in the case of parcellated landholding.

Chayanov correctly claims that for both Marx and himself the 'rents' associated with such high land prices are only nominal rents, because they cannot be economically supported simply on the basis of differential rent. However, although this claim to be similar to Marx is superficially correct, the basis of the high rent in each theory is different. With Marx it is related to the rate of interest, whereas with Chayanov it is an effect of overpopulation.

Chayanov does not examine land prices in terms of the rate of interest, since he considers that the concept of land price as the rent on the land capitalised at the current market interest rate on capital only applies to the capitalist farm (p. 233). So despite his acknowledgement of the existence of interest, and of 'rent-forming factors', land prices are not analysed in these terms. Land prices are considered in terms of the 'value' of land as determined by supply and demand. The reference to 'hunger rents' is thus an attempt to cope with phenomena which cannot be accounted for in terms of differential rent and developed capitalist credit. Kerblay remarks in his introduction (1966, p. liii) that Chayanov considers only differential rent, and (fn. 67) 'does not discuss absolute rent or scarcity rent that appears when all the land is occupied and when even marginal land produces rent'. Chayanov could 'legitimately' avoid discussing absolute rent, as Marx argues it does not exist among parcellated proprietors (it entails a separate class of landowners, and thus, like differential rent, must be an excess above the average rate of profit). However, absolute rent is not scarcity rent in Kerblay's sense, and Chayanov does in effect discuss the latter with his concept of 'hunger rent'. The 'correct' implication of Chayanov's concept of hunger rent is that even marginal land paying no differential rent has a price. Chayanov attributes this price simply to supply and demand, and fails to ask *why land becomes a commodity*. This failure is precisely a failure to escape from an economist explanation of rent. Thus Maslov is also guilty of economism – in this case, a failure to specify the political conditions of private ownership of land. All rent presupposes the monopolisation of certain sections of the globe. Even differential rent when land has been nationalised requires state monopolisation of the land, and the allocation of the land to different economic functions. Where there is a land market, the fact that marginal land which does not have differential rent still has a price is not necessarily an effect of *absolute* rent (the economic condition of existence of a separate class of landowners), it is simply an effect of private landownership.

There remain the points that for both Marx and Chayanov, production is not here regulated by a general rate of profit, and that differential rent is realised under more favourable conditions of labour. These points will be dealt with during an examination of Marx's text on parcellated farming which must also take up his views of land prices and the nominal nature of rent where land prices are high.

With Marx (*Capital*, vol. 3, p. 808), 'The price of land forms a weighty element of the individual unproductive costs of production or cost-price of the product for the individual producer'. It does not, however, contribute to the production of the rent itself (since it is not part of the capital employed on the farm) but merely establishes a claim to the rent. With parcellated farming, where land is the principal instrument of production and the indispensable field of employment for the peasant's labour and capital, the land price can be higher than the capitalised rent, since the 'rent' can comprise a portion of 'profit' and even of 'wages' because of the indispensability of the land to the peasant. Hence it forms a weighty element in the cost-price, but this conflicts with the fact that it does not enter into the price of production. Since capital 'invested' in purchasing land *ipso facto* cannot form part of the capital productively employed on the farm, it does not enter the price of production, and is therefore less easily recouped by the peasant. The peasant, Marx argues, is therefore subjected to the moneylender, since credit is not fully developed (whereas Chayanov treats interest as if credit were fully developed, despite his view that capitalist categories are not applicable in their usual sense to the peasant economy). This lack of development of credit means that, in contrast to capitalist farming, the price of land rises with the rate of interest. 'The price of land, this element foreign to production itself, may therefore rise to such a point that it makes production impossible' (*Capital*, vol. 3, p. 811). The price of land is an element foreign to production itself because it is an illusion to think (p. 810) 'that land itself possesses value and thus enters as capital into the price of production of the product, much as machines or raw material'.[24]

For Marx, then, it is the 'rent' associated with these high land prices that is the nominal rent, which comprises a portion of 'profit' and even a deduction from 'wages'. Marx is not arguing that differential rent as a source of revenue does not exist. On the contrary, it can and does exist among proprietors of land parcels, and is associated with commodity production. With parcellated land (*Capital*, vol. 3, pp. 804, 805) 'the greater portion of the agricultural product must be consumed as direct means of subsistence by the producers themselves, the peasants, and only the excess above that will find its way as commodities into urban commerce'. This implies that commodity production is necessary to peasant proprietorship of land parcels, since while the means of consumption are largely reproduced on the farm, the reproduction of the means of production entails commodity exchange. This is true even if no means of consumption are purchased as commodities, since the means of production cannot be entirely reproduced on the farm. Hence Marx's remark (p. 812) that here, as with capitalism, the producer depends upon the money-price of his product (whereas Chayanov's concept of the single labour income implies that the peasant does not).

Differential rent, then, even on parcellated land, is always associated with commodity prices (*Capital*, vol. 3, p. 805): 'No matter how the average market-price of agricultural products may here be regulated, differential rent, an excess portion of commodity prices from superior or more favourably located land, must inevitably exist here much as under the capitalist mode of production.' Even where no *general* market price has as yet been developed, there is still commodity production and hence market prices. Differential rent, then, is here an excess portion of commodity prices (or where no general market price exists, it is an 'excess surplus product'), that is, it is a separate category of revenue associated with market prices (and not therefore part of an income received in kind, as it is with Chayanov). Where there is no general market price, it is realised in an 'excess surplus-product', that is, more of the product is sold than on marginal land at the local market prices.

If differential rent appears here 'much as under the capitalist mode of production', what are the differences between this rent and capitalist rent? If a large portion of the agricultural product is consumed as means of subsistence, then much of the rest which is sold as commodities must be consumed as means of production. Labour is almost entirely necessary labour (necessary to reproduce the means of consumption and production, that is, necessary to reproduce the direct producer). Products are therefore sold at their value, but there is almost no surplus-value (embodying surplus-labour). Where it occurs, it must be realised in the form of differential rent. There is no profit in the sense of the surplus-value which supports a class of capitalists, and such surplus-value as occasionally arises is realised in the form of rent. Less labour-time per unit of the product is required on superior land, so a surplus-product can be more readily produced embodying surplus-labour and realised as surplus-value in the form of differential rent. Thus differential rent here is not an excess of surplus-value over the general rate of profit, since there is no general rate of profit supporting a class of capitalists.

Several consequences follow from this which do not appear to have been considered by Marx. Firstly, despite his talk of 'nominal' rents taking up a portion of 'profit' and 'wages', neither profit nor wages exist in parcellated land. The terms 'wages' and 'profit' only make sense in this context as 'shorthand' designating the product necessary to reproduce the means of consumption and production respectively, although the means of production are not replaced out of profit. Alternatively, profit could be an ideological category referring to differential rent, but this would only be a serious possibility where the capitalist mode of production predominates. In fact, much of Marx's treatment of parcellated proprietorship assumes that the capitalist mode of production is not well developed. Secondly, the peasant is not economically independent. If he depends on the market for the reproduction of the means of production, he does indeed, as Marx realises, depend on the money-price of his product. Consequently, peasant proprietorship of land parcels, precisely because of its inevitable association with commodity production, cannot form the basis of any mode of production. It can only ever be a subordinate or transitional form of production because the only way commodity production can become generalised is with capitalism, where the means of production, means of consumption and labour-power appear as commodities.

Hence there is a similarity between Marx and Chayanov in that production is not regulated by the general rate of profit. Yet while Chayanov says that profit properly speaking is absent (and while Marx *should have* said this), Chayanov has no conception of a general rate of profit, for reasons given above. The further apparent similarity that rent is realised under more favourable conditions of labour conceals the difference between on the one hand Chayanov, who considers rent here an undifferentiated income, realised in both products in kind and commodities, and on the other Marx, who treats it as a separate kind of revenue realised only in commodities (as surplus-value). While Marx says that it is realised in the 'excess surplus-product', it is in fact only realised in the surplus-product (sold as commodities to realise surplus-value). It is not realised in an excess of the surplus-value over the general rate of profit, since there is not only no general rate of profit regulating production, but also profit itself (like wages) is absent. The contrast between the two positions is evident. For Chayanov, differential rent is a revenue from land, an addition to gross income, but it is not a differentiated income in the peasant farm, since it is passed on to both commodities and 'natural' products, increasing thereby the single labour income. For Marx, differential rent is a differentiated revenue, deriving not from intrinsic features of the land giving it value (we have seen that he considers it an illusion to think that land itself possesses value), but from the monopolisation of certain sections of the globe and associated exclusively with commodity production. Consequently whereas Chayanov consciously analyses the effects of rent-forming factors on the labour – consumer balance in the same terms as his analysis of the effects of new machinery, Marx cannot treat differential rent and means of production in the same terms.

Having established that differential rent does exist here for Marx, the relation between differential rent and land prices must now be analysed. Whereas for Chayanov land prices could not be analysed in terms of the differential rent capitalised at the current rate of interest because rent *does not exist as a separate category*, for Marx the land prices are formed on a different basis from those under capitalism because of unusual factors affecting the rate of interest. The reason why land prices might make production impossible is that interest rates might rise to such a point that the entire differential rent, and possibly part of 'profit' and 'wages' as well, goes on interest payments. The reasons for this will be discussed in a moment, but first it is worth remembering that Chayanov misunderstands Marx on this point, thinking that Marx is referring to overpopulation as a reason for high land prices. How this misunderstanding can have arisen is something of a mystery. It may be connected with his misunderstanding of Marx's theory of interest. On p. 10, he counterposes Marx's general formula $M - C - M + m$ to his view that the market rate of interest is determined by the 'demand and supply, in that part of the nation's capital in the credit system'. Yet Marx does not analyse interest in terms of the formula cited. His view is that since capital *is* value (in an independent form) and therefore *has* no value, it is the one 'commodity' where the 'price' (rate of interest) is simply determined by demand and supply. For this reason, he thinks that interest rates will be high when there is a considerable demand for credit, but credit is poorly developed. He considers this to be the case with parcellated land, on grounds to be discussed in a moment, and it is in this context that he says (*Capital*, vol. 3, p. 811): '. . . the number of small buyers is large and the number of large buyers is small'. Perhaps Chayanov took this to be a reference to overpopulation, but it is a reference to the demand for credit.

Marx argues that land prices will be high because of the lack of development of the capitalist mode of production, in particular of the forms of credit. Because there is an insufficient supply of credit to force down usurious interest rates (a sufficient supply of credit would in Marx's view require the existence of a class of rich idle capitalists), the peasant pays a 'nominal rent', a rent higher than differential rent. Rather than land prices being determined by the differential rent capitalised at the going rate of interest (which would mean low land prices with high interest rates and vice versa), Marx argues that on parcellated land high land prices coincide with high interest rates. The existence of the nominal rent does not mean that differential rent does not exist. Marx is effectively arguing that the peasant may receive differential rent at existing market prices but he does not keep it because the demand for credit is high while the supply of credit is restricted. The demand for credit is high because the peasant has to pay off the lease or the purchase price of the land, which is a cost to the peasant, but does not enter the price of production for reasons already given. The supply of credit is short because the sources of credit on a large scale (in Marx's view, a class of rich idle capitalists) are not yet developed. The relatively large numbers of small peasants requiring such credit to purchase or lease land is too great for the available supply of credit, so that high interest rates are paid even though land prices are also high (because land is indispensable to the small peasant). This is not overpopulation in the sense of an incapacity of the available land to support the rural population on the basis of existing technology. The high land prices are produced by the lack of credit combined with the fact that (*Capital*, vol. 3, p. 807) 'possession of the land is a precondition for the labourer's ownership of the product of his own labour'.

It should be clear that if the peasant is forced to pay a nominal rent that exceeds his differential rent (as it inevitably must for all peasants on marginal land who receive no differential rent yet must own or lease their lands), then this 'rent' will be paid at the expense of 'wages' and 'profit', that is, at the expense of the means of consumption and production. Production, as Marx realised, would then become impossible if the means of production and consumption could not be reproduced, so such very high nominal rents cannot be an enduring feature of parcellated land. Indeed the whole discussion of the availability of credit refers to a state of affairs which has no necessary relationship to proprietorship of land parcels. Developed forms of credit do not necessarily require a class of rich idle capitalists. As Marx makes clear in Volume 2 of *Capital* (in his discussion of the circuits of capital), capitalism necessarily involves the precipitation and accumulation of money sums. Some development of banking and finance would suffice to make that money available for lending at interest. Hence Marx's remarks on the lack of development of credit (due to the lack of development of the capitalist mode of production) cannot be taken to refer to peasant proprietorship of land parcels *under all conditions*, for example when capitalism predominates in the rest of the economy. We shall see that they refer in fact to particular conjunctural conditions – the forms of landownership arising from the dissolution of feudal relations. For Marx, then, private landownership explains the existence of a land price, even where there is no differential rent (so long as the land price does not encroach on the means of production and consumption to such an extent that production becomes impossible), and the underdevelopment of credit explains why parcellated land prices *can* be higher than the capitalised differential rent. With Chayanov, by contrast, there is no explanation of the existence of land prices, and 'hunger rent' explains why the land price can be higher than capitalised differential rent, which does not in any case exist as a separate revenue.

Whatever the faults of Marx's brief text on parcellated land, the appearance of similarity between it and Chayanov's theory has now been largely dispelled. One cannot, as Chayanov seems to imagine, establish theoretical similarities by comparing various points in isolation. Rather such points must be evaluated in terms of the theory as a whole, and it is significant that Chayanov pays little attention to the major theoretical arguments of *Capital* in relation to the section on parcellated land. That this is absolutely necessary to evaluate the 'similarities' can be seen from an examination of the few remaining points which might create an impression of similarity between Marxism and Chayanov's position. One such point is that Marx, like Chayanov, treats independent peasant production (the form of organisation of the labour-process) as a single form which can exist in a wide variety of conditions – in particular, under several modes of production (*Capital*, vol. 3, p. 806): 'This form of free self-managing peasant proprietorship of land parcels as the prevailing, normal form constitutes, on the one hand, the economic foundation of society during the best periods of classical antiquity, and on the other hand, it is found among modern nations as one of the forms arising from the dissolution of feudal landownership. Thus, the yeomanry in England, the peasantry in Sweden, the French and West German peasants. We do not include the colonies here since the independent peasant there develops under different conditions.' On the following page, Marx also talks of the peasant being free or a vassal, which implies that this form of production can also exist under feudalism (not simply when feudal landownership is being dissolved). This is a genuine point of similarity between Marx's text and Chayanov's position, but it merely indicates that this text must be treated with caution, as could also be seen from his use of the terms 'wages' and 'profit' and his treatment of credit in relation to land prices.

The refusal to treat the independent peasantry in the colonies as the same phenomenon because of the different conditions of its existence is correct, but it should have led Marx to reconsider whether the independent peasantry in classical antiquity is the same as the independent peasantry 'as one of the forms arising from the dissolution of feudal landownership'. Even if the independent peasantry were wrongly conceded to be the economic foundation of society in classical antiquity, it could not be the same as the form arising from the dissolution of feudal relations, a form which Marx discusses in terms of the grave difficulties it has in reproducing itself. Marx's remarks about the lack of development of the capitalist mode of production, in particular the forms of credit, apply to this form. He is clearly discussing the peasantry in the transition from feudalism to capitalism, and as such his description (since it is by no means a full theoretical analysis) has only conjunctural, rather than general, significance. This description of the forms, arising from the dissolution of feudalism may well be correct, particularly if capitalist industry were expanding rapidly in scale and absorbing most of the existing credit based on the money sums it was itself precipitating and accumulating. If land prices really are a weighty element in this form of peasant proprietorship, production is being constantly threatened, as Marx says, and this analysis (even more than Chayanov's own remarks on 'hunger rent') stands in marked contrast to Chayanov's general conception of the peasant economy as a stable type resistant to change.

We have already seen that because of its inevitable association with commodity production, the peasant proprietorship of land parcels cannot form the basis of *any* mode of production, since commodity production can only be generalised as capitalism. Although Marx treats the independent peasantry as compatible with a variety of modes of production in a manner similar to Chayanov, this position of Marx is unacceptable. Nevertheless, Marx does at times treat the peasantry as a stable type of economy, or even as a 'mode of production' capable of existing in a wide variety of situations. For example, in *Capital*, (vol. 3, p. 807), Marx talks of the independent peasantry as a 'mode of production' in which 'the cultivator, be he free owner or vassal, always must produce his own means of subsistence independently as an isolated labourer with his family'. This appears to be very similar to Chayanov's discussion of the peasant economy existing even within feudalism, with the economically independent peasant family subject to non-economic constraint. In fact, Kerblay (1966, p. xxx) designates the peasant economy as a 'unique mode of production', but the apparent similarity is based on a failure to appreciate that Marx used the term 'mode of production' in two distinct senses in *Capital*. Firstly, it was used as a synonym for 'system of production', which refers to the organisation of the labour-process (that is, to the productive forces). Secondly, it was used in the full sense of mode of production, which refers to (a) an economy structured by the articulated combination of the relations and forces of production, (b) ideology and (c) where classes exist, politics. It is clear that he refers to independent peasant production as a 'mode of production' in the first sense. This can be seen in the above quotation from the fact that the cultivator only produces his own means of subsistence independently. He would have to produce his own means of production to be *economically* independent. Only with commodity production can the peasant reproduce his own means of production, and even then common lands may be necessary to raise cattle (*Capital*, vol. 3, p. 807). Since completely generalised commodity production only occurs with capitalism, parcellated peasant farming can only exist as a subordinate or transitional form of production; it cannot be the economic basis of a mode of production in the full sense. In addition, the peasantry under feudalism cannot be economically independent precisely because it does not appropriate the surplus-labour and cannot reproduce its own means of production except within certain limits (as Hindess and Hirst have shown (1975, chap. 5)). Even where the peasant engages in commodity production and pays money-rent to the feudal lord, this is not the same thing as the differential rent of the independent peasant proprietor. Whereas differential rent, although it forms the entire surplus-value here, only accrues to the peasants who are not on marginal land, feudal money-rent is not only in principle the entire surplus-labour, but is merely one form of feudal rent, the economic condition of existence of feudal landowners. As such, feudal money-rent has to be paid by all peasants, even those on marginal land, and the peasants consequently do not own the entire product of their labour. Occasionally feudal money-rent does not comprise all the surplus-labour, as Marx point out, since the very fact that the rent is money and therefore divisible may make it easier for the peasant to appropriate *part* of his surplus-labour. However, this is not the same as differential rent where, if the peasant retains it (and does not pay it out as interest), he is retaining his entire surplus-labour in the form of surplus-value. The peasant under feudalism is not economically independent and if he retains *part* of his surplus-labour, this only occurs as an effect of class struggle. As Hindess and Hirst (1975, p. 247) indicate, the class struggle can go badly for the direct producer, even with feudal money-rent, and the lord may be able to use feudal money-rent to tighten his control over the direct producer: 'Hence the falsity of the conception of commutation of labour services to money rents as a dissolution of feudal relations.'

There is therefore no such thing as a 'peasant mode of production' of which the independent peasantry forms the basis, since the independent peasantry can exist only with commodity production, and generalised commodity production entails the eclipse of the independent peasantry by capitalist farming. Nor can the 'independent peasantry' exist in the same form in different social formations such as feudal ones or those of classical antiquity. As we have seen, the peasantry paying feudal money-rent is not economically independent. Even with peasant proprietorship of land parcels, the peasant is not economically independent since the reproduction of the means of production depends on commodity prices, putting the peasant at the mercy of the structure of the wider economy.

Thorner is entirely correct when he remarks in his introductory essay (1966, p. xix) that Chayanov rejected the terms in which Marx analysed the peasant farm. Yet he accepts Chayanov's claim that he sometimes found Marx in agreement with him (p. xix, fn. 9). However, it can no longer be doubted that there is no real substance to such apparent agreement where Chayanov explicitly refers to it, and that what similarities there really are between Marx's text and Chayanov's position are explicable in terms of a few remarks by Marx that are not consistent with the main body of his theory.

The difficulties with Chayanov's theory of rent which have been demonstrated in this analysis seriously undermine its role in providing a link between the unit of production and the wider economy. One cannot proceed from the form of organisation of the unit of production (the forces of production) to the relations of production, since the latter must must be established at the level of the structure of the economy as a whole. Where classes exist, an analysis of the relations of production would entail an analysis of the political preconditions of those relations. Only when the structure of the economy as a whole has been analysed is it possible to specify the conditions of existence of a particular form of organisation of the production process, such as parcellated farming. Perhaps the clearest indication of the failure of Chayanov's analysis of rent in this respect is that it is impossible on the basis of an analysis of economic actors' perceptions even to *pose* the problem of why land becomes a commodity (which would require an analysis of the political level), let alone *solve* this problem of the existence of land prices.

CONCLUSION

The counterposing of the economy as a totality to the forms of consciousness of the economic actors (which in this particular theory takes the form of counterposing the national economy to the peasant family farm) creates problems with respect to the relationship between the two. The first problem is whether or not the structure of the economy can determine the categories available to the economic subjects for calculation, when the categories are compatible with a variety of economic systems. The second problem, related to the first, concerns the mechanism for ensuring that the available categories are indeed used by the economic subjects.

According to Chayanov, it is the presence or absence of certain categories due to the structure of the economy (for example, whether it is a natural economy or a commodity economy), or the structure of that sector of it within which the unit of production operates, which determines the applicability of certain forms of calculation on which economic action is based (for example, the labour – consumer balance or the price mechanism). Economic action is therefore not an effect of the individual's psychology (for example, a need for achievement) but of the categories available to the economic subject – in this case the family, which is a collective subject. This set of postulates has to be reconciled with the postulate that the form of calculation entailed in the labour – consumer balance can be sustained in a variety of economic systems, and is in a sense the predominant feature of those systems. The reconciliation is effected by means of setting up a peasant economy or sector within each of these systems which is to a certain extent insulated from any effects of those systems which would destroy the basis of the labour – consumer balance. The peasant economy is constituted basically by the aggregation of peasant family farms, that is, ultimately by the economic subjects. The subjects themselves maintain the structure of the peasant economy, since they constitute that structure by their actions. Since in this theory the rest of the economy and society are economically dependent upon (even if politically dominant over) the peasant economy, Chayanov can only sustain his (correct) claim that it is impossible to construct an entire system of national economy on the basis of subjective calculations by placing the non-peasant sector beyond the scope of his theory (ostensibly, on a temporary basis). But although the structure which is not determined by subjective assessment remains untheorised, it must nevertheless be compatible or consistent with the peasant economy. In this sense the peasant economy (which is not conceived as a structure, but as an aggregation of family farms) determines its own categories for economic action, since, whatever the structure of the total economy, it must be compatible with the continued existence of the peasant economy, and the 'structure' of the peasant economy is determined by its economic subjects.

To put it more simply, the rest of the economy and society bears an 'external' (and usually oppressive) relation to the peasant economy, a relation which is fundamentally determined by the peasant economy itself. Thus the economic subject, the family, constitutes the structure of the peasant family farm and the aggregation of these units of production forms the homogeneous peasant economy to which the rest of the economy must correspond. The variety of 'economic systems' within which the labour – consumer balance can operate is therefore limited to those which do not impede the formation of the categories necessary for the calculation of that balance. Slave societies and capitalist societies are excluded for precisely that reason. Once these categories are used by the subjects, it is difficult to see how an economic structure capable of generating different categories can develop, since in effect the peasant families are the constitutive agents of the predominant features of the economic system, and therefore of the very structure which is supposed to generate the categories available to them. The circular nature of this reasoning is evident. The only source of new categories is the non-peasant sector of the economy. Because this structure is not theorised, its compatibility with the peasant economy is fortuitous. Hence, if whatever 'objective factors' determining this structure happen to change it so that it becomes incompatible with the peasant economy, the possibility is opened up of the peasant economy itself being transformed. The difficulties which Chayanov faces when he tries to analyse this latter process in the case of a capitalist transformation of agriculture have already been illustrated.

While the first problem concerned the necessity for a basic compatibility between the untheorised structure and the sector determined by subjective assessment, as opposed to the ostensible determination of the subjective assessment by the structure, the second problem is that even if one accepted that the structure of the economy determined the categories available for economic calculation, how do these categories come to be used? The impossibility of calculating in monetary terms alone cannot *per se* ensure that economic activity will be a function of the labour – consumer balance. It has been argued, in fact, that Chayanov's detailed analysis designed to demonstrate this is unsuccessful. His analysis designed to show that, in the absence of monetary categories, the economic subject *immediately* forms a labour – consumer balance rests on a mere assertion that this is so. What is required, however, is a specification of the mechanism by which the categories available (as an effect of the structure of the economy) penetrate the consciousness of the economic subject. In the absence of a mechanism relating economy to consciousness,[25] there is potentially a whole range of possible motives for economic action.

Although the mere availability of concepts does not ensure that action is determined by calculation in terms of those concepts, there is no explicit analysis by Chayanov of a mechanism ensuring that this does occur. Clearly, such a mechanism would have to specify (a) how the actors came to learn or develop the concepts and (b) how the actors were motivated to use them. However, in a sense an implicit mechanism does exist, based on a variant of the familiar postulate of rational economic man. The difference from the usual notion is that whereas usually the activity of *homo oeconomicus* is restricted to the market, here he can operate without prices.[26] The precise nature of the human subject is what constitutes the peasant economy as a distinct type of economy. The essence of the subject, which centres on the choice of level of income, is founded on the articulation of rationality on biological needs. The rationality entails the use of the best categories available, and in the absence of the market, rational economic action designed to meet biologically determined consumption needs is thought to require the marginal analysis of the labour inputs as against the consumption needs. This is possible because labour inputs and consumption needs directly confront one another in the family farm. The organisational unity of production and consumption is a phenomenon of the human essence which makes it both possible and necessary to use the marginal analysis of the labour – consumer balance and motivates the family to use this as the basis of a sort of piece-rate system. Yet such a 'mechanism' based on the positing of a rational subject[27] effectively replaces any theoretical specification of a mechanism located in the social structure for ensuring that the categories supposedly generated by that structure are used by the subjects. It is clear that the subjects themselves in effect determine the categories used,[28] a position markedly inferior to the substantivist position (analysed in Alan Jenkins' paper in this volume), which at least attempts to analyse the motivation of economic action in terms of structurally located mechanisms, rather than merely the categories which a rational subject would use.

These two related problems concerning the relationship between the space of subjective determination and the space of structural determination (problems which are resolved in favour of the former) preclude the development of an adequate theoretical basis for the characterisation of the peasant economy as a distinct type of economy, since the social conditions of existence of this type of economy are not fully established. While Chayanov does not aim to give a complete theory of non-capitalist economic forms, recognising for example that the *oikos* does not fit into his framework (p. 22), he does give five main types of non-capitalist systems, plus communism (see the table on p. 123 above). There appear to be two main criteria in establishing this typology: firstly, whether or not commodity relations penetrate the unit of production, and secondly, non-economic constraint in the form of different types of legal ownership or non-economic coercion. If commodity relations *do* penetrate the unit of production, the result is, as with capitalism and slavery, that the owner of the unit of production himself (as opposed to the labourers) organises the unit of production on a large scale on the basis of rational calculation determined by objective market prices. Hence it is not simply the rationality of the economic actor which forms the basis for distinguishing the peasant economy. Rather the *absence* of penetration of commodity relations is an essential condition of the existence of the particular subject which constitutes the peasant economy by its action. If commodity relations do not penetrate the unit of production, as with the family labour farm, the quit-rent farm and the feudal peasant economy, then demographic factors are important in their effect on the labour – consumer balance, and the unit of production is organised on a small scale by the labourers themselves. The effect of non-economic constraint is to distinguish the main types of economy on a different basis, or rather two slightly different bases. The criterion of whether or not the labourer is owned distinguishes the family labour farm and capitalism on the one hand from quit-rent farms and slavery on the other. The feudal peasant farm paying labour rent is distinguished from the latter two merely by a slightly different form of non-economic constraint – possession of a coercive apparatus rather than legal ownership of the labourer.

The penetration or otherwise of commodity relations is clearly the more important criterion – Chayanov refers to the 'exterior legal similarities' between quit-rent farms and slave farms (p. 18). If the unit of production is a natural economy, then the labour – consumer balance is operative,[29] whatever the structure of the wider economy, or of the rest of society. Thus the real criterion for treating the peasant economy as a distinct type is the *absence* of any impediments to its existence, and it is the absence of structural determination that permits the existence of the labour – consumer balance established by the rational subject.

The constitutive rational subject as the essence of the economy is fundamentally distinct from the essence of capitalism and slavery, namely the market. While rational economic action is possible with the market, it is only possible on the basis of market categories. Chayanov thus conceives of types of economy basically in terms of only two essences: the family in a labour farm, and the market. This accounts for his failure to elaborate any theory of 'the natural economy of primitive people' (p. 2), of the *oikos* or of communism. These are recognised as different types of economy, but the reason why they are not analysed theoretically is evident from the attempt to discuss communism. The use of the labour – consumer balance cannot be sustained precisely because the unit of production is not identical with the unit of consumption, so that labour expenditure and consumption needs do not directly confront each other. That is why Chayanov considers it a problem to motivate the individual worker (pp. 22 and 23), since the planners can organise production nationally and balance it with aggregate consumption, but individual labour inputs bear no direct relation to individual consumption needs. On the other hand, if the units of production and consumption were reunited, this would entail a return to the peasant economy. Similarly, there is no basis for analysing the natural economy of primitive people or the *oikos* without positing (a) a rational subject (in which case they are indistinguishable from the peasant economy), or (b) a non-rational subject, in which case the rationality of the subject in the peasant economy would require further justification since the field would be open for the play of a whole range of possible motivations for economic action, or else (c) new essences other than the market which structurally determine the categories available to the economic actors. No such essences are proposed by Chayanov.

There is no necessary relationship between the various types of economy based on these two essences (and differentiated from each other by the presence or absence of particular kinds of non-economic constraint), so that Chayanov's typology is in no sense teleological. In this respect it may well differ from other theories of the peasant economy, but it shares its essentialism with these other theories. The claim that the peasant economy is compatible with a variety of economic systems is based on a definition of those systems in terms of non-economic constraint whose conditions of existence need not be theorised, since this type of theory does not merely set up an opposition between the peasant sector and other sectors of the economy, but between economy and society. Society (defined as the non-economic) is treated in an even more desultory and arbitrary descriptive manner than the non-peasant sector of the economy. It is a veritable *deus ex machina* from which all sorts of phenomena can appear to generate 'transitional forms' or even whole 'economic systems' (slavery, feudalism, capitalism, communism). In the last resort, this possibility of introducing concepts which are not adequately constructed within the discourse means that almost anything can be accounted for, even the commodity-producing family farm, but only at the cost of a complete reliance on a humanist essentialism with all its attendant difficulties.

NOTES

1. A. V. Chayanov was one of the leading exponents of the Organisation and Production School of agricultural thought in Russia at the time when it provided the major theoretical alternative to the agricultural views of the Bolsheviks in the 1920s. The members of the Organisation and Production School were also called neo-Narodniks, since their position was considered a development of the Narodnik (or Populist) theories which were influential in Russia at the turn of the century. As Jasny puts it (1972, p. 196), 'The neo-narodniks were almost completely dominant in the teaching of agricultural subjects and in writing about them, especially the peasant economy, until 1928 and even somewhat later'. Chayanov's major work, *Peasant Farm Organisation*, is of considerable interest since it contains an explicit defence of the neo-Narodnik position as against various Marxist criticisms, and draws attention to various aspects of the theory which Chayanov sees as similar to work by Marx. *Peasant Farm Organisation* was first published in English, together with an important article '*On the Theory of Non-Capitalist Economic Systems*', in a book entitled *The Theory of Peasant Economy* (1966). Page references in the text refer to this book unless otherwise stated. Quotations with American spelling have been changed to Queen's English.

2. In a speech delivered at the Conference of Marxist Students of the Agarian Question, 27 December 1929, published in Stalin (1942). In this speech Stalin attributes the continuing existence of various bourgeois and petty bourgeois theories on problems of the Soviet economy to the failure of the theoretical elaboration of economic problems by Marxism-Leninism to keep pace with practical successes. He attempts to demonstrate the unsoundness of some of these bourgeois theories. The main thrust of his attack on Chayanov is that the theoretical principles of Marx and Lenin on the theory of ground-rent in general, and absolute ground-rent in particular, had been brilliantly confirmed by practice in the work of Socialist construction in town and country (especially because of the effects of the nationalisation of the land). While it is beyond the scope of this paper to consider Stalin's analysis of Soviet agrarian policy, the question of the relation between Chayanov's theory of rent and the Marxist theory of rent will be taken up later.

3. Consideration of his influence on contemporary sociologists is beyond the scope of this examination of Chayanov's work, but an indication of the relation between Chayanov and Shanin may be found in the journal *Economy and Society*, vol. II, nos. 1–3 (1973). Chayanov's influence on Thorner can be seen, for example, in the fact that Thorner (1971, p. 205) describes the unit of production (the peasant family household) as the most fundamental of his five criteria of a peasant economy, although all five criteria are necessary in his view. It is clear that the terms 'peasant economy' and 'peasant society' are often interchangeable in this type of theory. For example, Thorner opens his discussion (1971, p. 202) with the remark: 'Peasant economies, we suggest, have been and still are a widespread form of organisation of human society.' Nevertheless, at other times the term 'peasant economy' refers to peasant economic action, as is noted in Harrison (1975a, pp. 392–3). For other assessments of Chayanov's influence, see Harrison (1975a, 1975b) and Hilton (1975, chap. 1).

4. Chayanov discusses 'economic categories' in a manner which conflates the conceptual and the real when he attempts to demonstrate the inapplicability of traditional economic concepts to the peasant farm (e.g. pp. 4 and 5). For the purpose of exposition this usage is followed here. It will be argued that commodity production means that the peasant farm is never a unit of production and consumption.

5. See Hindess & Hirst (1975) for an analysis of what are thought to be various pre-capitalist modes of production.

6. From the table on 'Economic Systems' there might appear to be an additional exception to the rule that there is a single labour income where the product is not sold as a commodity. This is the quit-rent serf economy, which is designated as a kind of hybrid (p. 16): 'The quit-rent farm, as a peculiar combination of a family labour farm, and a slave farm, is of extraordinary theoretical interest.' In the quit-rent farm there appear to be both commodities and a single labour income, but this is because the commodities only exist for the serf-owner. The serfs are thought to hand over their rent in kind, even in the quit-rent system. Thus the sole exception is the family labour farm producing commodities. While it is not explicitly designated as a combination of a natural economy family farm and a capitalist farm, such a view would-be consistent with this typology. However, as on the quit-rent farm, the labour — consumer balance is thought to remain intact despite the fact that, in this case, the *producers* sell the product as commodity.

7. Thorner (1966) argues in his introductory article ('Chayanov's Concept of Peasant Economy', p. xiii) that Chayanov 'contended that 90 per cent or more of the farms in Russia in the first quarter of the twentieth century had no hired labourers, that they were family farms in the full sense of the world'.

8. Chayanov's inability to theorise the transitional forms of developing capitalism explains his misunderstanding of the Marxist position on this point, although Chayanov does not openly criticise it. On p. 257 he says: 'The dynamic processes of agricultural proletarianisation and concentration of production, leading to large-scale agricultural production units based on hired labour, are developing throughout the world, and in the USSR in particular, at a rate much slower than was expected at the end of the nineteenth century.' Yet it is clear that in the case of Lenin at any rate there was no *prediction* of a rapid development along these lines. In *The Development of Capitalism in Russia*, Lenin argued that the penetration of commodity relations into agriculture was taking two main forms: (a) the capitalist differentiation of the peasantry, and (b) the internal transformation of the landlord economy latifundia into large-scale capitalist enterprises. There was no prediction that the capitalist differentiation of the peasantry would lead immediately to large-scale production with wage labour hired all year round. Nor was there any prediction that the path of the transformation of the landlord economy would necessarily predominate. The two roads, as Lenin called them, to a certain extent conflicted with each other, while at the same time reproducing each other, since each road was associated with definite agricultural products and rural industries necessary to the other road. The complicated class structure generated by the combination of these two roads illustrates how each conflicted with the other and retarded the development of the other. The landlord economy road involved the slow internal transformation of the landlords'

estates and therefore reproduced the peasant commune with the middle peasant owing his own implements and performing labour services on the estate. The capitalist peasantry road involved the creation of small-scale capitalists (called 'kulaks' or fists, since they were frequently also usurers) and landless agricultural wage labourers. If allowed to develop on its own, this latter road would have meant a comparatively rapid transition to capitalism which dissolved the repartitional peasant communes. However, as these communes were being reproduced by the landlords' transition with its different and slower processes of differentiation of capitalists and proletariat, there was no possibility of a simple prediction of a rapid transition to capitalism. All Lenin did was to indicate which road, if given free rein, would produce the quickest development of capitalism under the political conditions most favourable to the proletariat. This was the capitalist peasantry road, which did not, as Chayanov seems to think, immediately imply large-scale units of production and hired wage labour. In addition, even if the landlords' road had been miraculously eradicated overnight, this would not have implied that the transition to capitalism would have been all that rapid. Lenin cited other causes slowing down the transition to capitalism at the end of chap. 2 and of chap. 4 of *The Development of Capitalism in Russia*.

9. He admits this in the already cited passage where he distinguishes himself from the Austrian marginalists by not attempting to derive an *entire* system of national economy from subjective evaluations – a clear example of the counterposing of subject and structure. Thorner in effect shares this position in his 1971 article when he constructs four criteria in addition to the fundamental one of the peasant family farm in order to define 'peasant economy' as a structure encompassing whole societies.

10. Thorner (1971) also treats the structure in this way, although the quantitative nature of some of his description makes its *ad hoc* character even more clear than in the case of Chayanov's 'On the Theory of Non-Capitalist Economic Systems'.

11. These last remarks apply whether the structure is purely economic or also includes non-economic aspects of peasant societies. Thus Thorner, although defining the peasantry as a subject group, is able to say (1971, p. 206): 'In a sense the peasant in such economies is simultaneously subject and master.'

12. Chayanov's marginal analysis is virtually identical to that of neo-classical economics in its reliance on the effects of changing factor propotions. Sraffa (1963, Preface, p. v) points out that 'the marginal approach' requires attention to be focused on change, either in the scale of output or in the 'proportions of the factors of production'. Without such change there would be neither marginal product nor marginal cost. There is a clear difference, as Sraffa shows the marginalists themselves recognise, between such marginal elements and the use by the classical economists of margins, the most familiar case being the product of marginal land in the classical theory of rent. In the classical theory of rent, lands of different qualities are cultivated side by side. Consequently no question arises as to the variation or constancy of returns, unlike the marginalist position which analyses changes in scale or in factor proportions in relation to variations in returns. Sraffa places himself in the classical tradition rather than the marginalist one, and defines the classical economists as those from Smith to Ricardo, but Marx takes up a classical position in respect of the

theory of differential rent. The relation between Marx and Chayanov is discussed below, but it is already evident that Chayanov's marginalist theory is not based on the same premises as that of Marx on rent. Another implication of the classical position is that if the question of whether returns to factors of production are constant or variable is dropped, the possibility is opened up of a theory of rational economic calculation that is not based on marginalist concepts. Both Marx and Sraffa are critical of the concept of 'factors of production'. See Harrison (1975a, 1976) for analyses of Chaynov's marginalism and views of the relations between the 'factors of production'.

13. Yet there is clearly also pressure in these circumstances to become a rural semi-proletariat with the hiring-out of labour power, perhaps seasonally, although Chayanov does not discuss this or consider its implications for his theory. The reason for this is that Chayanov assumed that the labour market was virtually absent. Harrison notes this (1975a, p. 409), and draws attention to the main problems of this assumption (ibid., p. 412).

14. This abstinence theory of capital formation enables Chayanov to take into account evidence provided on p. 204 indicating that consumption may restrict capital formation. However, if as he says on p. 216 'the average peasant family on its farm is able to increase capital only in parallel with an increase in the personal budget' (rather than at the *expense* of the personal budget), it is clear that capital formation must be due not to abstinence but to an increase in gross farm income, which as Chayanov recognises is frequently the result of a favourable market situation. Harrison discusses the shift by Chayanov from a utility theory to a subsistence theory of savings decisions and capital formation (1975a, pp. 402–3.)

15. Such consistency, which would emphasise at this point the possibility of making a relatively objective estimate on the basis of roughly equivalent labour units and the income they would produce on the basis of past experience, would perhaps bring Chayanov uncomfortably close to a position he is at pains to distinguish himself from. On p. 215 he is arguing against critics who deny the need for the labour – consumer hypothesis and say that decisions to make capital expenditure can be made simply and objectively: if the use of capital gives an increase in net annual earnings per peasant family worker, the expenditure will be considered advantageous and, if resources are available, will be made. Chayanov in reply here emphasises the subjective evaluation of the *drudgery* of labour in the balancing of on-farm factors, but this position is impossible to sustain at this point when he has admitted earlier (p. 109) that the balance between agriculture and crafts and trades is determined by assessing the market situation, that is, on the basis of objectively given prices.

16. It is surprising in view of this remark that, although he cites Lenin in this context, he does not take seriously Lenin's argument that the hiring of wage labour is not an essential feature of the small rural bourgeoisie. Instead, he considers that the small commodity-producing farm cannot itself become capitalist, because he associates capitalism with large-scale production and wage labour hired all the year round. This is consistent with his view, already discussed, that if a certain category – wages – is absent, capitalism does not exist since capital, interest and rent are not applicable in their usual meanings.

17. The absurdity of treating demographic differentiation as an alternative to social (i.e. class) differentiation can be seen if one supposes that family labour

farms were to become the sole form of agricultural production (either in the Soviet Union or, if there were no political obstacles, in the world as a whole). In that case, with rising population and a finite land area, the point would ultimately be reached where it was technically impossible to establish new farms for new families, since the land area would be too small to sustain them on the basis of the established technical conditions of production. In such an ultimate case, demographic differentiation would by itself lead to the creation of a class of landless peasants. In the absence of capitalism, they would not become landless *wage labourers*, but it is difficult to see how Chayanov could avoid calling this social differentiation. Demographic differentiation is criticised at length in Harrison (1975b; also 1975a, 1976).

18. While this theory implies a transition from family labour farms engaging in some commodity production to farms conducting production almost on the basis of a technical commission, the latter farms would still be private property. In this case it is difficult to see how they could be economically sustained without commodity production.

19. This quotation is as it was translated from Russian in the Chayanov text. The reader may wish to compare it with p. 810 of the 1972 Lawrence & Wishart edition of *Capital*, vol. 3, which reads: 'here production to a large extent satisfies the producers' own wants and is carried on independently of regulation by the average rate of profit'.

20. The difficulties of this kind of theory are analysed by Marx in *Capital*, vol. 3, chap. 48.

21. A concept of surplus criticised in Hindess & Hirst (1975, chap. 1), and in the article by L. Culley in this volume.

22. That it is thought to derive from intrinsic properties of the land can best be seen from his distinction between land rent and 'water' rent, reported by Kerblay (1966, p. L).

23. The difficulties of a theory which conceives of value in terms of use-value and price in terms of supply and demand alone will be familiar to those who have read Marx's criticisms of classical political economy.

24. It has been shown that Chayanov's theory suffers from precisely this illusion, a conclusion that is reinforced by the fact that he consciously uses the same analysis of the labour – consumer balance for rent as he does to establish the profitability of a particular use of capital. It is hardly surprising that his analyses of the effects of rent and of a particular use of capital (e.g. new machinery) on the labour – consumer balance are identical in view of his failure clearly to distinguish profit and rent under capitalism.

Marx (*Capital*, vol. 3, p. 810) mentions only two cases where the price of land can enter as a determining factor into the price of agricultural products, and says that both are least of all the case with parcellated land. With Chayanov the land price is capital invested in the land which passes on its value to the product.

25. See Littlejohn (1973a) for a discussion of the conceptual couple economy/consciousness in Shanin (1972).

26. There is clearly a similarity between Chayanov's criticism of contemporary political economy and the substantivist's criticisms of the formal position (see the paper by Alan Jenkins in this volume) in that both Chayanov and the substantivists recognise the need for specific theoretical work on

different forms of economy. The basis for establishing a typology of economies is different in each case, though, despite substantivist references to Chayanov.

27. The rationality refers to the process of balancing labour expenditure with consumption needs; this does not preclude the evaluation of an acceptable equilibrium level being influenced by custom, habit and so on.

28. This conclusion represents a correlation to a remark on Chayanov in Little-john (1973a, fn. 3), where the view was taken that subjective assessments *were* an effect of the structure of the economy. As will be seen, this is only true to the extent that commodity relations penetrate the unit of production, so that subjective assessments within it are related to monetary calcu-lation – something which by definition does not occur in the peasant economy. In this respect, then, the positions of Chayanov and Shanin are very similar. The clearest evidence that Chayanov sees the structure of the peasant farm as subjectively determined occurs on p. 118.

29. This is carried to ludicrous lengths in his examination of communism, which is conceived of as one big unit of production – 'a single mighty economic unit of the whole people' (p. 23) – from which all market categories have been eliminated. Here the labour – consumer balance operates with the state planners as economic subjects (p. 23). See Harrison (1976, pp. 20 – 1) for a discussion of attempts by Chayanov to consider socialist planning. It appears that Chayanov's position did not change much over time on this problem. It has not been possible to discuss properly Harrison's work on Chayanov owing to the late date at which it came to my attention.

6 Humanism and Teleology in Sociological Theory

BARRY HINDESS

INTRODUCTION

This paper examines the conceptual structure of theoretical humanism and related theoretical positions and of teleology; it attempts to formulate both a rigorous general concept and a rigorous critique of both types of position. This objective takes us beyond the formal limits of a seminar on sociological theories of the economy. The scope of this paper is therefore more general than that of the other papers in this seminar. The presentation of a paper of this level of generality is justified on the ground that both theoretical humanism and related positions on the one hand and teleological conceptions on the other play a crucial role in sociological attempts to conceptualise the economy and social and economic change. Thus, whilst specific issues concerning these positions may be raised in several of the papers in the seminar, for example with respect to the work of Parsons or Weber, there is also a place for a more general discussion that is not restricted to a consideration of one particular school or author. The pragmatic justification of an examination of teleology is in any case clear given the pertinence of the economy as one of the principal locations of teleological conceptions in social theory, for example in theories of industrialisation, economic growth and development, and given the importance that is often attached in sociological theory to problems concerning the origins and development of capitalism. The case of theoretical humanism and related conceptions of action is a more general one, but its significance for this seminar can be argued on the grounds of its fundamental importance for the theoretical work of Parsons and Weber and for at least some aspects of the substantivist conception of the economy. I shall illustrate my arguments by reference to the work of Parsons and Weber, but it should be clear that my conclusions have a general significance for social theory.

Theoretical humanism is a form of social theory in which action is conceived as a function of the will and consciousness of the human individual. In the social sciences, theoretical humanism is based on an explicit or implicit philosophical anthropology which affirms the distinctive character of the object of social scientific investigation. It is a *philosophical* anthropology in the sense that the recognition of that distinctive character is thought to be not the *product* of scientific investigation but its *precondition*. Max Weber's definitions of sociology and social action in *Economy and Society* (Weber, 1968) represent a theoretical humanism in this sense. Sociology is defined as a science of human action. But the essential nature of action in general and of social action in particular is not something that may be established within sociology. Knowledge of the nature of action enables us to constitute sociology; it is not established within it. For example, in *The Methodology of the Social Sciences*, Weber refers to 'the transcendental presupposition of every cultural science', namely, 'that we are *cultural beings*, endowed with the capacity and the will to take a definite attitude toward the world and to lend it significance' (Weber, 1949, p. 81). Theoretical humanism proposes the reduction of the social realm to the will and consciousness of human actors. Social relations are intersubjective relations and social life is the product of the teleological action of individual human subjects: 'action . . . exists only as the behaviour of one or more individual human beings' (Weber, 1964a, p. 107).

In sociology, theoretical humanism has been challenged to some extent in the work of Durkheim[1] and in the later work of Parsons. In both cases, far from society being conceived as reducible to the will and consciousness of human individuals, these individuals are themselves conceived as subordinated to the functioning of more general and supra-individual mechanisms. The individual subject is no longer a 'free agent' in the sense of theoretical humanism. For example, in the later work of Parsons, personality systems are conceived as being necessarily integrated into a cybernetic heirarchy of control at a level below that of the social and cultural systems. There can be no personality system that is not part of such a hierarchy of control.

In this paper I show that both theoretical humanism and the anti-humanist positions developed in more rigorous forms of sociological theory are instances of a more general theoretical tendency which I shall call the rationalist conception of action. That conception is outlined in Part I. For purposes of this introduction it is sufficient to say that it postulates a realm of ideas (ultimate values, meanings, or whatever), a realm of nature, and a mechanism of action which effects the realisation of ideas in the realm of nature. This mechanism may be conceived as operating at the level of the individual actor, as in Weber's definition of sociology, or at a supra-individual level, as in Durkheim's work and in Parsons' theory of systems of action. Part I examines the theoretical properties of the rationalist conception of action in both its humanist and its anti-humanist forms. I argue that, whilst theoretical humanism in the social sciences has its own internal inconsistencies, the more general rationalist conception of action is ultimately and inescapably incoherent. There can be no coherent social theory based on the rationalist conception of action.

The question of teleology is discussed in Part II. I propose a minimal concept of teleology as combining a principle of temporal order with an essentialist conception of distinct forms. Such forms are conceived as the expression of a distinctive inner principle or essence and the essences are assigned a definite temporal order or hierarchy. At this level of generality, teleology subsumes both those positions which postulate a determinate immanent developmental tendency, for example an immanent tendency of 'rationalisation' or 'structural differentiation', and those apparently more limited forms which merely propose a principle of hierarchy, such as 'modernisation', 'industrialisation', or whatever, in terms of which differences between societies may be conceived. A particular teleology may well propose some form of historical necessity, but the crucial feature of the teleological postulate consists in its conceptualisation of the distinct forms as the realisation of their respective inner principles.[2]

There are two forms of teleology. A universal teleology subsumes the universe and all its parts; it encompasses everything that exists. A partial teleology, on the other hand, subsumes a part of the universe only. I argue that partial teleologies must be confronted by an irresoluble problem of double determination in which phenomena are conceived as subject to the coexistence of irreconcilable modes of effectivity since they postulate both that some part of the world is subject to the constraints of its natural or social conditions of existence and that it realises a determinate inner principle. Double determination in this sense involves partial teleology in conceiving of some social or natural process in terms of two incompatible and contradictory forms of constraint. This suffices to establish the incoherence of any partial teleology, that is, of any teleology which proposes to deal only with some limited part of the world, say human society or the development of Western civilisation. By subjecting only part of the world to its constraints, partial teleology ensures that the part of the world in question must also be subject to conditions of existence extraneous to the teleology itself. Teleology must either subsume the world and everything in it or it is incoherent. A universal teleology, on the other hand, can be shown to be theoretically vacuous since it provides no means of conceptualising the specificity of any determinate phenomena.

Before proceeding to these demonstrations, however, it is necessary to distinguish the arguments of this paper both from an influential form of critique of theoretical humanism which operates through the designation of humanism as an ideology and from a widespread critique of teleology on the basis of its manifest affinities with and representation in the idealist philosophies of history. Consider first the critique of theoretical humanism as an ideology. If humanism is an ideology, then theoretical humanism is merely an elaborated form of that ideology; it is a theoretical ideology, not a science. The best example of this form of critique may be found in

Althusser's critique of Political Economy in Part II of *Reading Capital* (Althusser & Balibar, 1970). Althusser represents Political Economy as a form of theoretical discourse that is constituted in part by the intervention of 'given', that is, extra-discursive, elements, by the intervention of a 'given' realm of economic facts. Now it is a consequence of Althusser's critique of the empiricist conception of knowledge that knowledge can never involve direct apperception of the real. The elements of knowledge must be conceived as constructed elements; they are never given by the real as such. In so far as 'given' elements appear in knowledge they are the product not of some mythical positivistic observation of the facts but rather of ideology. Elements constructed in ideology are *given* to theory prior to the operation of the theoretical knowledge process. In the case of Political Economy, Althusser argues, 'given' phenomena are constituted as *economic* by reference to the needs of human subjects: 'The peculiar theoretical structure of Political Economy depends on immediately and directly relating together a homogeneous space of given phenomena and an ideological anthropology which bases the economic character of the phenomena and its space on man as the subject of needs (the givenness of the *homo oeconomicus*)' (Althusser & Balibar, 1970, p. 162). Political Economy is constrained by its very definition to operate on a realm of 'given' economic phenomena. Since these are given by humanist ideology it follows that ideology must intervene at the most fundamental level of the discourse of Political Economy. Political Economy, therefore, cannot be scientific. It is easy to see that similar arguments could be advanced to establish that the sociology of a Durkheim, a Weber or a Parsons, perhaps sociology *tout court*, cannot be scientific because it pretends to operate with givens, for example with a mass of given empirical material that must be sorted and ordered by means of Weberian ideal types.[3]

I am not concerned here with the validity or otherwise of Althusser's identification of theoretical humanism as a fundamental element in the theoretical structure of Political Economy, but only with the form of critique of theoretical humanism which he proposes. I have examined this form of critique of what is alleged to be theoretical ideology elsewhere and have shown that it is logically invalid and theoretically ineffective.[4] For present purposes it is enough to note that the Althusserian critique of what it designates as theoretical ideology is based on a general *a priori* demarcation of discourses into sciences and ideologies such that, whilst the sciences are to be examined in terms of their concepts and relations between concepts, the theoretical ideologies are to be treated in an entirely different fashion. In the case of theoretical ideology, texts are to be examined for the signs of ideological contamination; in particular, empiricist formulations which refer to the given and humanist formulations are to be read as an index of the ideological character of the discourse in question. In the sciences, on the other hand, empiricist or humanist formulations must be treated as discrepant elements. For example, in *Reading Capital*, Part II, chap. 8, Althusser argues, correctly in my view, that whilst certain humanist formulations do appear in *Capital*, they can be shown to be incompatible with its basic concepts. This form of critique of what is thought to be theoretical ideology is ultimately dogmatic and therefore inconclusive since it presupposes precisely what it needs to establish, namely, that certain particular conceptions are indeed ideological and not scientific. The designation of theoretical humanism as an ideology may have some polemical significance but it cannot be theoretically effective.

In my examination of the Althusserian theory of science and theoretical ideology I have argued that the different modes of treatment of what are thought to be sciences and ideologies can have no rational justification. As far as their theoretical character is concerned, all discourses must be analysed in terms of the concepts and relations between concepts which are entailed in the positions developed in the discourse in question. What is significant from this point of view is not whether a particular concept or set of concepts can be said to represent some extra-theoretical interests or social forces, but rather their theoretical properties as concepts on the one hand and their location in particular discourses on the other. In this paper I am concerned with the concepts of theoretical humanism and the more general rationalist conception of action and with teleology. I have not attempted to demonstrate that particular theoretical discourses are indeed dominated by the rationalist conception of action or to establish their teleological character.[5] Those questions are taken up to some extent in other papers in this seminar. Instead I have taken the works of Weber and of Parsons as particularly clear examples of these tendencies for the purposes of illustration. If, as I argue, the rationalist conception of action and partial teleology are inescapably incoherent, it follows that any social or other theory in which one or both of these positions can be shown to play a fundamental part must also be incoherent. In part I of this paper I examine the particular set of concepts involved in theoretical humanism and, more generally, in the rationalist conception of action. It is on the basis of these concepts and the logical properties of the relations that obtain between them that I argue that theoretical humanism and the rationalist conception of action are fundamentally and inescapably incoherent.

As for teleology, it is hardly necessary to demonstrate the ubiquity of teleological conceptions in sociological theory, economic anthropology and in much of what passes for Marxism.[6] But is there any reason why social and economic change should not be conceptualised in teleological terms? The affinities of teleology with religion and its association with idealist philosophies of history are well known. These unsavoury associations may well lead us to view with some suspicion those conceptions that postulate a historical necessity or an explicit *ideal* principle of teleological order, but they cannot constitute adequate grounds for dismissing all teleologies out of hand. Accordingly, rather than present an argument for teleology's guilt by association with unsavoury theoretical companions, Part II examines the conceptual structure of teleology and its theoretical effects. It demonstrates that teleology cannot avoid either incoherence or vacuity.

PART I

HUMANISM AND THE RATIONALIST CONCEPTION OF ACTION

In this Part I examine the conceptual structure of the rationalist conception of action in both its humanist and its anti-humanist forms. I argue that, whilst theoretical humanism has its own particular inconsistencies, both this special case and the rationalist conception in general can be shown to be either completely vacuous or ultimately incoherent. After an outline of the basic structure of the rationalist conception of action I proceed to an examination of the particular features of theoretical humanism, with special reference to the work of Max Weber, and of anti-humanist forms of the rationalist conception of action, with special reference to the later work of Talcott Parsons. This Part closes with a demonstration of the fundamental theoretical indeterminacy of the rationalist conception of action and of its theoretical effects.

THE RATIONALIST CONCEPTION OF ACTION I

In its most general form the rationalist conception of action postulates a realm of ideas (values, representations, meanings), a realm of nature and a mechanism of the realisation of ideas in the realm of nature, namely human action. This mechanism may be defined at the level of the individual human subject, in which case it operates as a function of the will and consciousness of the subject, or at some supra-individual or social level of determination, in which case it subsumes the actions of individuals to its functioning. But whatever particular form the mechanism may be thought to take, its effect is to define some portion of nature as the product of ideal, extra-natural determinations. Thus the social or cultural sphere may be conceived as a sphere of both natural and extra-natural determinations. Where the one is the object of natural scientific investigation the other must be *understood*, that is to say, social or cultural phenomena must be referred back to the idéas (meanings, values, or whatever) which they express.

To describe this conception of action as rationalist is not to say that it must involve a rationalist epistemology. Rationalist epistemology conceives of the world as a rational order in the sense that its parts and the relations between them conform to concepts and the relations between them, the concept giving the essence of the real. Where rationalist epistemology presupposes a pre-given harmony between ideas and the world, the rationalist conception of action merely postulates a mechanism of the realisation of ideas in the world. The theological affinities of these conceptions are evident.

It is clear that Max Weber's concept of action represents a rationalism in this sense. 'In "action" is included all human behaviour *when and in so far as the acting individual attaches a subjective meaning to it*' (Weber, 1964a, p. 88; emphasis added). Both action and behaviour are events in nature but action is also something more: it is the expression of a *meaning* which is not part of nature. Weber's concept of action therefore postulates a realm of ideas (meanings and values), a realm of nature, and the will and consciousness of the human individual as the means of realisation of ideas in nature. For a very different example, consider *The Social System, Toward a General Theory of Action*, and the later works of Talcott Parsons. Parsons elaborates a rationalist conception of action which no longer accords primacy to the human individual but rather postulates a more complex social and cultural mechanism of the realisation of ideas. For Parsons, cultural systems consist of systems of ideas or beliefs, systems of expressive symbols and systems of value-orientations and they have a mode of existence that is different in kind from any other type of system: '*a cultural system is not an empirical system* in the same sense as a personality or social system, because it represents a special kind of abstraction of elements from those systems' (Parsons & Shils, 1962, p. 55; emphasis added). Cultural systems may be internalised in the orientation systems of actors and institutionalised in social systems, but they also have a different mode of existence. Thus we have a realm of ideas (the cultural system), a realm of nature and a complex mechanism of realisation of ideas in nature through the articulation of cultural systems on to social and personality systems. Similarly, Durkheim's conception of social facts as expressing 'states of the collective consciousness' also involves a rationalist conception of action functioning at a supra-individual level of determination.[7] Weber and Parsons will be discussed in more detail below. What should be noted here is that both Durkheim and Parsons, at least for Parsons' later work, have been criticised by representatives of theoretical humanism for their 'reification' of society, for their 'sociologism', and for elaborating an 'over-socialised conception of man'.[8] But the positions of Durkheim and Parsons and of their humanist critics may be subsumed under the same general concept. Whilst there are considerable differences between the theoretical humanism of Weber and the anti-humanism of Durkheim and of Parsons, they nevertheless share the fundamental problems of the rationalist conception of action. I discuss these problems in the last section of this Part of the paper.

Before proceeding to an examination of the particular features of the humanist and anti-humanist forms of the rationalist conception of action, it is necessary to consider some of the theoretical consequences of the basic postulates of this conception. Three consequences are of particular importance. First, the postulate of a mechanism of the realisation of ideas implies a capacity on the part of that mechanism to register discrepancies between the ideas and the situation in which action is to take place. More precisely, since ideas and the world are not strictly commensurable, the mechanism must be able to represent the situation of action in the realm of ideas and to compare that ideal representation with the ideas to be realised. In short, the mechanism must possess a *recognition structure* capable of constructing ideal representations of the natural conditions of action. Theoretical humanism clearly postulates such a capacity on the part of the human subject and it is for the same reason that Parsons insists on the necessity of a 'subjective point of view' in the analysis of all levels of action above that of the biological organism. Parsons' actor acts in terms of his conceptions:

> The actor's system of orientations is constituted by a great number of specific orientations. Each of these 'orientations of action' is a 'conception' (explicit or implicit, conscious or unconscious) which the actor has of the situation in terms of what he wants (his ends), what he sees (how the situation looks to him), and how he intends to get from the objects he sees to the things he wants (his explicit or implicit, normatively regulated 'plan' of action). (Parsons & Shils, 1962, p. 54)

Since Parsons insists that an actor may be either an individual or a collectivity, and since the category of collectivity includes societies, social systems and their functional sub-systems, we must conclude that social systems and sub-systems are endowed with recognition structures analogous to those which Parsons attributes to individual actors. In particular, the economy, as one of the major functional sub-systems of society, must have a recognition structure capable of registering discrepancies between its goals and the situation of action.[9]

Secondly, it is necessary to consider the sense in which the functioning of the postulated mechanism may be said to involve the realisation of ideas. Any form of the rationalist conception of action postulates firstly a system of ideas, ultimate values, rules, or whatever, in short an ideal totality, and secondly processes of realisation of the ideas of that totality. Ideas govern action in the sense that the actions are consistent with the ideas of the totality; for example, ultimate values govern action to the extent that actions conform to these values. In effect, the ideas govern action in at least the minimal sense of excluding actions which conflict with them. In addition, whatever particular mechanism of realisation may be postulated, its functioning is somehow constrained to conform to the prior determination of the ideal totality. We shall see that the rationalist conception of action runs into serious difficulties if it admits that ideal totalities may contain contradictory ideas, say, conflicting ultimate values, and that it becomes entirely vacuous if contradictory ideas are precluded.

The third point follows from the second. If the mechanism of realisation must be conceived as somehow constrained to conform to the primacy of ideas, it must also be conceived as involving processes in nature. There are three aspects of this point. The first is that what appears in nature is not the idea itself but rather its expression, its attempted realisation in action. Action must be accounted for by reference to the idea it attempts to realise, and the idea may be known only through its expressions and attempted realisation. The circular and speculative character of the relation between postulated ideas and its supposed expression is evident.[10] Secondly, the success of the mechanism in realising its ideas must be a function of the situation of action which, in certain respects, must be conceived as beyond the control of the acting mechanism itself. Parsons insists on this pertinence of the situation of action in his critiques of 'idealist emanationism'.[11] The third aspect is that the acting mechanism itself functions according to natural processes and is therefore subject to natural determinations. Thus, if contradiction is to be avoided on this point, the relevant parts of nature must be conceived as endowed with an immanent capacity to realise ideas. Whether contradiction can be avoided or not, the mechanism of realisation must be conceived as subject to two quite distinct and possibly conflicting modes of determination: on the one hand it is a thing in nature and subject to natural constraints; on the other hand it is constrained to conform to the prior determination of its ideal totality. In contrast to merely natural entities, the mechanisms of realisation of ideas must be regarded as free and undetermined; their actions go beyond natural determinations. In theoretical humanism this consequence appears in the form of the doctrine of the freedom of the will. For example, Weber conceives the behaviour of the human individual as a natural process subject to natural (physiological, biological, psychological) constraints, but in so far as it is endowed with meaning, behaviour is also constrained to conform to that meaning. Similarly, Parsons conceives social and personality systems as the embodiment of culture on the one hand and subject to their own internal conditions of existence as systems on the other. The rationalist conception of action cannot avoid postulating two antithetical forms of constraint and it is possible to reconcile them only by postulating a pre-given capacity on the part of the realm of nature to conform to the determination of ideas. The effect of that attempted reconciliation is to contradict the initial demarcation of the realms of nature and of ideas.

THEORETICAL HUMANISM: THE CASE OF WEBER

Weber's conception of action is a theoretical humanism; it postulates a mechanism of the realisation of ideas (called 'meanings' or 'ultimate values') which operate at the level of the individual human subject. Weber insists that social relationships and social collectivities are always reducible to the actions of individuals. Social collectivities 'must be treated as solely the resultants and modes of organisation of the particular acts of individual persons, since these alone can be treated as agents in a course of subjectively understandable action' (Weber, 1964a, p. 101). It follows, for example, that the investigation of a socialistic economy must be conducted in individualistic terms. It must begin with the question: 'What motives determine and lead the individual members and participants in this socialistic community to behave in such a way that the community came into being in the first place and that it continues to exist?' (ibid., p. 107).

In this brief discussion of Weber's position I shall consider two aspects of his theoretical humanism: the first concerns his conceptualisation of the mechanism of realisation of ideas,[12] and the second concerns the tension between the individualistic consequences of theoretical humanism and Weber's attempts to conceptualise forms of social action.

In Weber's definitions of sociology and in his methodological writings the mechanism of realisation of meanings and values is the human individual. On the one hand the human individual is a creature in nature subject to physiological, psychological and genetic determinations and on the other hand it is a free agent, a subject of will and consciousness. A recognition structure is entailed in the postulate of the consciousness of the human subject. Weber, in common with the bulk of theoretical humanism, does not elaborate on the mechanisms by which this recognition structure is supposed to function. The element of speculation entailed in the Weberian doctrine of interpretative understanding is well known. Interpretation may well strive 'for clarity and verifiable accuracy of insight and comprehension' (ibid., p. 90), but there is no means of knowing if it has been achieved. In no case does the 'meaning' attributed to a particular real or hypothetical actor 'refer to an objectively "correct" meaning or one which is "true" in some metaphysical sense' (ibid., p. 89) Values that are radically different from our own pose severe difficulties for the interpretative understanding of action:

> These difficulties apply, for instance, for people not susceptible to the relevant values, to many unusual acts of religious and charitable zeal; also certain kinds of extreme rationalistic fanaticism of the type involved in some forms of the ideology of the "rights of man" are in a similar position for people who radically repudiate such points of view. (ibid., p. 91)

The implications of this position are clear. We are compelled to speculate as to the meanings involved in the action of other actors and it is only when these values are reasonably close to our own that we have any chance of success. We can know their values only through our speculative interpretation of their actions. Since the action is defined by its meaning we can only classify and distinguish actions by reference to the meanings and values that we postulate in order to account for them. But the speculative effects of Weber's theoretical humanism go further than this. The behaviour of the human subject is a function of both natural and extra-natural determinations. In the latter case the behaviour is also an action. Action and behaviour may be distinguished by the meaning entailed in the one and the absence of meaning in the other. And how do we know in any particular case whether a meaning is involved at all? Since meanings can be known only through their expressions, we are compelled to speculate not only as to what is the meaning of a determinate item of behaviour but also as to whether it has any meaning at all. In these respects Weber's science of social action is a science of the speculative interpretation of what is speculatively identified as action.

In addition to its speculative effects, Weber's postulate of the realisation of ideas through human action poses the problem of the articulation of the natural and the extra-natural in man. The line between action and behaviour is very difficult to draw, and we are told that 'a very considerable part of sociologically relevant behaviour . . . is marginal between the two' (ibid., p. 90). The category of action that is marginal between action and behaviour plays a crucial part in Weber's sociology. In Section 2 of 'The Fundamental Concepts of Sociology' he distinguishes four basic types of social action according to their mode of orientation. Two of these are rational and the other two, traditional and affectual orientations, are on or 'very close to the borderline of what can justifiably be called meaningfully oriented action, and indeed often on the other side' (ibid., p. 116). In so far as they cease to be marginal they shade over into mere behaviour on the one side and into one or other of the rational types on the other. Action is essentially rational; it deviates from rationality only the extent that it is polluted by an admixture of behaviour, i.e. to the extent that it is the product of natural determinations. In effect, Weber's theoretical humanism imposes a threefold classification of human behaviour: rational action which conforms to meanings and values; mere behaviour which is the pure product of natural determinations; and non-rational action which is part action and part behaviour.[13] Human behaviour is rational if it conforms to meanings and values and non-rational if it does not. It is this essential rationality of action that leads to Weber's insistence on the construction of *rational* ideal types. The causal significance of all other elements in behaviour may then be interpreted 'as accounting for the deviations from this type' (ibid., p. 92). Weber adds that 'rational types' are only a methodological device, but it should now be clear that they have a theoretical necessity in the humanist form of the rationalist conception of action.

If we ask the question of what is the relative proportion of action and mere behaviour in a given society, it is clear that Weber's concepts preclude any empirical determination of that proportion. Meanings must be postulated but they cannot be empirically observed. Nevertheless, in his discussion of the relative role of 'mechanical and instinctive factors, as compared with that of the factors which are accessible to subjective interpretation' (ibid., p. 106), Weber tells us 'that *in the early stages of human development, the first set of factors is completely predominant*' (ibid., emphasis added). There are two levels in man, the rational and the animal, and in the early stages of human development the animal is predominant. Primitive men are closer to animals than the civilised and rational creatures of the West. For example, he describes some domestic animals as able to react to human commands in ways that are 'by no means purely instinctive and mechanical' and adds that 'there is no *a priori* reason to suppose that our ability to share the feelings of primitive men is very much greater' (ibid., p. 104).

Thus, in defining sociology as a science of *action*, Weber in no way denies the existence or significance of mere behaviour. But rationality, the capacity to realise meanings and values, is represented as what is specifically and essentially human. However, this rational essence is by no means always realised in human society. I refer above to his discussion of men in 'the early stages of human development', but the point is even clearer in Weber's studies of the economic ethics of the world religions. In his contrast between the rationalising development of Western civilisation and the ossification and stagnation of the East, Weber clearly conceives the development of the West as a process of realisation of the essence of man. In this sense the development of the West has '*universal* significance and value' (Weber, 1930, p. 18). The teleological character of this conception is evident.

The second aspect of Weber's position to be considered here concerns the attempted combination of a theoretical humanism with its clear individualistic implications on the one hand and a conception of social action on the other. In his definition of sociology, Weber defines social action as follows: 'Action is social in so far as, by virtue of the subjective meaning attached to it by the acting individual (or individuals), it takes account of the behaviour of others and is thereby oriented in its course' (ibid., p. 88). In fact, of course, it is not the *behaviour* but the *action* of others that is important here: action is social when and in so far as it takes account of the action of others. The conceptualisation of social action and of certain types of economic action takes us beyond the level of the individual actor. The very definition of particular forms of social and of economic action involves a necessary reference to the actions of others. It might seem that this poses a problem for Weber's theory, since he tells us: 'It is a monstrous misunderstanding to think that an "individualistic" *method* should involve what is in any conceivable sense an individualistic system of *values*.' (ibid., p. 107). A socialistic economy with socialistic values must nevertheless be understood in individualistic terms. But whether we are concerned with a socialistic or another type of economy, Weber's theory requires that some value or values be *shared*. It is difficult to see how the appearance of shared values could be accounted for in an individualistic theory except as an accidental and contingent occurrence.

But the problem with regard to the conceptualisation of social and economic action in Weber's theory goes much deeper. The existence of what Weber regards as theoretically the most significant types of social and economic action requires not only that a plurality of actors share similar values but also that their actions be socially structured and organised. Perhaps the clearest example of this point is given in Weber's discussion of the conditions of existence of modern capitalistic economic action in his General Introduction to the series of studies on the Economic Ethics of World Religons (published in English as the introduction to *The Protestant Ethic*), but the same type of problem would arise if we were to consider the major forms of political action. To say that a *state* exists is to say 'that there is or has been a probability that on the basis of certain kinds of known subjective attitude of certain individuals there will result in the average sense a certain specific type of action' (ibid., p. 119). The existence of each of the major types of political domination therefore implies a reference to a certain social distribution of the appropriate subjective attitudes among certain individuals. The problem here concerns how the distribution of appropriate subjective attitudes among a plurality of individuals is to be reconciled with the individualism of Weber's theory of action.

To return to the case of modern capitalism, Weber tells us that rational capitalistic economic action involves calculations in terms of capital: 'all that matters is that an actual adaptation of economic action to a comparison of money income with money expenses takes place, no matter how primitive the form' (ibid., p. 19). Rational capitalistic economic action presupposes the existence of money; its condition of existence cannot, then, be defined in individualistic terms.[14] But for *modern* rational capitalism a great deal more is required: the rational capitalistic organisation of formally free labour; the separation of business from the household; rational book-keeping; and last but not least, rational structures of law and administration: 'For modern rational capitalism has need, not only of the technical means of production, but of a calculable legal system and of administration in terms of formal rules. Without it . . . [there can be] no rational enterprise under individual initiative, with fixed capital and certainty of calculations' (ibid. p. 25). In short, modern rational capitalistic economic action presupposes what Weber calls 'the specific and peculiar rationalism of Western culture' and, above all, its realisation in the rational structures of law and administration and in 'the ability and disposition of men to adapt certain types of practical rational conduct' (ibid., p. 26).

The implication is clear: the existence of the most rational form of economic action presupposes the realisation of a rationality in the forms of organisation of society itself. Rational economic action on the part of the *individual* is possible only on condition of the rationalisation of his world. Rationality at the level of the individual is a function of the supra-individual level of society. In this case the functioning of Weber's postulated mechanism of realisation of ideas, namely, the human individual, is possible only on condition of the functioning of some supra-individual mechanism of realisation of ideas. Thus the whole Weberian theory of modern rational capitalism is incompatible with his insistence that the social world is reducible to the actions of individuals, that 'action . . . exists only as the behaviour of one or more individual human beings' (Weber, 1964a, p. 101). The realisation of the rational essence of man in modern Western civilisation is also the subordination of man to a supra-individual rationality in which the world becomes a meaningless sphere of merely instrumental rationality: 'For the last stage of this cultural development, it might well be truly said: specialists without spirit, sensualists without heart; this nullity imagines that it has attained a level of civilisation never before achieved (Weber, 1930, p. 182).

Although the incoherence of Weber's individualistic conception of social and economic action is most apparent in respect of his conception of rational economic action, it is clear that precisely similar conclusions could be reached with regard to the other forms of social and economic action.[15] In particular, if rational economic action presupposes the rationalisation of the world, then other forms of economic action involve the realisation of those spiritual obstacles to the development of rationality which 'have in the past been among the most important formative influences on conduct' (ibid., p. 27).

THEORETICAL ANTI-HUMANISM: THE CASE OF PARSONS

If humanist forms of the rationalist conception of action locate the primary mechanism of the realisation of ideas in the will and consciousness of the human individual, the anti-humanisms subordinate the action of the individual to the functioning of a supra-individual mechanism of realisation. Where theoretical humanism falls into incoherence in its attempt to conceptualise social and economic action, the anti-humanist forms of the rationalist conception of action have at least the merit of being able to avoid that particular problem. Since there is no necessity for social life to be reduced to the action of individuals, there is no necessary contradiction between an individualistic conception of action and the supra-individual reference involved in the conceptualisation of social action. The more general problems of the rationalist conception of action remain; the distinction between idea and its realisation or expression imposes the necessity for a speculative mode of 'reading' of the forms of social life, of social actions and of expressive symbols for the 'ideas' that are assumed to underlie them, and the supra-individual mechanism of realisation remains subject to the double determination of the natural on the one hand and the ideal on the other.

A relatively undeveloped form of this position is involved in the substantive view of the economy elaborated by Polanyi and his associates, but Parsons is undoubtedly its most rigorous exponent in the contemporary social sciences. In spite of his insistence on the importance of the 'subjective point of view' Parsons devotes little attention to the problems of the 'reading' or 'interpretation' of action involved in his conception of social life. But, at least in his post-war writings, he does elaborate a complex and sophisticated conception of the mechanism of realisation of ideas. It is this aspect of his work that I consider here. Parsons proposes a form of the rationalist conception of action in which ideas are thought to be realised in and through the articulation of cultural, social and personality systems on to human biological organisms. The three systems are interdependent and interpenetrating and none can exist without the other two. In particular there can be no personality or social system without a cultural system. Culture, in Parsons' sense, consists of systems of ideas and beliefs, systems of expressive symbols and systems of value-orientations. Elements of the cultural system may be institutionalised in social systems and internalised in personalities, and some elements will be involved in the definitions of the goals of individual or collective actors.

Any mechanism of realisation of ideas in nature must function by means of natural processes. In Parsons' theory, all action involves on the one hand an orientation to the attainment of specific ends and on the other the expenditure of energy which has its source in the energy potential of the physiological organism. In action, 'ideas' in the form of actors' conceptions and orientations must be articulated on to the sources of energy of physiological organisms in such a way that the behaviour of organisms is a function of these 'ideas'. The structure of human physiological organisms must therefore be such as to allow for its expenditure of energy to be governed by its conceptions: 'In addition to the specific viscerogenic needs and the wider discrimination between gratification and deprivation, the human organism has *a constitutional capacity to react to objects*, especially other human beings, *without the specific content or form of the reaction being in any way physiologically given*. (Parsons & Shils, 1962, p. 10; emphasis added). The human organism has an *innate* capacity to act 'in terms of' ideas.

In *The Structure of Social Action* (Parsons, 1949a) 'normative orientation' occupies a position of unique importance since it is both an element of action that is irreducible to the other elements and an element whose intervention is decisive whenever action is not uniquely determined by the other elements. In Parsons' later work the decisive and primary importance of value-orientations in action is retained at least with regard to all levels of action above the merely physiological. Action is a function of motivational orientation on the one hand and of value-orientation on the other. One provides the energy for action and the other provides its control. The energy for action is derived from the gratification structure of the organism and the direction or objective of action is given by its orientations. Because of the necessary articulation of orientation on to the gratification structure of the organism, it follows that orientation must always involve both cognitive and cathectic modes:

> One cannot 'orient' without discriminating objects, one cannot discriminate an object without its arousing some interest either by virtue of its intrinsic gratificatory significance, or by virtue of its relationships to other objects. Similarly, one cannot make a choice without 'cognising' the alternatives; and also one cannot select except on the basis of the cathectic interest aroused by the alternatives. (ibid., p. 68)

In addition, since the situation of action and gratification structure do not in general uniquely determine action, there must be a comparison of the gratification – deprivation balance presented by possible alternative courses of action and an orientation to 'ideas', in the shape of standards of value-orientation, which is decisive in the choice among these alternatives.

Although the ultimate source of energy is to be found in the physiological organism, the combination of motivational orientation with value-orientation is a necessary feature of all actors, of human individuals and of collectivities. Thus, for Parsons, collectivities, including social systems and their functional sub-systems, must be characterised by some equivalent to the gratification structure of the physiological organism and by a recognition structure in the sense of a capacity for cognitive orientation towards the situation of action.[16] The gratification structure of the actor is implicated in the forms of his cognition since objects are discriminated by virtue of their cathectic significance. There is therefore a double articulation of the level of ideas and the level of the natural or social: the organisation of ideas is in part a function of a gratification structure which provides the source of energy in action, and the expenditure of energy in action is a function of an organisation of ideas in the orientations of the actor. A major source of inconsistency and incompleteness in the cultural system is therefore to be found in the exigencies of the internalisation of culture in personalities and its institutionalisation in social systems.

Action is organised into systems which are defined either at the level of the individual organism (the personality system) or at the level of the interaction of two or more actors (the social system). Each type of system is dependent on the other and both are dependent on the existence of a cultural system on the one hand and physiological organisms on the other. Elements of the cultural system may be internalised in personalities in the form of a relatively stable system of orientations articulated on the gratification structure of individuals and they may be institutionalised in social systems in the form of systems of rules and role-expectations, collectivities and social institutions.

Now, although they are interdependent and interpenetrating, cultural, social and personality systems must each be conceived as relatively autonomous from the other two; as *systems* they each have their own functional exigencies and conditions of existence. Thus, personality and social systems cannot be treated as mere emanations of ideas since they are also subject to determinate conditions of existence of systems. For example, a social system consists of the relatively stable interactions of the incumbents of socially organised roles. The existence of the system therefore depends on the performance of its roles (or at least of a high proportion of them) and this implies a fundamental set of problems of allocation: the system must allocate human capacities and resources among tasks by assigning individuals to roles; it must allocate the facilities necessary for the performance of roles (including both physical objects on the one hand and rights and obligations on the other), and it must allocate the rewards necessary to the maintenance of an appropriate pattern of motivation among role-incumbents—if need-dispositions are not gratified, then the performance of role-incumbents may be impaired.[17] If it fails to resolve its problems of allocation to a satisfactory degree, then role-performance will be unable to continue and the social system will not survive. Similarly, social systems must achieve adequate solutions to their other functional problems and personality systems must resolve theirs if they are to continue in existence. Finally, the very definition and classification of the functional prerequisites of the three types of system itself presupposes their relative autonomy and independence as systems: 'action systems are structured about three integrative foci, the individual actor, the interactive system, and a system of cultural patterning. Each implies the others and therefore *the variability of any one is limited by its compatibility with the minimum conditions of functioning of the other two*' (Parsons, 1951, p. 27; emphasis added).

Thus, in Parsons' theory, social and personality systems as mechanisms of the realisation of ideas are subject to the type of double determination indicated at the beginning of this Part of the paper, namely, one involving the coexistence of irreconcilable modes of effectivity. On the one hand they have determinate functional exigencies as systems and if they fail to achieve a satisfactory resolution of the fundamental systems problems then they cannot survive. On the other hand the role of ideas in action is primary: if the situation of action or the physiological structure of the organism do not completely determine action, then the orientation of the action is decisive. This double determination is of fundamental importance for the formation of the major substantive concepts of Parsons' sociological theory. But, as Stephen Savage and I have shown elsewhere,[18] the conception of the relative autonomy of the cultural, social and personality systems is incompatible with the primacy of ideas in Parsons' concept of action. Systems of action cannot be conceived as truly autonomous on the one hand and as constrained by the immanent necessity to realise ideas on the other. Parsons' theory is impossible without the conjunction of the concept of action on the one hand and the concepts of autonomous systems of action on the other, and it is logically incoherent as a theory because of their conjunction.

In his most recent work Parsons has tended to conceive the personality, social and cultural systems in a different fashion both as the functional sub-systems of the General System of Action and as organised into a definite hierarchy of controlling and conditioning elements. The effect of these changes is to overcome, at least in part, the incompatibility of the concepts of the systems and the primacy of ideas in action by denegating both the autonomy of the systems and the specificity of their functional exigencies. The cultural, personality and social systems no longer appear as the interdependent and irreducible systems which occupy a central place in much of Parsons' substantive theory; they are now merely different aspects of the realisation of ultimate reality in the realm of nature. In this latest position the three levels of action occupy intermediate positions between the ultimate controlling elements (called 'ultimate reality') and the ultimate conditions of action in the physical and organic environment. Cultural, social and personality systems are effects of the intervention of ultimate reality in the world of nature.[19] These changes may well avoid the incoherence entailed in Parsons' major substantive theory since they postulate an immanent capacity in nature, i.e. in the human organism as the highest product of biological evolution, to respond to the call of ultimate reality, but, as we shall see, they do not escape the more general problems and the ultimate incoherence of the rationalist conception of action.

THE RATIONALIST CONCEPTION OF ACTION. II

So far I have merely considered certain problems that arise within two particular cases of the rationalist conception of action. But there are two more general problems which are sufficient to ensure that any form of the rationalist conception of action must be either vacuous or incoherent. Consider first the implications of the postulate of a mechanism of realisation of ideas for the conceptualisation of the realm of nature. We have seen that nature, or some part of it, must be subject to a double determination. The mechanism of realisation must be constrained to conform to the primacy of ideas and it must be implicated in processes in nature; it is subject to ideal constraints on the one hand and to natural constraints on the other. For example, Weber's actor is a rational being acting in accordance with meanings and values *and* it is a human biological organism subject to physical, biological and psychological determinations.

Similarly, in Parsons' theory of the systems of action the personality and social systems are the means of realisation of ideas through internalisation and institutionalisation and action to realise goals *and* they are subject to determinate functional exigencies as systems. In his most recent work, the General System of Action is subject to the constraints of ultimate reality on the one hand and of the physical and organic environment on the other. If this double determination of the mechanism of action is not to involve the rationalist conception in the contradiction of postulating the coexistence of irreconcilable modes of effectivity, then it is necessary to suppose an immanent capacity for the order of nature to correspond to the order of ideas; it is necessary to suppose a pre-established harmony between the order of ideas and the order of nature. Nature has a pre-given capacity to realise ideas and some such capacity must be postulated as the fundamental condition of existence of any rationalist mechanism of action. Nature must therefore be conceived as endowed with a purpose, namely, to realise its capacity to realise ideas, for example through the process of natural evolution. The price of avoiding immediate contradiction in the notion of the double determination of the mechanism of action is the conception of nature as subject to a universal teleology.[20]

The second problem concerns the ideas themselves and their relation to the mechanism of their realisation. Any form of the rationalist conception of action postulates first an ideal totality, a system of ideas, ultimate values, meanings, rules, or whatever, and some process of realisation of those ideas. Ideas govern action in the sense that actions must be consistent with the system of ideas in question. Action that fails to conform is either precluded by the ideas or else it is a *mistake*, i.e. not a product of the ideas at all. Whatever particular process of realisation may be postulated, its functioning must be somehow constrained to conform to the prior determination of the ideal totality. So far so good. Now what happens if elements of the ideal totality, say two ultimate values or two rules, conflict and therefore entail conflicting forms of action? The authors of *Toward a General Theory of Action*, for example, tell us: 'Very close approximations to complete consistency in the patterns of culture are practically never to be found in large complex social systems' (Parsons & Shils, 1962, p. 22). What are the effects of inconsistency for the conceptualisation of action?

Let us suppose that in a given situation one rule or ultimate value entails action A and that the other entails action B. Since A and B conflict and we are concerned with a given situation of action, it is impossible for both A and B to appear in that situation. The problem here is that if one, say action A, appears then its appearance cannot be accounted for by reference to *its* rule or ultimate value alone, because some further explanation is required to explain why that rule or value is realised and not the other, conflicting, rule or value. Thus if inconsistency is possible within the ideal totality which is alleged to govern action, then some further mechanism must be called in to account for the realisation of one of the conflicting ideas in a given situation and not the other. The rationalist conception of action must either concede that ideas govern action only by courtesy of some other mechanism, that is, that they do not *govern* action at all, or else it must adopt the relativisitic tactic which denies that contradiction within the ideal totality can arise at all.

We have seen that the possibility of logical inconsistency is clearly recognised in Parsons' theory of action. Ideas, in this case value-orientations, have a certain primacy in the theory of action in that they are decisive whenever the other elements (situation, motivational orientation, etc.) do not completely determine action. In effect, value-orientations must be called in to account for action that cannot be accounted for as the resultant of the other elements. If conflict at the level of value-orientations is possible, then the realisation of one value-orientation rather than another cannot be accounted for by reference to the other elements of action since value-orientation is pertinent only when the effect of those other elements is indeterminate. In the event of inconsistency in the cultural system, action would seem to be theoretically indeterminate, that is to say, inexplicable in terms of Parsonian theory. Since neither value-orientations nor the remaining elements of action suffice to achieve theoretical determinacy, the only possible recourse for Parsons is to call on ultimate reality itself to ensure that one value-orientation rather than another is realised in any determinate situation of action. But since ultimate reality is specifically defined by Parsons as lying beyond the realm of scientific knowledge, theoretical indeterminacy cannot be overcome by calling on ultimate reality to do its turn.

As an example of the relativistic manoeuvre, namely, the effective denial of logical inconsistency, consider the writings of Peter Winch. In *The Idea of a Social Science*, Winch (1958) argues that human conduct is a matter of the following of rules. Now it is clear that the coexistence of inconsistent rules within a given system of rules must introduce an element of indeterminacy into Winch's system unless they are subsumed under the primacy of a more general rule which acts so as to prevent inconsistency from arising. Winch invokes precisely this possibility in 'Understanding a Primitive Society', where he argues that 'many contradictions we might expect to appear in fact do not in the context of Zanda thought, *where provision is made for avoiding them*' (Winch, 1970, p. 91; emphasis added). Inconsistencies are avoided by subordinating apparently conflicting rules to a super-rule which specifies the conditions in which each rule may be called upon to take effect. This device, however, does not entirely overcome the problem for there remains the possibility that what is inconsistent to us is consistent to the society in question:

the forms in which rationality expresses itself in the culture of a human society cannot be elucidated *simply* in terms of the logical coherence of the rules according to which activities are carried out in that society. For

. . . *there comes a point where we are not even in a position to determine what is and what is not coherent in such a context of rules,* without raising questions about the point which following those rules has in that society. (ibid., p. 93; emphasis added).

So much for the possibility of inconsistency. But this relativistic dissolution of the notion of logical coherence merely gives rise to another problem. If conduct never deviates from the super-rule which avoids contradiction, then the notion of rule-governed conduct is simply vacuous because to specify the super-rule is merely to describe whatever conduct takes place. Winch avoids that result by means of the notion of 'mistake': 'the notion of following a rule is logically inseparable from the notion of *making a mistake*' (Winch, 1958, p. 32). But if mistakes are conceivable, then the situation is again indeterminate: the rule is followed in all cases except those in which it is not followed. Thus Winch's relativistic conception of action is either vacuous or theoretically indeterminate.

The rationalist conception of action is either vacuous or indeterminate. It can avoid those alternatives only by invoking some other, non-rationalist, mechanism to account for action, that is, it can avoid them only at the cost of theoretical incoherence.

PART II

TELEOLOGY

The problem of teleology can now be dealt with without difficulty, partly because its basic features have been touched on in a different context in Part I of this paper and partly because several particular teleologies are discussed in other papers in this seminar. I propose a general concept of teleology in the form of a minimal definition which subsumes both those positions which postulate a determinate immanent developmental tendency, such as Parsons' 'rationalisation' and 'structural differentiation', and those apparently more limited positions which merely propose a principle of hierarchy, such as 'development', 'modernisation', *'Gemeinschaft/Gesellschaft'*, etc., in terms of which differences between societies may be conceived. In this second case the teleological postulate need involve no *necessary* process of realisation of the forms in the hierarchy. I argue that teleological theories must be confronted by an irresolvable problem of double determination similar to that identified above with respect to the rationalist conception of action, and I show that this suffices to establish the incoherence of teleology.

As a minimal definition we can say that a teleology combines an essentialism with a principle of temporal order. To say that it involves an essentialism is to say that phenomena are conceived as the expression or realisation of a determinate inner principle, the principle being the essence of the phenomena expressing it. The essentialist relation between essence and phenomena is clearly represented in Althusser's definition in *Reading Capital* of expressive causality as a mode of conceptualising the relations between a whole and its elements:

> But it presupposes in principle that the whole in question be reducible to an *inner essence*, of which the elements of the whole are then no more than the phenomenal form of expression, the inner principle of the essence being present at each point in the whole, such that at each moment it is possible to write the immediately adequate equation: *such and such an element* (economic, political, legal, literary, religious, etc., in Hegel) = *the inner essence of the whole*. (Althusser & Balibar, 1970, pp. 186–7)[21]

A teleology postulates a number of such 'wholes', for example a number of distinct political or economic forms, each with its own distinctive essence, and it assigns a definite temporal order or hierarchy to these essences. In effect, each form is the expression of its position in the hierarchy. My analysis and critique will be concerned mainly with the consequences of the essentialism of teleology and not with the notion of a temporal sequence as such. It should be noted that while teleologies may well postulate a *necessary* process of realisation of the hierarchy of forms, it is possible for them not to do so. The movement from one form to the next need not be conceived as the necessary effect of the lower form, and it is well known that Weber explicitly repudiates such a conception.[22] The crucial and most problematic feature of the teleological postulate is not historical necessity but rather the conceptualisation of the distinct forms as the realisation or expression of their position in the hierarchy. It is clear that the rationalist conception of action is teleological in this sense, since any given action involves a hierarchy of at least two distinct forms, namely, the starting-point and the goal to be realised in action, with possibly several intermediate stages. While that teleology is ubiquitous in sociology, another quite distinct type of teleology is normally present in sociological attempts to conceptualise social and economic change. For example, sociological theories of industrialisation, modernisation or development involve teleologies which are, in general, irreducible to the teleology of *action*. Much of sociology is therefore characterised by two teleologies: a teleological conception of action and a more general teleology of history. Thus, Weber and Parsons elaborate both a rationalist conception of action and a further teleology in the processes of rationalisation, structural differentiation and increasing adaptive capacity.

To postulate any form of teleology is to postulate a principle of ranking in terms of which the forms in the hierarchy may be ordered. The principle itself may take many forms. It may take the form of an *ideal*, say, of the goal or purpose of historical development that is postulated in the idealist philosophies of history. For example, Kant in his 'Idea for a Universal

History' postulates a purpose in 'Nature's secret plan' which is to bring about the full realisation of human capacities in the process of history, and it is well known that Hegel conceives of history as a process of realisation of the Idea. But the principle of teleology need not be represented in the form of an ideal. Many teleological versions of Marxism propose a principle of ranking in terms of the articulation of relations and forces of production. In its simplest forms this involves an immanent tendency of the forces of production to expand subject only to temporary constraints imposed from time to time by the relations of production. History is therefore a process of expansion of productive forces with occasional interruptions where the class struggle succeeds in transforming relations of production so as to allow further expansion of productive forces.[23] These teleological distortions of Marxist theory have been criticised by Paul Hirst and me in *Pre-Capitalist Modes of Production* (Hindess & Hirst, 1975). A different type of example which is particularly prevalent in sociology is provided by those teleologies which light upon some alleged feature of the present as their ranking principle: for example, the teleologies of modernisation, development or industrialisation, the dichotomies of *Gemeinschaft/Gesellschaft*, or of the pattern-variables and the continua of rationalisation or structural differention in which societies are ranked according to their divergence from the alleged features of 'modern society', 'industrial society', 'structurally differentiated society', or whatever. Teleological conceptions of this kind play a crucial role in Parsons' and Weber's theories of the economy and they may also be found in Polanyi's treatment of the differences between market and non-market economies.

But if it is hardly necessary to demonstrate the ubiquity of teleological conceptions in sociological theories of the economy, in much of what passes for Marxism and in economic anthropology, it is necessary to pose the question of what, to put it bluntly, is wrong with teleology. Is there any reason why social and economic *change* should not be conceptualised in essentialist and therefore teleological terms? The association of teleology with the idealist philosophies of history and with religion is, of course, well known. But whilst that association may lead us to view with some suspicion those conceptions which postulate a historical necessity or an explicit *ideal* principle of hierarchy, it cannot provide sufficient grounds for dismissing all teleologies – in the sense of my minimal definition – out of hand.

Accordingly, rather than dwell on its idealist and religious affinities, I propose to examine the conceptual structure of teleology and its theoretical effects. It will be convenient for this purpose to distinguish between a universal and a partial teleology. A universal teleology subsumes the world and all its parts; it encompasses everything that exists. Hegel's philosophy is perhaps the best-known example. A partial teleology on the other hand subsumes a part of the world only, such as natural evolution[24] or human history or even just the process of modernisation. A universal teleology will, of course, include many partial teleologies but these appear merely as different aspects of the one universal teleology. I shall concentrate here on partial teleologies because these are by far the most prevalent form. We shall see that the conceptual structure of a partial teleology entails a necessary inconsistency whether or not it postulates any historical necessity. A universal teleology, however, cannot avoid the postulate of historical necessity; its principle of hierarchy is also a principle of movement. Such a position may well be consistent but, like relativistic forms of the rationalist conception of action, it is consistent only if it is also vacuous.

Any partial teleology must confront one of the major problems of the rationalist conception of action discussed in Part I. On the one hand it conceives of a determinate hierarchy of forms such that each form is defined by its position in the hierarchy. The form is the realisation or expression of its place in the hierarchy of forms. On the other hand, as part of the world, each form is subject to determinate real conditions of existence. The conceptual structure of partial teleology reproduces the problem of double determination characteristic of the rationalist conception of action. In the social sciences this situation is further complicated by the ubiquity of the rationalist conception of action. In effect a historical teleology is compounded with a teleology of action so that we have three distinct levels of determination: a particular natural process or situation is subject to the determination of its natural conditions of existence, it serves to realise an idea and it expresses a position in a hierarchy of historical forms. For ease of exposition it will be convenient to overlook the particular difficulties of the ·rationalist conception of action and to contrast determination by the teleology of history on the one hand with the determination of action and of nature on the other. It should be clear that the consistency or otherwise of partial teleology does not depend on taking this further complication into account. The fundamental problem of the double determination postulated by the partial teleologies and by the rationalist conception of action is that the two determinations can be reconciled only by the further postulate of a pre-given harmony between them. Otherwise they will in general be inconsistent and incompatible. A partial teleology must therefore either presuppose a universal teleology or lapse into inconsistency.

These points may be illustrated by reference to the works of Parsons and Weber. The teleological character of their sociological theories and, in particular, of their conception of the economy has been shown in other papers in this seminar and I need not repeat those arguments here. Consider first the work of Parsons. In *The Social System, Toward a General Theory of Action*, and in much of his subsequent work, Parsons has elaborated a theory of three or four relatively autonomous systems of action, each with its own determinate functional prerequisites, its conditions of existence as a system. A society, as a social system, is therefore confronted by four major types of functional problems the resolution of which at some level of adequacy is indispensable for the continued existence of the system. But in addition to the determination of social systems according to their functional conditions of existence, Parsons proposes an immanent directional tendency or tendencies in the form of rationalisation and structural differentiation. (The relation between these tendencies does not concern us here.)[25] Let us take the case of structural differentiation. The effect of postulating such an immanent tendency is to subject any society to a double determination by its conditions of existence on the one hand and by its immanent tendency on the other. Change in the society is a function of changes in its conditions of existence and it is a function of this immanent tendency. The conflict between these two determinations is clearly demonstrated in Savage's paper: societies are conceived as determinate systems of action with determinate structural forms and subject to determinate conditions of existence and they are also conceived in terms of their *difference* from a structurally differentiated society. In effect, for Parsons, modern differentiated societies are conceived in one way and the rest are conceived in the other. Less differentiated societies are conceived primarily *as* less differentiated and not according to their structural forms and functional exigencies as systems. This position is clearly formulated in *Economy and Society*:

> We hold that our generalised theoretical scheme, for the analysis of a society and of the economy as one of its subsystems, is *not* bound to any particular structural type of society or economy. The analytical elements . . . are distinguishable as elements in *any* society, indeed in any social system. *These analytical elements are not, however, equally closely related to the concrete structure of collectivities and roles in all societies. In general our functional subsystem categories correspond more closely to organisationally differentiated sectors of the social structure as the society approaches greater structural differentiation.* But even here the correspondence is only approximate. Furthermore, the categories of economic theory apply more directly to the concrete social structure of a differentiated society and its processes as adaptive or economic values approach greater primacy over others. Only in societies which meet both these criteria do many of the more technical parts of economic theory apply directly to empirical analysis, e.g. in the analysis of price determinations in specific markets. (Parsons & Smelser, 1956, pp. 83–4; emphasis added)

Societies may therefore be conceived in terms of the degree to which they realise the elements of 'our generalised theoretical scheme'. The more differentiated may be analysed in terms of our scheme and the less differentiated in terms of their distance from it. In this conception Parsons' teleological principle is accorded primacy over the conception of a society as a determinate social system with determinate system exigencies. An equivalent teleological principle is invoked in Parsons' more recent treatment of 'evolutionary universals' and his rank-ordering of primitive, intermediate and modern societies. Indeed, in 'Evolutionary Universals in Society', Parsons argues for an essential continuity between organic and cultural evolution. The 'new relativity' proposed in that paper assumes that

> the watershed between sub-human and human does not mark a cessation of developmental change, but rather a stage in a long process that begins with many pre-human phases and continues through the watershed into our own time, and beyond. Granting a wide range of variability of types at all stages, it assumes that levels of evolutionary advancement may be empirically specified for the human as well as the pre-human phases. (Parsons, 1967, p. 491)

Here societal evolution is subsumed under a more general teleological process. The development of the human brain at the highest level of natural evolution provides the organic foundation of culture in the human capacity to learn and manipulate symbols. Thereafter culture takes over: 'cultural innovations, especially definitions of what man's life *ought* to be, replace Darwinian variations in genetic constitution' (ibid., pp. 494–5). The highest level of natural evolution establishes the conditions for 'ultimate reality' to intervene directly in the realm of nature through the cybernetic hierarchy of cultural, social and personality systems which it controls. In taking these positions Parsons effectively displaces the partial teleology of rationalisation and structural differentiation in favour of a universal teleology of nature.

The case of Weber appears to be more complex for two reasons. One is that he explicitly repudiates the notion of a necessary developmental tendency in history. Whereas Parsons postulates an immanent tendency in the process of rationalisation and structural differentiation, Weber appears not to do so. For example, in the introduction to his studies on the Economic Ethics of the World Religions, Weber poses the problem of the development of the West as follows:

> A product of modern European civilisation, studying any problem of universal history, is bound to ask himself to what combinations of circumstances the fact should be attributed that in Western civilisation, and in Western civilisation only, cultural phenomena have appeared which (as we like to think) lie in a line a development having *universal* significance and value. (Weber, 1930, p. 13)

In this paragraph we find a hierarchical principle of order with respect to social and cultural forms, namely, 'a line of development', together with the proposal that movement through that hierarchy be accounted for by reference to 'a combination of circumstances'. We have seen in Part I that

Weber's 'line of development' may be conceived as the realisation of the rational essence of man – hence its 'universal significance and value'. Weber's position represents a teleology in the sense of the minimal definition proposed above. The present, in the shape of modern rational capitalism, provides a principle of the ranking of all other societies, and distinct social and cultural forms are conceived as the realisation or expression of their position in the hierarchy of forms established by that principle. In this respect, Weber's theory of the rationalisation of the West epitomises the structure of those sociological theories of development, modernisation, or whatever, which on the one hand rank social forms according to one or more dichotomies or continua and on the other appear to pose the problem of movement along the hierarchy of forms in terms of 'a combination of circumstances'.

The second complication is that Weber, in line with his theoretical individualism, fails to elaborate a rigorous conception of the structures and conditions of existence of societies and social systems. In this respect too, Weber epitomises much of sociological theory. The effect of this failure to conceptualise the conditions of existence of determinate social forms is to obscure the problem of double determination which appears so clearly in Parsons' work. Social forms are ranked according to their position in the postulated hierarchy, but the question of their conditions of existence appears not to arise. However, the fact that the teleological problem of double determination does not appear explicitly in the text does not enable these minimal teleologies to avoid inconsistency in their concepts. The issue may be ignored in these positions but it does not thereby cease to exist.

We have seen that, on Weber's theory, the existence of the most rational forms of economic action presupposes the realisation of a rationality in the forms of organisation of society itself. Rational economic action on the part of the individual presupposes the rationalisation of his world. Thus Weber's whole theory of modern rational capitalistm is incompatible with his insistence that the social world is reducible to the actions of individuals. But if modern Western civilisation is conceived as the realisation of an essentially spiritual rationality, then other social forms may be conceptualised in terms of their divergence from the embodiment of rationality, that is, as the embodiment of those 'magical and religious forces, and the ethical ideals based upon them' (ibid, p. 27) which Weber conceives as the major spiritual obstacles to the development of rationality. Consider, to take just one example, Weber's explanation of why capitalism failed to develop in China:

> the varied conditions which externally favoured the origin of capitalism in China did not suffice to create it. . . . Many of the circumstances which could or had to hinder capitalism in China similarly existed in the Occident and assumed definite shape in the period of modern capitalism. . . . Circumstances which are usually considered to have

been obstacles to capitalistic development in the Occident had not existed for thousands of years in China. (Weber, 1964b, pp. 248–9)

Weber therefore concludes that 'external', that is, non-spiritual, conditions have not proved decisive obstacles in the development of capitalism in China. What remains, of course, is the Chinese 'ethos' or 'mentality' and the 'practical attitude toward the world' based upon them. Whilst these must be considered in relation to economic and political realities, nevertheless 'in view of their autonomous laws, one can hardly fail to ascribe to these attitudes effects strongly counteractive to capitalist development' (ibid., p. 249). There we have it. In spite of his talk about the 'combination of circumstances' responsible for the unique development of the West, Weber discovers, to nobody's very great surprise, that the decisive obstacle to the rationalisation of the East lies in its failure to embody the essential rationality of the West. Modern rational capitalism developed in the West because it embodied the spirit of modern rational capitalism and it failed to develop in the East because the East embodied a spirit alien to that of modern rational capitalism.

Thus the fundamental condition of existence of modern rational capitalism is precisely the spirit of capitalism which it is alleged to embody, and the realisation of that spirit in turn presupposes, as we saw in Part I, the general rationalisation of the world. Other social and material conditions of existence may be mentioned by Weber, but their significance is ignored. Capitalism requires the spirit of capitalism and the more general rationalisation of the world. Other conditions of existence of capitalism are either reduced to the level of expressions of rationality – the rational organisation of formally free labour, rational book-keeping, rational systems of law and administration – or they are ignored. Weber's myth of the putter-out and the spirit of capitalism illustrates this last point perfectly. Once upon a time in the Continental textile industry things were organised in a traditionalistic fashion. We are asked to consider

> the spirit which animated the entrepreneur: the traditional manner of life, the traditional rate of profit, the traditional amount of work, the traditional manner of regulating the relationships with labour, and the essentially traditional circle of customers and the manner of attracting new ones. (Weber, 1930, p. 67)

Then one day a process of rationalisation set in with the result that the 'idyllic state [of traditionalism] collapsed under the pressure of a bitter competitive struggle' (ibid., p. 68). What had happened was this:

> some young man from one of the putting-out families went out into the country, carefully chose weavers for his employ, greatly increased the rigour of his supervision of their work, and thus turned them from

peasants into labourers. (ibid., p. 67)

At the same time he transformed his marketing techniques and 'began to introduce the principle of low prices and large turnover' (ibid., p.68). What is significant in this story for Weber is that a new spirit –

> the spirit of modern capitalism had set to work. The question of the motive forces in the expansion of modern capitalism is *not in the first instance a question of the origin of the capital sums* which were available for capitalistic uses, *but, above all, of the development of the spirit of capitalism.* Where it appears and is able to work itself out, *it produces its own capital and monetary supplies as the means to its ends* but the reverse is not true. (ibid., pp. 68–9; emphasis added)

In the myth of the putter-out and the spirit of capitalism we must also suppose that the new spirit produced its own raw materials and means of production and a market for its product so that 'the *principle* of low prices and large turnover' could be realised. Where the spirit of capitalism is at work the appearance of its social and material conditions is truly miraculous.

Finally, since Weber utterly fails to conceptualise the conditions of existence of determinate social and economic forms but conceives them rather as the expression of a determinate spirit, the spirit of capitalism, the Chinese ethos, or whatever, his explanations of the movement from one form to another reduce to a single elementary form. Traditional economic life embodies the spirit of tradition and modern capitalist economic life embodies the spirit of capitalism and a more general rationality. The movement from one economic form to the other is explained quite simply by the supersession of the one spirit by the other. From time to time in human history a new spirit and new ultimate values appear from nowhere and transform society in their image. No 'external', non-spiritual conditions can stand in their way.

All partial teleologies must subject some part of the world, say human society, to a contradictory double determination. On the one hand, as part of the world, any given human society, any given social or economic form, has determinate social and natural conditions of existence which must be secured if that society or form is to survive. On the other hand, in a partial teleology, it is the expression of a determinate inner principle, namely, its position in the teleological hierarchy of forms. This combination of two antithetical forms of determination in a partial teleology entails an inescapable logical inconsistency. The problems posed by the social and natural conditions of existence of societies and social and economic forms may be ignored, as they tend to be by Weber, but they do not thereby cease to exist.

Now if partial teleology entails a necessary theoretical incoherence, the only alternatives for social theory would seem to be either the development of non-teleological conceptions of distinct social and economic forms or the insertion of partial teleology into a wider universal teleology. Neither alternative is much favoured by sociological theory. Although, as we have seen, Parsons tends towards a universal teleology in his most recent work, sociological theory is dominated by crude dichotomies and continua in its attempts to conceptualise social change. The beginnings of a non-teleological conception of distinct social forms may be found in the Marxist theory of modes of production – although it can hardly be denied that teleology abounds in much of what passes for Marxist theory. In the 1857 introduction to *A Contribution to the Critique of Political Economy*, Marx rejects the utility of the notion of 'production in general' and proposes instead the concept of distinct and specific modes of production as determinate and theoretically specific structures. Apart from the theory of the capitalist mode of production in *Capital*, there are brief indications of other possible modes of production in the writings of Marx and Engels. Paul Hirst and I have developed non-teleological concepts of several non-capitalist modes of production and of the transition from one mode of production to another in *Pre-Capitalist Modes of Production*.

But what of the other alternative? If a partial teleology is necessarily incoherent, that is precisely because its partial character entails the invocation of two antithetical forms of determination. A universal teleology avoids at least that problem. There can be no question of my attempting an analysis of the theoretical structure of universal teleology in the present paper, but the fundamental difficulty with universal teleology may be simply shown by considering first the structure of an elementary partial teleology. Consider a teleology of action involving just two states of the world, the starting-point of action and the state in which the goal of action is realised. In this case the goal of action provides a hierarchical principle of ranking of the two states. The two states of the world may be conceived as the non-realisation and realisation of the goal respectively. So far so good. But if we consider those phenomena not directly pertinent to the action in question, it is clear that the teleological principle provides no means of conceptualising the specificity of those phenomena. They must be conceptualised, if they are conceptualised at all, in terms of the non-teleological determinations entailed in the concept of a partial teleology. In a universal teleology non-teleological determinations cannot appear: there is a hierarchy of forms and nothing else. Each state of the universe, and anything within it, is the expression of its position in the hierarchy. No other determinations are possible. Two consequences follow from this. First, the hierarchical principle of a universal teleology is also the principle, the cause, of movement through the hierarchy, since no other determinations are possible. Secondly, the teleology provides no theoretical means of conceptualising the specificity of phenomena. At any given position in the hierarchy all phenomena are equally the expressions of that position. All differences must therefore be 'unreal' with regard to the inner principle which all phenomena express. The result is that the specificity of phenomena has no theoretical foundation in the teleology itself. Specificity may be retained, then, either by denying its reality or else by positing it at the level of the teleological principle itself so that every position in the hierarchy is defined as consisting of each and every one of the phenomena which are to be conceived as its expression. If partial teleology offers nothing but incoherence, then a universal teleology can offer nothing but a complete and exhaustive description of one hierarchical form after another.[26]

CONCLUSION

This paper has examined the conceptual structure of the rationalist conception of action, including theoretical humanism as a particular case of that conception, and of teleology. The rationalist conception of action was considered in Part I. It postulates a realm of ideas, values, meanings, or whatever, a realm of nature and a mechanism of the realisation of those ideas in nature, namely, human action. If the mechanism is defined at the level of the individual human subject then we have a theoretical humanism which conceives of the realisation of ideas as a function of the will and consciousness of the subject. Otherwise the mechanism is defined at some supra-individual social level of determination and it subsumes the human individual to its functioning. But whatever particular mechanism may be postulated, its effect is to define some portion of nature as the product of ideal, extra-natural determinations, as the social or cultural sphere in which phenomena may be objects of natural scientific investigation but must first and foremost be *understood* by reference to the ideas they may be alleged to express. I have shown that the rationalist conception of action is fundamentally and inescapably incoherent and that, in addition to this general incoherence, the specifically humanist forms are subject to a further inconsistency in their attempts to conceptualise those forms of action which involve some supra-individual or social reference. Part II examined teleology defined in terms of the minimal postulate that combines an essentialist conception of distinct forms with a principle of temporal order. The forms of teleology pertinent to the social sciences are *partial* teleologies in the sense that, far from attempting to subsume the universe as a whole to their teleological principle, they claim to subsume only part of the universe, namely, human society or particular social and economic forms. I have shown that all partial teleologies are necessarily incoherent and I have suggested that a universal teleology must be theoretically vacuous. I have not attempted to demonstrate that particular theoretical discourses are indeed dominated by the rationalist conception of action or to establish their teleological character, but I have taken the works of Weber and Parsons as particularly clear examples of these tendencies for the purposes of illustration. Since the rationalist conception of action and partial teleology are inescapably incoherent, it follows that any social or other theory in which one or both of these positions plays a fundamental part must also be incoherent. To the extent that they depend on rationalist or teleological positions, its demonstrations must be theoretically ineffective and its conclusions can have no rational or coherent foundation.

NOTES

1. See Hirst (1975a) for a discussion of the limits and significance of Durkheim's anti-humanism.

2. In his review of Anderson (1974), Hirst proposes the term 'genealogy' to refer to teleologies which postulate a historical necessity in the limited sense that the existence of any one form in the hierarchy requires that lower forms have been realised.

3. This form of argument has been used by Paul Hirst and myself to show that the academic social sciences cannot be scientific. See especially the introduction and conclusion to Hindess & Hirst (1975).

4. See 'The Critique of Empiricism and the Analysis of Theoretical Discourse', chap. 7 of Hindess (1977).

5. To avoid a possible misunderstanding at this point, it is necessary to insist that my analysis is concerned solely with properties of the order of concepts of certain discourses. An analysis of this kind must be clearly distinguished from those positions which treat determinate discourses as the products of extra-discursive systems of ideas so that, for example, teleological discourses would be treated as the product of a teleological world-view or set of presuppositions, of a teleological problematic, or whatever. Such positions involve a rationalist conception of the production of discourse that is merely a special case of the more general rationalist conception of action and is subject to the same fundamental critique. (See the introduction and chap. 7 of Hindess, 1977.) In the case of Weber, for example, I argue that teleology and theoretical humanism are *properties* of his discourse; I do not claim that his discourse is the *product* of teleological and humanist presuppositions.

6. See Hindess & Hirst (1975) for a critique of teleological distortions of Marxism.

7. Cf. the discussion in Hirst (1975a) chap. 5.

8. e.g. the critiques of Douglas (1967) or Wrong (1961).

9. See Savage's paper in this volume for further analysis on this point.

10. This point is elaborated in the introduction to Hindess (1977). It is this consequence of the rationalist conception of action that Lukács attempts to overcome with the postulate of the working class as subject and object of history.

11. e.g. *The Structure of Social Action*, pp. 82, 446.

12. On this point see chap. 1 of Hindess (1977).

13. While theoretical humanism must imply the possibility of border line cases in this sense, it is clearly impossible to derive the specific categories of traditional and affectual action from theoretical humanism alone.

14. Cf. the discussion of 'sociological categories of economic action' in *Economy and Society*, where money is defined as an artefact which enjoys 'a significant degree of conventional or legal, agreed or imposed, formal value *within the membership of a group of persons* or within a territorial area' (Weber, 1964a, p. 174; emphasis added). The absurdity of an individualistic conception of money is brought out very clearly in Parsons' critique of Homans (Parsons, 1964).

15. Similar points may be made with regard to attempts to conceptualise language as a function of the creative activity of the human individual. See Volosinov (1973).

16. This aspect is developed in Savage's paper in this volume.

17. Parsons & Shils (1962) pp. 197 f.

18. See Hindess & Savage (1977).

19. See especially *Societies*, chap. 2

20. Alternatively, ideas may be conceived as essentially conforming to the order of nature, that is, as epiphenomenal manifestations of natural processes. The effect of this manoeuvre is merely to establish a teleology of nature that is independent of the postulate of a supra-natural realm of ideas.

21. Like his earlier papers, 'Contradiction and Overdetermination' and 'On the Materialist Dialectic' (both in Althusser, 1969), much of *Reading Capital*, part II, is concerned to establish a demarcation between the 'Hegelian' conception of the social totality (i.e. that of Hegel's lectures on the philosophy of history and Hegelian interpretations of Marxism) and that of Marxist theory. In the discussion of causality in chap. 9, his main concern is to distinguish the structural causality which he attributes to Marxist theory from the expressive causality which he attributes to Hegel rather than to elaborate a theoretical critique of expressive causality as such. In fact his concept of structural causality involves an essentialism that is little different in principle from that of expressive causality. See the discussion in Hindess & Hirst (1975) chap. 6.

22. For a different and more rigorous example, see *Reading Capital*'s proposals for an anti-teleological science of history. The teleological character of these proposals is demonstrated in Hindess & Hirst (1975), esp. chap. 6 and the Conclusion.

23. One of the clearest examples is the conception of history outlined in Stalin's *Dialectical and Historical Materialism* (Stalin, 1972).

24. I do not intend to suggest that evolutionary theory in biology is teleological, but it is frequently interpreted in a teleological fashion. See, for example, Parsons' treatment in 'Evolutionary Universals in Society' (Parsons, 1967).

25. But see Savage's paper in this volume.

26. Since the best known and most rigorous of all teleologies is elaborated in the work of Hegel, it may be necessary to add that the few lines I have devoted to universal teleologies in this paper do not suffice for the dismissal of Hegel. I cannot attempt to analyse the conceptual structure of Hegel's work within the limits of this paper, but it may be noted that Hegel makes use of both devices given in the text in his attempts to conceptualise the specificity of phenomena.

Bibliography

Albrow, M. (1970). *Bureaucracy*. London: Macmillan.
Althusser, L. (1969). *For Marx*. London: Allen Lane, The Penguin Press.
—— & Balibar, E. (1970). *Reading Capital*. London: New Left Books.
Anderson, P. (1974). *Passages from Antiquity to Feudalism* and *Lineages of the Absolutist State*. London: New Left Books.
Arensberg, C. (1957). 'Anthropology as History', in Polanyi *et al.* (eds.) (1957).

Baren, P. (1973). *The Political Economy of Growth*. Harmondsworth: Penguin Books.
—— & Sweezy, P. (1970). *Monopoly Capital*. Harmondsworth: Penguin Books.
Bendix, R. (1956). *Work and Authority in Industry*. New York: John Wiley.
—— (1960). *Max Weber: An Intellectual Portrait*. London: Heinemann.
Bettelheim, C. (1972). 'Theoretical Comments', in A. Emmanuel, *Unequal Exchange*. London: New Left Books.
Black, M. (ed.) (1961). *The Social Theories of Talcott Parsons*. Englewood Cliffs, N.J.: Prentice-Hall.
Blau, P. & Scott, W. R. (1963). *Formal Organisations*. London: Routledge & Kegan Paul.
Bohannan, P. (1963). *Social Anthropology*. New York: Holt, Rinehart & Winston.
—— & Dalton, G. (1962). Introduction to *Markets in Africa*. Evanston, Ill.; Northwestern University Press.
Böhm-Bawerk, E. (1973). *Value and Price*. South Holland, Ill.: Libertarian Press.
Booth, D. (1975). 'André Gunder Frank: An Introduction and Appreciation', in Oxaal *et al.* (eds.) (1975).

Caplow, T. (1962). *The Sociology of Work*. Minneapolis: University of Minnesota Press.
Chayanov, A. V. (1966). *The Theory of Peasant Economy*, ed. D. Thorner, B. Kerblay & R. E. F. Smith. Homewood, Ill.: Irwin.

Dalton, G. (ed.) (1967). *Tribal and Peasant Economies*. New York: Natural History Press.
—— (ed.) (1968). *Primitive, Archaic and Modern Economies: Essays of Karl Polanyi*. New York: Anchor Books.
—— (1971). *Economic Anthropology and Development*. New York: Basic Books.
Dobb, M. (1960). *Political Economy and Capitalism*. London: Routledge & Kegan Paul.
—— (1973). 'The Trend of Modern Economics', in E. K. Hunt & J. G. Schwartz (eds.), *A Critique of Economic theory*. Harmondsworth: Penguin Books.
Douglas, J. (1967). *The Social Meanings of Suicide*. Princeton, N. J.: Princeton University Press.

Firth, R. (1951). *Elements of Social Organisation*. London: Watts.
—— (1966). *Primitive Polynesian Economy*, rev. ed. London: Routledge & Kegan Paul.
—— (ed.) (1967). *Themes in Economic Anthropology*. London: Tavistock Press.
Frank, A. G. (1970). *Latin America: Underdevelopment or Revolution*. London & New York: Monthly Review Press.
—— (1971). *Capitalism and Underdevelopment in Latin America*. Harmondsworth: Penguin Books.
—— (1972). *Lumpenbourgeoisie and Lumpendevelopment: Dependence, Class and Politics in Latin America*. London and New York: Monthly Review Press.
Fusfield, D. B. (1957). 'Economic Theory Displaced: Livelihood in Primitive Society', in Polanyi *et al.* (eds.) (1957).

Gerth, H. H. & Mills, C. W. (eds.) (1970). *From Max Weber: Essays in Sociology*. London: Routledge & Kegan Paul.
Giddens, A. (1973). *The Class Structure in the Advanced Societies*. London: Hutchinson.
Godelier, M. (1970). *Rationality and Irrationality in Economics*. London: New Left Books.
Goldthorpe, J. H. *et al.* (1968). *The Affluent Worker: Industrial Attitudes and Behaviour*. Cambridge: Cambridge University Press.
Goodfellow, P. M. (1939). *Principles of Economic Sociology*. London: Routledge & Kegan Paul.
Gouldner, A. W. (1955). *Patterns of Industrial Bureaucracy*. London: Routledge & Kegan Paul.

Habermas, J. (1971). *Toward a Rational Society*. London: Heinemann.
Harrison, M. (1975a). 'Chayanov and the Economics of the Russian Peasantry', *Journal of Peasant Studies*, vol. II, no. 2.
—— (1975b). 'Resource Allocation and Agrarian Class Formation: The Problem of Social Mobility Among Russian Peasant Households, 1880 – 1930', Warwick Economic Research Papers No. 66.
—— (1976). 'The Peasant Mode of Production in the Work of A. V. Chayanov', unpublished.
Herskovits, N. J. (1952). *Economic Anthropology*. New York: Knopf.
Hilton, R. H. (1975). *The English Peasantry in the Later Middle Ages*. Oxford: Clarendon Press.
Hindess, B. (1973). 'Models and Masks: Empiricist Conceptions of the Conditions of Scientific Knowledge', *Economy and Society*, vol. II, no. 2.
—— (1977). *Philosophy and Methodology in the Social Sciences*. Brighton: Harvester Press.
—— & Hirst, P. Q. (1975). *Pre-Capitalist Modes of Production*, London: Routledge & Kegan Paul.
—— & Savage, S. P. (forthcoming). 'Talcott Parsons and the Three Systems of Action', in H. Martins (ed.), *Structural Functionalism: A Reappraisal*. London: Macmillan.
Hirst, P. Q. (1975a). *Durkheim, Bernard and Epistemology*. London: Routledge & Kegan Paul.
—— (1975b). 'The Uniqueness of the West', *Economy and Society*, vol. IV, no. 4.
—— (1976). Review of Sahlins (1974), *Journal of Peasant Studies*, vol. II, no. 2.

Homans, G. (1972). 'Bringing Men Back In', in Turk & Simpson (eds.),

Isajiw, W. W. (1968). *Causation and Functionalism in Sociology*. London: Routledge & Kegan Paul.

Jasny, N. (1972). *Soviet Economists of the Twenties: names to be remembered*. Cambridge: Cambridge University Press.

Kaldor, N. (1958). Review of *Monopoly Capital, American Economic Review*, vol. 48, Mar. pp. 164–70.
Kant, I. (1963). 'Idea for a Universal History', in L. W. Beck (ed.) *Kant on History*, Indianapolis: Bobbs-Merrill.
Kerblay, B. (1966). 'A. V. Chayanov: Life, Career, Works', in Chayanov (1966).
Keynes, J. M. (1936). *The General Theory of Employment, Interest and Money*, London: Macmillan.
Kolko, G. (1959). 'A Critique of Max Weber's Philosophy of History', *Ethics*, vol. LXX, pp. 21–36.

Laclau, E. (1971). 'Feudalism and Capitalism in Latin America', *New Left Review*, no. 67.
Lange, O. (1963). *Political Economy*, vol. 1. Oxford: Pergamon Press.
LeClair, E. & Schneider, K. (eds.) (1968). *Economic Anthropology*. New York: Holt, Rinehart & Winston.
Lenin, V. I. (1964). *The Development of Capitalism in Russia (Collected Works*, vol. III). London: Lawrence & Wishart.
Lessnoff, M. H. (1968). 'Parsons' System Problems', *Sociological Review*, vol. XVI, no. 2, pp. 185–215.
Levine, D. P. & Levine L. S. (1975). 'Social Theory and Social Action', *Economy and Society*, vol. IV, no. 2.
Littlejohn, G. (1973a). 'The Peasantry and the Russian Revolution', *Economy and Society*, vol. II, no. 1.
—— (1973b). 'The Russian Peasantry: A Reply to Teodor Shanin', *Economy and Society*, vol. II, no. 3.
Lubitz, R. (1971). 'Monopoly Capitalism and Neo-Marxism', in D. Bell, & I. Kristol, (eds.), *Capitalism Today*. New York: Basic Books.

Malinowski, B. (1922). *Argonauts of the Western Pacific*. London: Routledge & Kegan Paul.
Marcuse, H. (1968). *Negations: Essays in Critical Theory*. London: Allen Lane, The Penguin Press.
Marshall, A. (1925). *The Principles of Economics*. London: Macmillan.
Martindale, D. (1961). *The Nature and Types of Sociological Theory*. London: Routledge & Kegan Paul.
Marx, K. (1968). 'Critique of the Gotha Programme', in Marx & Engels, *Selected Works*. London: Lawrence & Wishart.
—— (1971). Introduction to *A Contribution to the Critique of Political Economy*. London: Lawrence & Wishart.
—— (1972). *Theories of Surplus Value*, 3 vols. London: Lawrence & Wishart.
—— (1974). *Capital*, 3 vols. London: Lawrence & Wishart.

Mauss, M. (1954). *The Gift*. Glencoe, Ill.: The Free Press.
Menger, K. (1950). *Principles of Economics*. Glencoe, Ill.: The Free Press.
Mommsen, W. (1974). *The Age of Bureaucracy*. Oxford: Blackwell.

Nash, M. (1966). *Primitive and Peasant Economic Systems*. San Francisco: Chandler.
Neale, W. C. (1957a). 'Reciprocity and Redistribution in an Indian Village'.
—— (1957b) 'The Market in Theory and History', both in Polanyi *et al*. (eds.)
(1957)
Nove, A. (1974). 'On Reading André Gunder Frank', *Journal of Development Studies*,
vol. x.

O'Brien, P. (1975). 'A Critique of Latin American Theories of Dependency', in
Oxaal *et al*. (eds.) (1975).
Oxaal, I., Barnett, T. & Booth, D. (eds.) (1975). *Beyond the Sociology of Development*.
London: Routledge & Kegan Paul.

Pareto, V. (1935). *The Mind and Society*. London: Cape.
Parsons, T. (1932). 'Economics and Sociology: Marshall in Relation to the
Thought of His Time', *Quarterly Journal of Economics*, vol. XLVI, pp. 316–47.
—— (1949a). *The Structure of Social Action*. New York: The Free Press.
—— (1949b). 'The Motivation of Economic Activities', in *Essays in Sociological
Theory*, rev. ed. New York: The Free Press.
—— (1951). *The Social System*. London: Routledge & Kegan Paul.
—— (1961). 'Introduction to 'Culture and Social Systems', in Parsons *et al*. (eds.),
Theories of Society, New York: The Free Press.
—— (1964). 'Levels of Organisation and the Mediation of Social Interaction',
Sociological Inquiry, vol. XXXIV.
—— (1966). *Societies: Evolutionary and Comparative Perspectives*. Englewood Cliffs,
N. J.: Prentice-Hall.
—— *(1967)*. 'Evolutionary Universals in Society', in *Sociological Theory and Modern
Society*. New York: The Free Press.
—— (1971). *The System of Modern Societies*. Englewood Cliffs, N. J.: Prentice-Hall.
—— & Shils, E. A. (eds.) (1962). *Toward a General Theory of Action*. New York:
Harper Torchbooks.
—— & Smelser, N. J. (1956) *Economy and Society*. London: Routledge & Kegan
Paul.
Pearson, H. W. (1957a). 'The Secular Debate on Economic Primitivism'.
—— (1957b). 'Parsons and Smelser on the Economy'.
—— (1957c). 'The Economy Has No Surplus', all in Polanyi *et al*. (eds.)(1957).
Polanyi, K. (1944). *The Great Transformation*. New York: Holt, Rinehart &
Winston.
—— (1957a). 'The Economy as Instituted Process'.
—— (1957b). 'Aristotle Discovers the Economy', both in Polanyi *et al*. (eds.)
(1957).
—— (1966). *Dahomey and the Slave Trade*. Seattle: Washington University Press.
Polanyi, K., Arensberg, C. & Pearson, H. W. (eds.) (1957). *Trade and Markets in the
Early Empires*. Glencoe, Ill.: The Free Press.
Poulantzas, N. (1973). *Political Power and Social Classes*, London: Sheed & Ward and
New Left Books.

—— (1975). *Classes in Contemporary Capitalism*. London: New Left Books.

Rex, J. (1969) *Key Problems in Sociological Theory*. London: Routledge & Kegal Paul.
—— & Moore, R. (1971). *Race, Community and Conflict*. London: Oxford University Press.

Sahlins, M. (1974). *Stone Age Economics*. London: Tavistock Press.
Savage, S. P. (forthcoming). *The Sociological Theories of Talcott Parsons: Modes of Critique and the Analysis of Discourse*.
Shanin T. *(1972)*. *The Awkward Class: Political Sociology of Peasantry in a Developing Society – Russia, 1910 – 1925*. London: Oxford University Press.
—— (1973). 'Gray Littlejohn's Review of T. Shanin, *The Awkward class, Economy and Society*, vol. II, no. 2.
Smelser, N. J. (1959a). 'A Comparative View of Exchange Systems', *Economic Development and Cultural Change*, no. 7.
—— (1959b). *Social Change and the Industrial Revolution*. Chicago: University of Chicago Press.
—— (1963). *The Sociology of Economic Life*. Englewood Cliffs, N. J.: Prentice-Hall.
—— (ed.) (1965). *Readings in Economic Sociology*. Englewood Cliffs, N. J.: Prentice-Hall.
Sraffa, P. (1963). *Production of Commodities by Means of Commodities*. Cambridge: Cambridge University Press.
Stalin, J. (1942). 'Problems of Agrarian Policy in the USSR', in *Leninism*. London: Lawrence & Wishart.
—— (1972). *Dialectical and Historical Materialism*. New York: International Publishers.
Stammer, O. (ed.) (1971). *Max Weber and Sociology Today*. Oxford: Blackwell.
Stanfield R. (1973). *The Economic Surplus and Neo-Marxism*. Boston: Heath.

Tax, S. (1963). *Penny Capitalism*. Chicago: University of Chicago Press.
Thorner, D. (1966). 'Chayanov's Concept of Peasant Economy', in Chayanov (1966).
—— (1971). 'Peasant Economy as a Category in Economic History', in T. Shanin (ed.), *Peasants and Peasant Societies*. Harmondsworth: Penguin Books.
—— & Thorner, A. (1962). *Land and Labour in India*. London: Asia Publishing House.
Thurnwald, R. C. (1932). *Economics in Primitive Communities*. London: Oxford University Press.
Turk, H. & Simpson, R. L. (eds.) (1972) *Institutions and Social Exchange: The Theories of George Homans and Talcott Parsons*. Indianapolis: Bobbs-Merrill.

Volosinov, V. (1973). *Marxism and the Philosophy of Language*. London and New York: Seminar Press.

Warren, B. (1973). 'Imperialism and Capitalist Industrialisation', *New Left Review*, no. 81.
Weber, M. (1930). *The Protestant Ethic and the Spirit of Capitalism*. London: Allen & Unwin.
—— (1949). *Methodology of the Social Sciences*. New York: The Free Press.

—— (1964a). *The Theory of Social and Economic Organisation*. New York: The Free Press.
—— (1964b). *The Religion of China*. New York: The Free Press.
—— (1968). *Economy and Society*. New York: Bedminster Press.
Winch, P. (1958). *The Idea of a Social Science*. London: Routledge & Kegan Paul.
—— (1970). 'Understanding a Primitive Society', in B. Wilson (ed.), *Rationality*. Oxford: Blackwell.
Wrong, D. (1961). 'The Oversocialized Conception of Man', *American Sociological Review*, vol. XXVI.

Index